SO-CTH-362

WITHDRAWN

ARTHUR C. CLARKE

a primary and secondary
bibliography

Masters of
Science Fiction and Fantasy

Advisory Acquisitions Editor

Marshall B. Tymn

The Author

   Known internationally for his scholarly and critical writings on science fiction, fantasy, and utopian literature, Professor Samuelson received his Ph.D. in comparative literature from the University of Southern California in 1969. Author of <u>Visions of Tomorrow: Six Journeys from Outer to Inner Space</u> (Arno, 1974), he has taught courses in this area since 1969 and has participated in numerous local, national, and international academic conferences. His articles and reviews have been published in specialty periodicals in the United States and England, in collections of essays and reference volumes, and in the <u>Los Angeles Times</u> and other major newspapers.

Contents

Library of Congress Cataloging in Publication Data

Samuelson, David N.
   Arthur C. Clarke : a primary and secondary
bibliography.

   (Masters of science fiction and fantasy)
   Includes indexes.
   1. Clarke, Arthur Charles, 1917-   —Bibliography.
   I. Title: II. Series.
Z8174.6.S25   1984   [PR6005.L36]   016.823'914   84-10762
ISBN 0-8161-8111-X

This publication is printed on permanent/durable acid-free paper
MANUFACTURED IN THE UNITED STATES OF AMERICA

ARTHUR C. CLARKE

a primary and secondary bibliography

DAVID N. SAMUELSON

G.K.HALL &CO.

70 LINCOLN STREET, BOSTON, MASS.

Preface

This bibliography provides access to over 900 primary works by Arthur C. Clarke and almost 300 pieces of secondary material (annotated) in English about Clarke through 1980. It also includes a tabular listing of over 800 reviews of his books, but it does not pretend to contain references to everything ever written by or about Clarke. Books have been restricted to American and British first editions, hardbound and paper, and variant editions in English with revisions and/or changes in prefatory material.

Journals are also limited to English-language periodicals, which include several in Sri Lanka and some in other Asian countries. Science fiction fanzines are included, and some movie journals which are little less fugitive. In addition, I have documented Clarke's grammar school publications and contributions to British "comic papers." But published letters are generally omitted, except for some reprinted in the Congressional Record, a couple of technical pieces on communication satellites and breathing in vacuum, and a controversy over interpretation of a Clarke work in an American scholarly publication.

The checklist is divided into five sections, with four appendixes and three indexes.

Primary Material

Section A (Fiction) consists of Clarke's novels, stories, and collections of both, plus one anthology of fiction edited by him. Citations include books by Clarke, science fiction magazines, newspapers, general interest magazines, amateur publications, anthologies, and even textbooks.

Section B (Miscellaneous Media) consists of two (published) poems, as well as films, scripts, recordings, and adaptations of Clarke's work by himself and others (most of which are recordings for the blind).

Section C (Nonfiction) consists of books, essays, book and film reviews, interviews, a very small number of letters, supplementary materials to his and others' books (forewords, introductions, after-words, prefaces, author's notes, and acknowledgments), and auto-biographical statements directly attributed to Clarke. There are also a few pieces which might almost equally be classified as fiction (e.g., interviews and reviews of imaginary persons and books).

All three sections of primary material include grammar school and fanzine publications, and all reprints and title changes that could be verified.

Secondary Material

Section D includes and annotates biographical profiles (some-times approaching or even involving interviews), unattributed résumés in reference books (even though they may be supplied by the author), critical explorations of Clarke's works in general, introductions to his books (written by other people), bibliographical surveys, and other writings and recorded presentations about him and his work. Book reviews are included only if they involve more than one book, or both the book and movie versions of 2001: A Space Odyssey. An-notated entries regarding that film (selected from over 400 articles and film reviews not included for reasons of space) emphasize Clarke's contributions.

Section E lists in tabular form all book reviews locatable through standard reference sources (see Appendix 2). Others exist, especially in smaller newspapers, many of which have been supplied to Clarke or his brother Fred by their clipping service, but some limits are needed here as well.

Appendixes

Appendix 1 lists collections of typescripts and manuscripts. Appendix 2 identifies resource persons, institutions, and publications of assistance in the compiling of this checklist. Appendix 3 con-sists of Clarke's honorary degrees and other awards. Appendix 4 is a partial accounting of his radio and television appearances.

Indexes

Since the main listings are in chronological order, alphabetical indexes offer an alternate means to find a given author or title.

Index 1 includes all titles assigned to Clarke's works, (includ-ing editors' titles for excerpts from his work), as well as titles of books (articles, talks) he has reviewed. It also gives titles of sections of multi-part works which have not been given individual item numbers in the main bibliography. Index 1 corresponds to Sections A-C, Primary Material.

Index 2, which corresponds to Section D, Secondary Material, lists titles of published works (written or recorded) concerning Clarke's life and work.

Index 3 (Register of Names) includes Clarke's pseudonyms, collaborators, people whose work he has written about (usually in book reviews), people who have written about him (also including book reviews), and readers who have recorded his work. Where more than three people are credited with a book or essay, however, only the name of person whose name first appears is given. An attempt has been made, moreover, to ascertain the names behind initials, wherever possible. In Sections A-D, this is generally indicated by square brackets, a practice carried over into Index 3. In Section E, brackets are only occasionally used; thus the names of a considerable number of reviewers are more completely cited than in the original publications.

One kind of information is conspicuously absent in the indexes. The titles of anthologies (and the names of their editors) in which Clarke's work is reprinted are readily available elsewhere (e.g., William G. Contento, Index to Science Fiction Anthologies and Collections [Boston: G.K. Hall, 1978]) and would only add many unnecessary pages to this volume.

Time Limit

This checklist includes only items published by 31 December 1980, which preceded the official end of Clarke's "retirement" (although reference sources through 1982 and into 1983 were consulted). That date may yet prove only a half-way house in the Clarke industry. If he does not write several hundred more pieces, surely more will be written about him (e.g., a 1983 book by John Hollow). Foreign-language editions, unindexed book reviews, movie reviews and critiques, a more comprehensive listing of manuscripts (in addition to those in the two major collections), and more complete information on broadcast appearances, could easily amount to another volume of comparable size.

HOW TO USE THE CHECKLIST

General organization

Numbered items in Sections A-D follow chronological sequence by year. A (Fiction) and C (Nonfiction) are also arranged chronologically

within a given year (book and serial publication dates are inte-
grated).

   Section B (Miscellaneous Media) is alphabetical by title within
the year, because many media productions are impossible to date pre-
cisely (dates ascertained are indicated in brackets). Numbers for
recordings, slideshows, and filmstrips are those assigned by the
manufacturers or by the Library of Congress, Division for the Blind
and Physically Handicapped (formerly the National Library Service).

   Section D (Bibliography, Biography, Criticism) is alphabetical
within the year by last name of author, where available. If no
author is cited, listing is usually alphabetized by title of article
or by editor's name. Listing is by book title, however, for annual
reference books, in which only Clarke's first appearance is listed.

   Section E (Book Reviews) is first alphabetized by the titles of
Clarke's books, then chronological for each title. For access by
name of reviewer, see Index 3 listings with E prefixes.

Chronology of entries

   In a given year, a periodical with a monthly appearance date is
assumed to have been published before the first day of that month.
Similarly, a weekly publication normally precedes a daily periodical
with the same date. Seasonal or quarterly periodicals are treated
as if they were published at the calendar beginning of the season,
that is, between the 20th and 21st of March, June, September, or
December (unless a journal explicitly indicates Winter is part of
the new year, in which case it precedes 1 January).

   Within these conventions, if two publications have the same
posted date, they are alphabetized by periodical title; multiple
items from the same issue are arranged by page precedence. Anything
without a specific date assigned to it is listed at the end of the
year or (if totally undated) of its section.

Within a numbered entry

   For entries, the usual order for primary materials is title(s),
date(s), page(s), in keeping with MLA format. For journals, issue
numbers usually are not given, and if volume numbers are available,
page numbers follow the month (or quarter) without a "p." or "pp."

   Reprints of a numbered item are also given in chronological
order by year. Within the year the following sequence is observed:
collections of Clarke stories, dated periodicals, anthologies alphabetized by editor.

Preface

<u>Symbols and other conventions</u>

Publications of limited availability are so indicated in square brackets (e.g., [fanzine] or [in-house publication]). Square brackets are also used for other incidental information (e.g., Clarke's byline if other than the usual "Arthur C. Clarke," and my authority for citations of those few items I have not seen personally or in photocopy--any such item is also identified with an asterisk). Authorities are abbreviated, their initials identified at the end of the Preface.

Alternate titles for Clarke writings are given their own numbers, unless the change is insignificant (e.g., addition or omission of a definite or indefinite article). In some cases, several reprints under each title may exist. Variant texts with the same title are also given, to help the researcher follow the tangled publication history.

"A," "an" and "the" are always indicated at the beginning of a Clarke title or an anthology, though they are not counted in alpha-betizing (e.g., in the indexes). "The" as part of a journal title, however, is always omitted.

Cross-referencing is fairly complete for Primary Material (Sections A-C), including nonfiction items in fiction books and vice versa. Cross-fertilization obviously occurred between Clarke's fiction and nonfiction, and to some extent between the writer and his audience(s). Repetition and overlap of material is inevitable, and I have tried to indicate exact excerpts and expansion established by direct textual comparison. It is also possible that some passages were slipped across between stories and essays, but I have not tried to crosscheck every piece of fiction with its opposite numbers in nonfiction.

ACKNOWLEDGMENTS

Many people have contributed to this effort, most notably my wife, Marilee, who has proofread, encouraged, and endured. Without the brothers Clarke, however, there might have been no book. Arthur opened the way to the files of others, called me from Sri Lanka, had his secretary copy (in longhand) his publication records, corresponded with me on details, and obtained from officials in Sri Lanka coopera-tion and even photocopies (no mean feat, even for a distinguished resident). One door opened to Fred's house in London, where I spent the daylight hours for almost four weeks in 1978. Since then, he and his new wife have spent additional hours tracing errant texts and rec-ords, welcomed me again for a week in their new house in Somerset in 1983, and returned several long-distance calls for last-minute emer-gencies.

David Higham Associates, Arthur's London agents, opened their records for three days of furious copying. Patrick Codd supplied a couple of dozen items otherwise unlocatable. Dozens of people helped me search: multiple entries were provided by Forrest Ackermann, Bill Contento, Alex Eisenstein, Bruce Pelz, Leslie K. Swigart, and Marshall B. Tymn. And Gregory Benford allowed me the use of his word processor during 1982 and 1983, for complete revisions of several sections.

California State University, Long Beach, my employer, was helpful in numerous ways. I would have been lost without the Interlibrary Loan Department, specifically Barbara Barton, Tony Dumas, Dale Guerrero, Catherine L. Ida, Juanita Knox, Charlene La Forge, Suzanne Latauska, and Teddy Varvares. Some pages of manuscript were typed (and retyped) by English Department secretaries Paula Cataldo, Margie Chavez, Ellen Fritz, and Marilyn Therrien. And student assistant money paid for the clerical and typing services of Ann Calhoun, Jean Davis, Ellen Lindsay, Jill Cary Martin, Chris McCabe, Lisa Valencia, and Susan Wodarczyk.

ABBREVIATIONS

ACC	Arthur C. Clarke	DH	David Higham Associates
BC	William G. Contento	SM	Sam Moskowitz [D34]
FC	Fred Clarke	RR	R[obert] Reginald [D105]
LC	Library of Congress (Talking Book Topics)	ES	Erwin Strauss (MIT Science Fiction Index)
PC	Patrick Codd	DT	Donald H. Tuck [D8]
TC	Tom Craven	MT	Marshall B. Tymn
WC	Wallace Coyle [D267]		

Introduction

Space propagandist, underwater explorer, communications expert, futurist, and general popularizer of science, Arthur Charles Clarke is surely the best-known writer of science fiction since H.G. Wells. Perennially ranked at the top of science-fiction reader polls along with Isaac Asimov and Robert A. Heinlein, he is compared by critics not only to Wells, Jules Verne, and his avowed master, Olaf Stapledon, but also to such visionaries as the theologian Pierre Teilhard de Chardin and the architect Paolo Soleri, as an influence on contemporary thought, literature, and society.

Clarke's publications include 15 novels (one rewrite), almost 200 short stories, and 26 books of nonfiction (including 2 anthologies and 8 collaborations). Co-author of the screenplay for the most acclaimed science-fiction film of all time, he has made countless appearances in radio, television, and movies. In on the ground floor during the development of radar, he originated but could not patent the conception of communications satellites in geosynchronous orbit. A familiar face, name, even voice around the world, he has received numerous prizes for science and science-fiction writing.

Born 16 December 1917, in England--the village of Minehead in the farming county of Somerset--he soon sought wider horizons. Interested as a child in paleontology and astronomy, he broadened his sense of space and time still more by reading whatever fantasy and science fiction he could find in those days. Today he acknowledges debts to dozens of writers, from Melville and Tennyson to Dunsany and Maugham, but then he read American pulp science-fiction magazines widely and fairly indiscriminately.

Going to London as a very junior civil servant, he met others who shared his interests, and found outlets for his scientific and literary aspirations in the fledgling British Interplanetary Society and science-fiction fan publications. Those days are recorded not only in his nonfiction, but also in a young man's vision of London captured in the technological utopia of Diaspar in Against the Fall of Night (rewritten as The City and the Stars). In this short novel, which occupied him on and off for almost twenty years, Clarke's

alter ego, young Alvin, finds his destiny in uniting apparent oppo-
sites: past and future, earth and space, mind and matter, nature and
technology, adventure and story-telling.

World War II made Clarke an experimenter and instructor in the
infant science of radar, memorialized later in the novel, Glide Path.
Returning to London for his Bachelor of Science in physics and mathematics, he expanded his participation in the BIS, the British Astronomical Association, and fan activities, and began to sell both fiction and nonfiction. Three times president of the BIS, he advanced
its cause and his own in lecture halls, newspapers, books, and magazines, closely paralleling his early novels in many respects. Four
years after his first professional sale, selection of The Exploration
of Space by the American Book-of-the-Month Club won him prestige and
money enough to quit his job, useful though it was to both of his
writing pursuits, as assistant editor of Science Abstracts.

The 1950s were his peak years for sheer volume: he published
eight novels, four collections of short stories, and ten nonfiction
books (six on space, four on the sea) in that decade. His reputation
was made, as a scholar, as a tireless popularizer of scientific
knowledge and speculation, and as a story-teller, by turns sober
(Prelude to Space), visionary (Childhood's End), and whimsical (Tales
from the White Hart).

These were also the years he discovered the world, on land,
under the sea, and through the air. A fateful love affair began--
much longer-lived than his ill-starred marriage--with the tropical
island nation of Sri Lanka (then Ceylon). It has been his home since
1956, whenever he could find the time to stay there. Visitors often
came to this home base a world away from his birthplace and most of
his audience, and Clarke himself made frequent trips to England,
Europe, and the United States, where his greatest renown came in the
late 1960s.

Lured to New York by filmmaker Stanley Kubrick, he spent much of
1965 in a hotel room, hammering out draft after draft of the screenplay for 2001: A Space Odyssey to meet the director's specifications.
Even then there were changes (see The Lost Worlds of 2001), and
Clarke was involved peripherally up to and even after the film's
release in April 1968.

Whether he fully understood the film (did anyone?) is open to
question. His novel, an "interpretation" drawn from the endingless
screenplay and largely unedited rushes, is far more prosaic than the
film, although Kubrick's meticulous attention to surfaces, details,
and verisimilitude mirrors Clarke's, and the ending finally shot
owes more to Childhood's End than either author admitted in print.
If the novel was not the filmguide many perplexed viewers hoped for,
it was still a commercial success, though dwarfed by the popularity
and canonical status attained by the movie. Along with his pioneer

championing of spaceflight, it made him a natural choice for a network commentator on American telecasts of NASA space efforts.

In demand as a public speaker, he published as well as delivered during the 1960s and 1970s several standard speeches with varying emphases on the future. He also made audio recordings and films, while finding some time for Sri Lanka, for skin-diving, for writing, and for himself. Although only three new novels appeared in that decade, their quality was appreciated by both large and demanding audiences, as the academic industry of science-fiction scholarship and criticism expanded. Clarke was a certain choice for the first volumes of Taplinger's "21st Century Writers" series, and two shorter books on his work were published.

With The View from Serendip (1977), a collection of nonfiction pieces with autobiographical commentary, and The Fountains of Paradise (1978), his supposedly last novel, Clarke announced his retirement from travel, fiction, and nonfiction. This triple threat was short-lived. More articles began appearing, a sequel to 2001 was published in 1982 (leading to another movie contract), and a revision of Profiles of the Future appeared in 1983. Plans for 1984 include a novelization of a screenplay based on an earlier story, a retrospective assemblage of his uncollected science articles, another volume of occasional pieces, and another television series. At least two more whirlwind tours of Europe and the United States have already taken place, an autobiography is underway, and yet another novel is taking shape in the word processor whose role is credited in 2010: Odyssey Two (1982).

Primary Material

Part A: Fiction

1932

A1   "Correspondence." [One-Time Sixth Former, pseud.]. <u>Huish</u>
    <u>Magazine</u> 21 (Autumn):51-52. [Letter from a fictitious
    graduate of Huish Grammar School (now Richard Huish Col-
    lege) concerning rigors of work in an extreme environment.
    Sequels: A2-3, 5-6.]

1933

A2   "Our Correspondence Column." [A Real Old 6th Former, pseud.].
    <u>Huish Magazine</u> 22 (Spring):42-43. [See A1.]

A3   "News from the Torrid Zone." [Ex-Sixth Former, pseud.].
    <u>Huish Magazine</u> 22 (Christmas):34-35. [See A1.]

1935

A4   "The Fate of Fu-Manchu." [Clericus, pseud.]. <u>Huish Magazine</u>
    24 (Spring):33-37.

A5   "Letters to the Editor." [A. Munchhausen, pseud.]. <u>Huish</u>
    <u>Magazine</u> 24 (Spring):39-40. [See A1.]

A6   "Letters to the Editor." [De Profundis, pseud.]. <u>Huish</u>
    <u>Magazine</u> 24 (Summer):50-52. [See A1.]

1936

A7   "Things to Come (?)." [Court, pseud.]. <u>Huish Magazine</u> 25
    (Spring):36-43.

1937

A8   "Travel by Wire!" <u>Amateur Science Stories</u> [fanzine] 1
     (December):9-11.

        In <u>The Best of Arthur C. Clarke</u>, 1973. [Erroneously cited
           on title page as from <u>Amateur Science Fiction Stories</u>.]
           A209

1938

A9   "How We Went to Mars." <u>Amateur Science Stories</u> [fanzine] 1
     (March):2-6, 13.

A10 "Retreat from Earth." <u>Amateur Science Stories</u> [fanzine] 1
     (March):7-13.

        In <u>The Best of Arthur C. Clarke</u>, 1973. [Erroneously cited
           on title page as from <u>Amateur Science Fiction Stories</u>.]
           A209
        <u>Speed and Power</u> no. 14 (21-28 June 1974), pp. 26-28 (pt.
           1); no. 15 (28 June-5 July 1974), pp. 26-28 (pt. 2,
           subtitled "Secret of the Sphere," A213).

1939

A11 "Into the Past." <u>Satellite</u> [fanzine] 3 (December):3-6.

1940

A12 "At the Mountains of Murkiness, or Lovecraft-into-Leacock."
     <u>Satellite</u> [fanzine] 3 (February):2-7. [Year not indicated.]

        George Locke et al. <u>At the Mountains of Murkiness and
           Other Parodies</u>. London: Ferret Fantasy, 1973, paper.

A13 "Ego's Review" [of nonexistent books]. <u>Gargoyle</u> [fanzine] 1
     (April):7-9.

A14 "Court News." <u>Gargoyle</u> [fanzine] 2 (June):3-8.

1941

A15 "A Short History of Fantocracy--1948-1960." [Bylined Arthur
     Ego Clarke.] <u>Fantast</u> [fanzine] 2 (December):6-8 (pt.
     1); 3 (April 1942):21-24 (pt. 2); 3 (July 1942):8-11 (pt.
     3).

1942

A16 "The Awakening." <u>Zenith</u> [fanzine], no. 4 (February), pp. 57–
    59. [Text cannibalized for "Exile of the Eons," 1950,
    A34; and "The Awakening," 1952, A52.]

    In <u>The Best of Arthur C. Clarke</u>, 1973. A209

A17 "Whacky." [Ego, pseud.]. <u>Fantast</u> [fanzine] 3 (July):25–26.

    In <u>The Best of Arthur C. Clarke</u>, 1973. [Variant text,
    omits one line, section numbers; erroneously cited as
    from <u>Fantasy.</u>] A209

1946

A18 "Loophole." <u>Astounding Science Fiction</u> 37 (April):57–61.

    Groff Conklin, ed. <u>A Treasury of Science Fiction.</u> New
      York: Crown, 1948.
    In <u>Expedition to Earth</u>, 1953. A66
    Damon Knight, ed. <u>First Flight: Maiden Voyages in Space
    and Time.</u> New York: Lancer, 1963, paper.
      Same as <u>Now Begins Tomorrow.</u> New York: Lancer, 1969,
      paper.
    In <u>An Arthur Clarke Omnibus</u>, 1965. A178
    Jane Hipolito, and Willis E. McNelly, eds. <u>Mars, We Love
    You.</u> Garden City, N.Y.: Doubleday, 1971.
      Same as <u>The Book of Mars.</u> London: Futura, 1976, paper.

A19 "Rescue Party." <u>Astounding Science Fiction</u> 37 (May):36–60.

    Groff Conklin, ed. <u>A Treasury of Science Fiction.</u> New
      York: Crown, 1948.
    Frederik Pohl, ed. <u>Beyond the End of Time.</u> Garden City,
      N.Y.: Permabooks, 1952, paper.
    In <u>Reach for Tomorrow</u>, 1956. A82
    Donald A. Wollheim, ed. <u>The End of the World.</u> New York:
      Ace, 1956, paper.
    In <u>Across the Sea of Stars</u>, 1959. A141
    In <u>The Nine Billion Names of God</u>, 1967. A185
    Robert Silverberg, ed. <u>Alpha 3.</u> New York: Ballantine,
      1972, paper.
    Bonnie L. Heintz et al., eds. <u>Tomorrow, and Tomorrow, and
    Tomorrow. . . .</u> New York: Holt, Rinehart & Winston,
      1974, paper.
    Robert Silverberg, and Martin Harry Greenberg, eds. <u>The
    Arbor House Treasury of Modern Science Fiction.</u> New
      York: Arbor House, 1980.

A20 "Technical Error." Fantasy: The Magazine of Science Fiction
        1 (December):56-68.

        Retitled "The Reversed Man," 1950. A36
        In Reach for Tomorrow, 1956. A82
        In Across the Sea of Stars, 1959. A142
        Frederik Pohl, Martin Harry Greenberg, and Joseph Olander,
            eds. Science Fiction of the 40's. New York: Avon,
            1978, paper.

                                1947

A21 "Castaway." [Charles Willis, pseud.]. Fantasy: The Magazine
        of Science Fiction 1 (April):72-76.

        Sam Moskowitz, and Roger Elwood, eds. Strange Signposts.
            New York: Holt, Rinehart & Winston, 1966.
        Peter Haining, ed. The Future Makers. New York: Belmont,
            1971, paper.
        Included in Science Fiction Special 5. London:
            Sidgwick & Jackson, 1971. [Source: BC]
        In The Best of Arthur C. Clarke, 1973. A209

A22 "The Fires Within." [E.G. O'Brien, pseud.]. Fantasy: The
        Magazine of Science Fiction 1 (August):72-77.

        Startling Stories 20 (September 1949):121-25, 142.
        [Charles Willis, pseud.]. Eagle 4 (August 1950):12-13.
            [Variant text.]
        Groff Conklin, ed. The Science Fiction Galaxy. Garden
            City, N.Y.: Permabooks, 1950, paper.
        August Derleth, ed. Worlds of Tomorrow. New York:
            Pelligini & Cudahy, 1953.
            Partially reprinted as New Worlds for Olds. London:
                Four Square, 1963, paper.
        In Reach for Tomorrow, 1956. A82
        *Science World 5 (19 March 1957):18-21. [Source: ACC]
        In Across the Sea of Stars, 1959. A142
        In Of Time and Stars, 1972. A206
        Speed and Power, no. 50 (28 February-7 March 1975), pp.
            26-28 (pt. 1); no. 51 (7-14 March 1975), pp. 26-28 (pt.
            2).
        Mike Ashley, ed. The History of the Science Fiction Maga-
            zines: Part 3, 1946-1955. London: New English
            Library, 1976.

A23 "Inheritance." [Charles Willis, pseud.]. New Worlds 1
        ([October]):54-57.

        Astounding Science Fiction 42 (September 1949):145-52.

In <u>Expedition to Earth</u>, 1953. A66
In <u>Across the Sea of Stars</u>, 1959. A142
In <u>An Arthur Clarke Omnibus</u>, 1965. A178

A24 "Nightfall." <u>King's College Review</u> 46 (December):9-10.

Retitled "The Curse," 1953. A65

1948

A25 "Against the Fall of Night." <u>Startling Stories</u> 18 (November): 11-70.

Expanded, <u>Against the Fall of Night</u>, 1953. A63

A26 "The Forgotten Enemy." <u>King's College Review</u> 47 (December): 20-24.

<u>New Worlds</u> 2 ([September] 1949):48-52.
<u>Avon Science Fiction and Fantasy Reader</u> 1 (January 1953): 17-23.
William Sloane, ed. <u>Stories for Tomorrow</u>. New York: Funk & Wagnalls, 1954.
In <u>Reach for Tomorrow</u>, 1956. A82
Brian W. Aldiss, ed. <u>More Penguin Science Fiction</u>. Harmondsworth: Penguin, 1963, paper.
Included in <u>The Penguin Science Fiction Omnibus</u>. Harmondsworth: Penguin, 1973, paper.
In <u>Prelude to Mars</u>, 1965. A180
Edmund Crispin, ed. <u>The Stars and Under</u>. London: Faber & Faber, 1968.
In <u>Of Time and Stars</u>, 1972. A206.
<u>Speed and Power</u>, no. 39 (13-20 December 1974), pp. 26-28 (pt. 1); no. 40 (20-27 December 1974), pp. 26-28 (pt. 2).
Edmund J. Farrell et al., eds. <u>Science Fact/Fiction</u>. Glenview, Ill.: Scott, Foresman, 1974, paper.
Harry Harrison, ed. <u>SF: Author's Choice 4</u>. New York: G.P. Putnam's Sons, 1974.
Bryan Newton, ed. <u>Points of View (Book I)</u>. London: Ward Lock Educational, 1980, paper.

1949

A27 "Critical Mass." <u>Lilliput</u> 24 (March):43-45.

In <u>Tales from the White Hart</u>, 1957. A99
<u>Space Science Fiction</u> 1 (August 1957):122-28.
In <u>Prelude to Mars</u>, 1965. A180

A28 "History Lesson." Startling Stories 19 (May):137-41.

>   Retitled "Expedition to Earth," 1954. A73
>   Science Fantasy 1 (Winter 1950):67-74.
>   Groff Conklin, ed. Omnibus of Science Fiction. New York:
>   Crown, 1952.
>   Partially reprinted as Science Fiction Omnibus. New
>   York: Berkley, 1956, paper.
>   In Expedition to Earth, 1953. A66
>   In Across the Sea of Stars, 1959. A142
>   Cordelia T. Smith, ed. Great Science Fiction Stories.
>   New York: Dell, 1964, paper.
>   Tony Licata, ed. Great Science-Fiction. Chicago: Three
>   Star Books, 1965, paper.
>   Richard J. Hurley, ed. Beyond Belief. New York:
>   Scholastic Book Services, 1966, paper.
>   Dick Allen, ed. Science Fiction: The Future. New York:
>   Harcourt Brace Jovanovich, 1971, paper.
>   Social Education 36 (March 1972):250-54.
>   In The Best of Arthur C. Clarke, 1973. A209
>   SF Monthly 1 (July 1974):10-12.
>   Bernard C. Hollister, ed. Another Tomorrow. Dayton,
>   Ohio: Pflaum, 1974, paper.
>   Daniel Roselle, ed. Transformations II: Understanding
>   American History Through Science Fiction. Greenwich,
>   Conn.: Fawcett, 1974, paper.
>   Sheila Schwartz, ed. Earth in Transit: Science Fiction
>   and Contemporary Problems. New York: Dell, 1976,
>   paper.

A29 "Transience." Startling Stories 19 (July):125-28.

>   Everybody's, 15 July 1950, pp. 21, 24.
>   Milton Lesser, ed. Looking Forward. New York: Beechhurst
>   Press, 1953.
>   In The Other Side of the Sky, 1958. A132
>   In From the Ocean, From the Stars, 1961. A156
>   In The Nine Billion Names of God, 1967. A186

A30 "The Wall of Darkness." Super Science Stories 5 (July):66-
     78.

>   Sam Moskowitz, ed. Editor's Choice in Science Fiction.
>   New York: McBride, 1954.
>   In The Other Side of the Sky, 1958. A132
>   In From the Ocean, From the Stars, 1961. A156
>   In The Nine Billion Names of God, 1967. A186
>   Robert Silverberg, ed. Other Dimensions. New York:
>   Hawthorne, 1973.
>   Speed and Power, no. 31 (18-25 October 1974), pp. 26-28
>   (pt. 1); no. 32 (25 October-1 November 1974), pp. 26-28

(pt. 2); no. 33 (1-8 November 1974), pp. 26-28 (pt. 3); no. 34 (8-15 November 1974), pp. 26-28 (pt. 4).

A31 "The Lion of Comarre." Thrilling Wonder Stories 34 (August): 44-69.

   In The Lion of Comarre and Against the Fall of Night, 1968. A191

A32 "Hide and Seek." Astounding Science Fiction 44 (September): 68-77.

   In Expedition to Earth, 1953. A66
   William Sloane, ed. Space, Space, Space. New York: Franklin Watts, 1953.
   John Carnell, ed. Gateway to Tomorrow. London: Museum Press, 1954.
   In Across the Sea of Stars, 1959. A142
   Brian N. Ball, ed. Tales of Science Fiction. London: Hamish Hamilton, 1964.
   In An Arthur Clarke Omnibus, 1965. A178
   In The Nine Billion Names of God, 1967. A186
   In Of Time and Stars, 1972. A206
   In The Best of Arthur C. Clarke, 1973. A209
   Harry Harrison, and Brian W. Aldiss, eds. The Astounding-Analog Reader. Vol. 2. Garden City, N.Y.: Doubleday, 1973.
   Speed and Power, no. 48 (14-21 February 1975), pp. 26-28 (pt. 1); no. 49 (21-28 February 1975), pp. 26-28 (pt. 2).

A33 "Thirty Seconds--Thirty Days." Thrilling Wonder Stories 35 (December):106-22.

   Retitled "Breaking Strain." A55
   Samuel S. Mines, ed. The Best from Startling Stories. London: Holt, 1953.
   Same as Startling Stories. London: Cassell, 1954.
   Argosy 15 (June 1954):33-50.
   H.G. Stenzel, ed. 2001 and Beyond. Hong Kong: Longman, 1975, paper. [Text adapted by Anthony Laude.]

1950

A34 "Exile of the Eons." Super Science Stories 6 (March):86-96. [Cannibalized from "The Awakening," 1942, A16.]

   Retitled "Nemesis," 1954. A74
   In Expedition to Earth, 1953. A66
   In Prelude to Mars, 1965. A180

Alden H. Norton, ed. <u>Award Science Fiction Reader</u>. New
    York: Award Books, 1966, paper.
Alden H. Norton, ed. <u>Futures Unlimited</u>. New York:
    Pyramid, 1969, paper.

A35 "Guardian Angel." <u>Famous Fantastic Mysteries</u> 11 (April):98-
     112, 127-29. [Text altered by James Blish. Cf D10.]

     <u>New Worlds</u> 3 (Winter 1950):2-29. [Minor revisions.]
     In <u>Childhood's End</u>, 1953. [More minor revisions, expan-
         sion.] A64
     William F. Nolan, and Martin Harry Greenberg, eds. <u>Sci-
         ence Fiction Origins</u>. New York: Fawcett, 1980. [New
         Worlds text.]

A36 "The Reversed Man." <u>Thrilling Wonder Stories</u> 36 (June):43-51.

     Originally "Technical Error," 1946. A20

A37 "Time's Arrow." <u>Science Fantasy</u> 1 (Summer):31-42.

     In <u>Reach for Tomorrow</u>, 1956. A82
     In <u>Across the Sea of Stars</u>, 1959. A142

A38 "A Walk in the Dark." <u>Thrilling Wonder Stories</u> 36 (August):
     134-40.

     Groff Conklin, ed. <u>Possible Worlds of Science Fiction</u>.
         New York: Vanguard Press, 1951.
     In <u>Reach for Tomorrow</u>, 1956. A82
     Groff Conklin, ed. <u>Great Stories of Space Travel</u>. New
         York: Tempo, 1963, paper.
     In <u>Prelude to Mars</u>, 1965. A180
     *<u>Great Science Fiction Stories</u>, no. 3 (1966), pp. 30-36.
         [Source: ES.]
     In <u>The Nine Billion Names of God</u>, 1967. A186
     Robert Silverberg, ed. <u>To the Stars</u>. New York: Hawthorne,
         1971.
     John L. Foster, ed. <u>Science Fiction Stories</u>. London:
         Ward Lock Educational, 1975, paper.
     Bryan Newton, ed. <u>Points of View (Book I)</u>. London: Ward
         Lock Educational, 1980, paper.

A39 "Silence, Please!" [Charles Willis, pseud.]. <u>Science
     Fantasy</u> 1 (Winter):47-56.

     In <u>Tales from the White Hart</u>, 1957. [Revised text, no
         punctuation in title.] A99
     In <u>Across the Sea of Stars</u>, 1959. [Revised text and
         title.] A142
     Groff Conklin, ed. <u>13 Great Science Fiction Stories</u>.

Greenwich, Conn.: Fawcett, 1960, paper. [Original
text and title.]

1951

A40 "Holiday on the Moon." [Charles Willis, pseud.]. Heiress
     (January), pp. 38-43 (pt. 1); (February), pp. 27-30, 60-
     61 (pt. 2); (March), pp. 40-44, 66 (pt. 3); (April), pp.
     58-61, 74 (pt. 4).

A41 Prelude to Space. New York: World Editions. [Magazine
        format; "Galaxy Novel #3"; subtitle, A Compellingly
        Realistic Novel of Interplanetary Flight, omitted in sub-
        sequent editions.]

     Retitled Master of Space, 1961. A155
     Retitled The Space Dreamers, 1969. A193
     London: Sidgwick & Jackson, 1953. [Revised text used for
        all subsequent editions.]
     New York: Gnome Press, 1954.
     New York: Ballantine, 1954, paper. [Includes "About
        Arthur C. Clarke," C187.]
     London: Pan, 1954, paper.
     Excerpts [prologue; part III, chapter 3, most of chapter
        13]. A.E.M. Bayliss, and J.C. Bayliss, eds. Science
        in Fiction. London: University of London Press, 1957.
     In An Arthur Clarke Omnibus, 1965. A178
     In Prelude to Mars, 1965. [Includes "Foreword," C348.]
        A180
     New York: Harcourt, Brace & World, 1970. [Includes
        "Post-Apollo Preface," C536.]
     New York: Lancer, 1970, paper. [Includes "Post-Apollo
        Preface," C536, and "Preface to the 1962 (sic) Edition,"
        C539.]
     New York: Ballantine, 1976. [Includes revised "Preface,"
        C537.]
     In The Sands of Mars/Prelude to Space, 1980. A225

A42 "The Men in the Flying Saucer." Lilliput 28 (February):73-
     78.

     Retitled "Captain Wyxtpthll's Flying Saucer," 1951. A45
     Retitled "Trouble with the Natives," 1956. A83

A43 "Seeker of the Sphinx." Two Complete Science Adventure Books
     1 (Spring):106-42.

     Retitled "The Road to the Sea," 1962. A167
     Everett F. Bleiler, and T.E. Dikty, eds. Year's Best
        Science-Fiction Novels: 1952. New York: Frederick
        Fell, 1952.

A44   "Sentinel of Eternity." <u>Ten Story Fantasy</u> 1 (Spring):41-47.

      Retitled "The Sentinel," 1954. A68
      Retitled "Peak of Promise," 1968. A189

A45   "Captain Wyxtpthll's Flying Saucer." <u>Marvel Science Stories</u>
      3 (May):101-10.

      Originally "The Men in the Flying Saucer," 1951. A42
      Retitled "Trouble with the Natives," 1956. A83

A46   "Earthlight." <u>Thrilling Wonder Stories</u> 38 (August):56-86.

      Expanded, <u>Earthlight</u>, 1955. A76

A47   "Second Dawn." <u>Science Fiction Quarterly</u> 1 (August):104-30.

      In <u>Expedition to Earth</u>, 1953. A66
      In <u>An Arthur Clarke Omnibus</u>, 1965. A178
      In <u>Prelude to Mars</u>, 1965. A180
      In <u>The Best of Arthur C. Clarke</u>, 1973. A209

A48   "Superiority." <u>Magazine of Fantasy and Science Fiction</u> 2
      (August):3-11.

      In <u>Expedition to Earth</u>, 1953. A66
      August Derleth, ed. <u>Worlds of Tomorrow</u>. New York:
         Pellegrini & Cudahy, 1953.
         Partially reprinted as <u>Worlds of Tomorrow</u>. London:
            Four Square, 1963, paper.
      Clifton Fadiman, ed. <u>Fantasia Mathematica</u>. New York:
         Simon & Schuster, 1958.
      In <u>Across the Sea of Stars</u>, 1959. A142
      In <u>An Arthur Clarke Omnibus</u>, 1965. A178
      In <u>The Nine Billion Names of God</u>, 1967. A186
      Martin Harry Greenberg, and Patricia S. Warrick, eds.
         <u>Political Science Fiction: An Introductory Reader</u>.
         Englewood Cliffs, N.J.: Prentice-Hall, 1974.
      Martin Harry Greenberg, and Joseph Olander, eds. <u>Inter-</u>
         <u>national Relations Through Science Fiction</u>. New York
         and London: New Viewpoints, 1978, paper.
      Reginald Bretnor, ed. <u>The Future at War</u>. New York: Ace,
         1980, paper. Vol. 3, <u>Orion's Sword</u>.

A49   "If I Forget Thee, Oh Earth. . . ." <u>Future Science Fiction</u> 2
      (September):66-69. [Reprints place quotation marks around
      title.]

      Retitled "Exiles from Earth," 1974. A215

> Evening News, 15 January 1953. [No page on clipping. "O" in title.]
> World Digest (May 1953). [No volume no. or page on clipping; condensed.]
> In Expedition to Earth, 1953. A66
> In Across the Sea of Stars, 1959. A142
> In An Arthur Clarke Omnibus, 1965. A178
> In The Nine Billion Names of God, 1967. A186
> In Of Time and Stars, 1972. A206
> Thomas D. Clareson, ed. A Spectrum of Worlds. Garden City, N.Y.: Doubleday, 1972. ["O" in title, ellipsis marks omitted.]
> Brian W. Aldiss, ed. Evil Earths. London: Weidenfeld & Nicholson, 1975.

A50 "Broken Circuit." Sketch 240 (7 November):484.

A51 The Sands of Mars. London: Sidgwick & Jackson.

> New York: Gnome Press, 1972. [Omits "The" in title.]
> London: Corgi, 1954, paper.
> New York: Pocket, 1954, paper. [Omits "The" in title.]
> In Prelude to Mars, 1965. [Omits "The" in title on dust jacket only.] A180
> New York: Harcourt, Brace & World, 1967. [Includes "Fore-word," C470.]
> In An Arthur C. Clarke Second Omnibus, 1968. [Omits "The" in title on dust jacket and flyleaf, retains on pages of text.] A190
> In The Sands of Mars/Prelude to Space, 1980. A225

1952

A52 "The Awakening." Future Science Fiction 2 (January):83–85. [Text cannibalized from "The Awakening," 1942 (A16).]

> Sunday Chronicle, 5 September 1954, p. 2.
> In Reach for Tomorrow, 1956. A82
> In Prelude to Mars, 1965. A180
> Tom Boardman, Jr., ed. An ABC of Science Fiction. New York: Avon, 1968, paper.
> Robert Silverberg, ed. The Ends of Time. New York: Hawthorne, 1970.
> Alan L. Madsen, ed. Tomorrow: Science Fiction and the Future. New York: Scholastic Book Services, 1973, paper.
> H.G. Stenzel, ed. 2001 and Beyond. Hong Kong: Longman, 1975, paper. [Text adapted by Anthony Laude.]
> Gerry Goldberg, ed. Strange Glory: Awakening Man's Latent Powers. New York: St. Martin's, 1977.

A53 "All the Time in the World." <u>Startling Stories</u> 26 (July):69-
     76.

       Donald A. Wollheim, ed. <u>Prize Science Fiction</u>. New York:
         McBride, 1953.
         Same as <u>Prize Stories of Space and Time</u>. London:
           Weidenfeld, 1953.
       <u>Wonder Stories</u> 45 (1957):40-50.
       In <u>The Other Side of the Sky</u>, 1958. A132
       In <u>From the Ocean, From the Stars</u>, 1961. A156
       <u>Wonder Stories</u> 45 (1963):32-39, 47.
       <u>Science Fiction Yearbook</u>, no. 2 (1968), pp. 26-33.
       Ross R. Olney, ed. <u>Tales of Time and Space</u>, Racine, Wis.:
         Western Publishing, 1969.
       In <u>Of Time and Stars</u>, 1972. A206

A54 <u>Islands in the Sky</u>. Philadelphia: Winston. [Includes
     introduction, "Cities in Space," C161, omitted by other
     publishers.]

       London: Sidgwick & Jackson [1952].
       <u>Popular Science</u> 162 (June 1953):140-59. [Abridged.]
       New York: New American Library, 1956, paper.
       New York: Holt, Rinehart & Winston, 1958. ["Cities in
         Space" revised, C265a.]
       London: Sidgwick & Jackson, 1971. [With a new introduc-
         tion by Patrick Moore, D116.]
       Hong Kong: Oxford University Press, 1976, paper. [Retold
         by Susan Davies.]
           No connection with C133.

A55 "Breaking Strain." In <u>No Place Like Earth</u>. Edited by John
     Carnell. London: T.V. Boardman, pp. 57-89.

       Originally "Thirty Seconds--Thirty Days," 1949. A33
       In <u>Expedition to Earth</u>, 1953. A66
       In <u>Across the Sea of Stars</u>, 1959. A142
       Amabel Williams-Ellis, and Mably Owen, eds. <u>Out of this
         World 1</u>. London: Blackie & Son, 1960.
       In <u>An Arthur Clarke Omnibus</u>, 1965. A178

                            1953

A56 "The Possessed." <u>Dynamic Science Fiction</u> 1 (March):85-88.

       In <u>Reach for Tomorrow</u>, 1956. A82
       Ivan Howard, ed. <u>Novelets of Science Fiction</u>. New York:
         Belmont, 1963, paper.
       In <u>Prelude to Mars</u>, 1965. A180
       In <u>The Nine Billion Names of God</u>, 1967. A186
       Brian W. Aldiss, ed. <u>Galactic Empires</u>. Vol. 1. London:
         Weidenfeld & Nicolson, 1976.

A57   "The Nine Billion Names of God." In <u>Star Science Fiction</u>
        <u>Stories</u>. Edited by Frederik Pohl. New York: Ballantine,
        pp. 195-202.

        Retitled "Twilight in Tibet," 1973. A207
        William Sloane, ed. <u>Stories for Tomorrow</u>. New York:
           Funk & Wagnalls, 1954.
        In <u>The Other Side of the Sky</u>, 1958. A132
        Edmund Crispin, ed. <u>Best SF Two</u>. London: Faber & Faber,
           1956.
        G.D. Doherty, ed. <u>Aspects of Science Fiction</u>. London:
           John Murray, 1959.
        In <u>From the Ocean, From the Stars</u>, 1962. A156
        Clifton Fadiman, ed. <u>The Mathematical Magpie</u>. New York:
           Simon & Schuster, 1962.
        In <u>The Nine Billion Names of God</u>, 1967. A186
        Amabel Williams-Ellis, and Mably Owen, eds. <u>Out of this</u>
           <u>World 6</u>. London: Blackie & Son, 1967.
        Damon Knight, ed. <u>One Hundred Years of Science Fiction</u>.
           New York: Simon & Schuster, 1968.
        Leon Stover, and Harry Harrison, eds. <u>Apeman, Spaceman:</u>
           <u>Anthropological Science Fiction</u>. Garden City, N.Y.:
           Doubleday, 1968.
        Robert Silverberg, ed. <u>Science Fiction Hall of Fame</u>.
           Vol. 1. Garden City, N.Y.: Doubleday, 1970.
        Mayo Mohs, ed. <u>Other Worlds, Other Gods: Adventures in</u>
           <u>Religious Science Fiction</u>. Garden City, N.Y.: Double-
           day, 1971.
        In <u>Of Time and Stars</u>, 1972. A206
        Leslie A. Fiedler, ed. In <u>Dreams Awake: A Historical-</u>
           <u>Critical Anthology of Science Fiction</u>. New York: Dell,
           1975, paper.
        Patricia Warrick, and Martin Harry Greenberg, eds. <u>The</u>
           <u>New Awareness: Religion Through Science Fiction</u>. New
           York: Delacorte, 1975.
        Abbe Mowshowitz, ed. <u>Inside Information: Computers in</u>
           <u>Fiction</u>. Reading, Mass.: Addison-Wesley, 1977, paper.
        Donald Lawler, ed. <u>Approaches to Science Fiction</u>. Boston:
           Houghton Mifflin, 1978, paper.

A58   "The Parasite." <u>Avon Science Fiction and Fantasy Reader</u> 1
        (April):118-28.

        In <u>Reach for Tomorrow</u>, 1956. A82
        In <u>Prelude to Mars</u>, 1965. A180

A59   "Jupiter Five." <u>If</u> 2 (May):4-28, 75.

        In <u>Reach for Tomorrow</u>, 1956. A82

15

In Across the Sea of Stars, 1959. A142
Robert Silverberg, ed. Explorers of Space. Nashville,
    Tenn.: Thomas Nelson, 1975.
Mike Ashley, ed. The Best of British SF 1. London:
    Futura, 1977, paper.

A60 "Encounter in the Dawn." Amazing Stories 27 (June–July):4–16.

Retitled "Expedition to Earth," 1953. A67
Retitled "Encounter at Dawn," 1959. A143
In Expedition to Earth [U.K. edition], 1954. A66
In Arthur Clarke Omnibus, 1965. A178
Amazing Stories 40 (June 1966):72–83.
John L. Foster, ed. Science Fiction Stories. London:
    Ward Lock Educational, 1975, paper.
Donald Lawler, ed. Approaches to Science Fiction. Boston:
    Houghton Mifflin, 1978, paper.

A61 "The Other Tiger." Fantastic Universe Science Fiction 1
     (June–July):116–18.

August Derleth, ed. Portals of Tomorrow. New York:
    Rinehart, 1954.
Isaac Asimov, Martin Harry Greenberg, and Joseph D.
    Olander, eds. Microcosmic Tales: 100 Wondrous Science
    Fiction Short-Short Stories. New York: Taplinger,
    1980.

A62 "Publicity Campaign." Evening News, 9 June, p. 6.

Satellite Science Fiction 1 (October 1956):109–12.
In The Other Side of the Sky, 1958. A132
In From the Ocean, From the Stars, 1961. A156

A63 Against the Fall of Night. New York: Gnome Press.

Expanded from "Against the Fall of Night," 1948. A25
Revised, The City and the Stars, 1956. A81
New York: Pyramid, 1960, paper. [Includes "Publisher's
    Note," D22.]
In The Lion of Comarre and Against the Fall of Night,
    1968. A191
New York: Jove, 1978, paper. [Includes "Arthur C.
    Clarke," D220.]

A64 Childhood's End. New York: Ballantine. Simultaneous hard-
     cover and paper. [Includes "About Arthur C. Clarke," C187.]

Expanded from "Guardian Angel," 1950. A35
London: Sidgwick & Jackson, 1954.
London: Pan, 1956, paper.

In <u>Across the Sea of Stars</u>, 1959. A142
In <u>An Arthur Clarke Omnibus</u>, 1965. A178
New York: Ballantine, 1967, paper. [Includes "Arthur C.
    Clarke," C336.]
Ontario, Canada: Nelson, 1968. [School edition with
    study materials by Roy Bentley.]
New York: Harcourt, Brace & World, 1970. [Omits sentence
    on copyright page: "The opinions expressed in this
    book are not those of the author.]
New York: Ballantine, 1976, paper. [Includes "Arthur C.
    Clarke," C625.]

A65 "The Curse." <u>Cosmos Science Fiction</u> 1 (September):82-84.

Originally "Nightfall," 1947. A24
In <u>Reach for Tomorrow</u>, 1956. A82
In <u>Prelude to Mars</u>, 1965. A180
*James Goldie Brown, ed. <u>From Frankenstein to Andromeda</u>.
    London: Macmillan, 1966. [Source: DT.]
In <u>The Nine Billion Names of God</u>, 1967. A186
Peter Haining, ed. <u>The Nightmare Reader</u>. Garden City,
    N.Y.: Doubleday, 1973.
Anthony Adams, and Esmor Jones, eds. <u>Storymakers 3</u>.
    London: Harrap, 1974.

A66 <u>Expedition to Earth</u>. New York: Ballantine. Simultaneous
    hardcover and paper. ["Second Dawn," A47; "'If I Forget
    Thee, Oh Earth. . . ,'" A49; "Breaking Strain," A55;
    "History Lesson," A28; "Superiority," A48; "Exile of the
    Eons," A34; "Hide and Seek," A32; "Expedition to Earth,"
    A67; "Loophole," A18; "Inheritance," A23; "The Sentinel,"
    A68; "About Arthur C. Clarke," C187.]

London: Sidgwick & Jackson, 1954. [Three story titles
    changed: from "History Lesson" to "Expedition to Earth,"
    A73; from "Exile of the Eons" to "Nemesis," A74; from
    "Expedition to Earth" back to "Encounter in the Dawn,"
    A60.]
London: Corgi, 1959, paper. [1954 contents.]
In <u>An Arthur Clarke Omnibus</u>, 1965. [1954 contents.] A178
London: Sidgwick & Jackson, 1968. [As <u>Expedition to</u>
    <u>Earth and Other Science Fiction Stories, Including</u> "The
    Sentinel."]
New York: Harcourt, Brace & World, 1970. [1953 contents,
    includes "Preface," C534.]
In <u>The Lost Worlds of 2001/Expedition to Earth</u>, 1980. A226

A67 "Expedition to Earth." In <u>Expedition to Earth</u>, pp. 125-37.
    A66

Originally "Encounter in the Dawn," 1959. A60

Retitled "Encounter at Dawn," 1959. A143

A68 "The Sentinel." In Expedition to Earth, pp. 155-65. A66

Originally "Sentinel from Eternity," 1951. A44
Retitled "Peak of Promise," 1968. A189
New Worlds Science Fiction 8 ([April] 1954):47-55.
In Across the Sea of Stars, 1959. A142
Kingsley Amis, and Robert Conquest, eds. Spectrum III.
    London: Victor Gollancz, 1963.
In An Arthur Clarke Omnibus, 1965. A178
In The Nine Billion Names of God, 1967. A186
Damon Knight, ed. Worlds to Come. New York: Harper &
    Row, 1967.
Practical English 46 (14 March 1969):8-12.
Jerome Agel, ed. The Making of Kubrick's 2001. New York:
    New American Library, 1970, paper. D95
Robert Silverberg, ed. The Mirror of Infinity: A Critics'
    Anthology of Science Fiction. New York: Harper & Row,
    1970.
In The Lost Worlds of 2001, 1972. A200
In Of Time and Stars, 1972. A206
In The Best of Arthur C. Clarke, 1973. A209
Sylvia Z. Brodkin, and Elizabeth J. Pearson, eds. Science
    Fiction. Evanston, Ill.: McDougal, Littell & Co.,
    1973, paper.
Robert Pierce, and Murray Suid, eds. Science Fiction 3.
    Boston: Houghton Mifflin, 1973.
Jack C. Wolf, and Gregory Fitz Gerald, eds. Past, Present,
    and Future Perfect. Greenwich, Conn.: Fawcett, 1973,
    paper.
Speed and Power, no. 55 (4-11 April 1974), pp. 26-28 (pt.
    1); no. 56 (11-18 April 1974), pp. 26-28 (pt. 2).
Brian W. Aldiss, ed. Space Odysseys. London: Weidenfeld
    & Nicolson, 1974.
Bonnie L. Heintz et al., eds. Tomorrow, and Tomorrow, and
    Tomorrow. . . . New York: Holt, Rinehart, Winston,
    1974, paper.
Charles W. Sullivan III, ed. As Tomorrow Becomes Today.
    Englewood Cliffs, N.J.: Prentice-Hall, 1974, paper.
H.G. Stenzel, ed. 2001 and Beyond. Hong Kong: Longman,
    1975, paper. [Text adapted by Anthony Laude.]
James Gunn, ed. The Road to Science Fiction #3: From
    Heinlein to Here. New York: New American Library,
    1979, paper.
William Kittridge, and Steven M. Krauzer, eds. Stories
    Into Film. New York: Harper & Row, 1979.
Jim Wynorski, ed. They Came From Outer Space: 12 Classic
    Science Fiction Tales that Became Major Motion Pictures.
    Garden City, N.Y.: Doubleday, 1980.

1954

A69   "The Deep Range."   In <u>Star Science Fiction Stories 3</u>.   Edited
      by Frederik Pohl.   New York: Ballantine, pp. 36-45.

         Expanded as <u>The Deep Range</u>, 1957.   [First chapter, revised.]
            A112
         <u>Argosy</u> 19 (February 1956):34-52.
         Frederik Pohl, ed.   <u>Star of Stars</u>.   Garden City, N.Y.:
            Doubleday, 1960
            Same as: <u>Star Fourteen</u>.   London: Ronald Whiting &
               Wheaton, 1966.
         *James Goldie Brown, ed.   <u>From Frankenstein to Andromeda</u>.
            London: Macmillan, 1966.   [Source: DT.]
         Groff Conklin, ed.   <u>Giants Unleashed</u>.   New York: Grosset
            & Dunlap, 1965.
            Same as <u>Minds Unleashed</u>.   New York: Tempo, 1970, paper.
         Damon Knight, ed.   <u>Beyond Tomorrow</u>.   New York: Harper &
            Row, 1965.
         Isaac Asimov, ed.   <u>Where Do We Go From Here?</u>   Garden City,
            N.Y.:   Doubleday, 1971.
         Jane Yolen, ed.   <u>Zoo 2000</u>.   New York: Seabury, 1973.
         Robert Silverberg, ed.   <u>The Infinite Web: Eight Stories
            of Science Fiction</u>.   New York: Dial, 1977.

A70   "Armaments Race."   <u>Adventure</u>, April, pp. 34-36, 57-58.

         In <u>Tales from the White Hart</u>, 1957.   A99
         In <u>Across the Sea of Stars</u>, 1959.   A142

A71   "No Morning After."   In <u>Time to Come</u>.   Edited by August
      Derleth.   New York: Farrar, Straus & Young, pp. 75-85.

         <u>Magazine of Fantasy and Science Fiction</u> 11 (July 1956):122-
            27.
         In <u>The Other Side of the Sky</u>, 1958.   A132
         In <u>From the Ocean, From the Stars</u>, 1961.   A156
         In <u>The Nine Billion Names of God</u>, 1967.   A186
         In <u>Of Time and Stars</u>, 1972.   A206
         R[onald] Chetwynd-Hayes, ed.   <u>Tales of Terror from Outer
            Space</u>.   London: Fontana, 1975, paper.

A72   "The Secret Weapon."   <u>Adventure</u>, June, pp. 36-37, 77-79.

A73   "Expedition to Earth."   In <u>Expedition to Earth</u>, pp. 77-86.
      [U.K. edition.]

         Originally "History Lesson," 1949.   A28
         In <u>An Arthur Clarke Omnibus</u>, 1965.   A178

A74   "Nemesis."   In <u>Expedition to Earth</u>, pp. 99-115.   [U.K. edition.]

Originally "Exile of the Eons," 1950.

A75 "The Invention." Adventure, November, pp. 34-37, 85-86.

Retitled "Patent Pending," 1957. A101

1955

A76 Earthlight. New York: Ballantine. Simultaneous hardcover
and paper. [Dedicated "To Val who massacred the second draft
and Bernie who slaughtered the third--but particularly to
Marilyn who spent the advance before I got to Chapter 2."]

Expanded from "Earthlight," 1951. A46
London: Frederick Muller, 1955.
London: Pan, 1957, paper.
In Across the Sea of Stars, 1959. A142
In An Arthur C. Clarke Second Omnibus, 1968. A190
New York: Ballantine, 1971, paper. [8th printing, deletes
mention of Marilyn from dedication.]
New York: Harcourt Brace Jovanovich, 1972. [Includes
"Preface," C578, new dedication "To Dave Scott and Jim
Irwin, the first men to enter this land, and to Al
Worden, who watched over them in orbit."]
New York: Ballantine, 1977, paper. [18th printing, new
dedication.]

A77 "?" [contest story]. Magazine of Fantasy and Science Fiction
9 (July):114-24.

Retitled "This Earth of Majesty," 1956. A80
Retitled "Royal Prerogative," 1957. A98
Retitled "Refugee," 1958. A133

A78 "The Star." Infinity Science Fiction 1 (November):120-27.

In The Other of the Sky, 1958. A132
Ceylon Observer, 12 June 1960, p. 9.
In From the Ocean, From the Stars, 1961. A156
Isaac Asimov, ed. The Hugo Winners. [Vol. 1.] Garden
City, N.Y.: Doubleday, 1962.
Damon Knight, ed. A Century of Science Fiction. New York:
Simon & Schuster, 1962.
Edmund Crispin, ed. Best SF 5. London: Faber & Faber,
1963.
Short Story International 2 (January 1965):7-13
G.D. Doherty, ed. Second Orbit. London: John Murray,
1965.
Terry Carr, ed. Science Fiction for People Who Hate Sci-
ence Fiction. Garden City, N.Y.: Doubleday, 1966.

In <u>The Nine Billion Names of God</u>, 1967. A186
S[amuel] H[olroyd] Burton, ed. <u>Science Fiction</u>. London:
    Longman's, Green, 1967.
Robert Hoskins, ed. <u>Infinity One</u>. New York: Lancer,
    1970, paper.
*<u>Swank</u>, May 1973, pp. 4, 39, 86. [Source: ACC.]
In <u>The Best of Arthur C. Clarke</u>, 1973. A209
Thomas E. Sanders, ed. <u>Speculations: An Introduction to
    Literature Through Fantasy and Science Fiction</u>. Beverly
    Hills, Calif.: Glencoe Press, 1973, paper.
Edmund Crispin, ed. <u>Outwards from Earth: A Selection of
    Science Fiction</u>. London: Faber & Faber, 1974.
Norman Spinrad, ed. <u>Modern Science Fiction</u>. Garden City,
    N.Y.: Anchor, 1974, paper.
Brian W. Aldiss, and Harry Harrison, eds. <u>Decade, the
    1950s</u>. London: Macmillan, 1976.
Terry Carr, ed. <u>To Follow a Star: Nine Science Fiction
    Stories About Christmas</u>. New York: Thomas Nelson, 1977.

                              1956

A79 "What Goes Up. . . ." <u>Magazine of Fantasy and Science Fiction</u>
     10 (January):26-34. [Reprints omit ellipses.]

     In <u>Tales from the White Hart</u>, 1957. A99
     In <u>Prelude to Mars</u>, 1965. A180

A80 "This Earth of Majesty." In <u>The Best from Fantasy and Sci-
     ence Fiction, 5th series</u>. Edited by Anthony Boucher.
     Garden City, N.Y.: Doubleday, pp. 45-48. [Epigraph from
     Richard II, i, i, unique to this version.]

     Originally "?" [contest story], 1955. A77
     Retitled "Royal Prerogative," 1957. A98
     Retitled "Refugee," 1958. A133
     Hans Stefan Santesson, ed. <u>Rulers of Men</u>. New York:
         Pyramid, 1965, paper.

A81 <u>The City and the Stars</u>. New York: Harcourt, Brace. [In-
     cludes "Preface," C224.]

     Revision of <u>Against the Fall of Night</u>, 1953. A63
     London: Frederick Muller, 1956. [Omits preface.]
     New York: New American Library, 1957, paper.
     London: Corgi, 1957, paper. [Omits preface.]
     In <u>From the Ocean, From the Stars</u>, 1961. [Omits preface.]
         A156
     Abbe Mowshowitz, ed. In <u>Inside Information: Computers in
         Fiction</u>. Reading, Mass.: Addison-Wesley, 1977, paper.
         [Excerpt from chapters 5 and 7.]

In <u>Four Great SF Novels</u>, 1978. [Omits preface.]   A221

A82   <u>Reach for Tomorrow</u>. New York: Ballantine, simultaneous
        hardcover and paper. ["Preface," C227; "Rescue Party,"
        A19; "A Walk in the Dark," A38; "The Forgotten Enemy," A26;
        "Technical Error," A20; "The Parasite," A58; "The Fires
        Within," A22; "The Awakening," A52; "Trouble with the
        Natives," A83; "The Curse," A65; "Time's Arrow," A37;
        "Jupiter Five," A59; "The Possessed," A56.]

        London: Victor Gollancz, 1962.
        New York: Harcourt, Brace & World, 1970. [New preface,
          C535.]

A83   "Trouble with the Natives." In <u>Reach for Tomorrow</u>.   A82

        Originally "The Men in the Flying Saucer," 1951. A42
        Retitled "Captain Wyxtpthll's Flying Saucer," 1951. A45
        In <u>Prelude to Mars</u>, 1957. A180
        In <u>Of Time and Stars</u>, 1972. A206
        <u>Speed and Power</u>, no. 36 (22–29 November 1974), pp. 26–28
          (pt. 1); no. 37 (29 November–6 December 1974), pp. 26–
          28 (pt. 2); no. 38 (6–13 December 1974), pp. 26–28 (pt.
          3).

A84   "Double-Crossed in Outer Space." <u>Evening Standard</u>, 23 May,
        p. 17.

        Retitled "The Starting Line," 1956. A94
        See "Venture to the Moon," 1956. A90

A85   "Saved! . . . by a Bow and Arrow." <u>Evening Standard</u>, 24 May,
        p. 17.

        Retitled "Robin Hood, F.R.S.," 1956. A95
        Retitled "Robin Hood on the Moon," 1975. A217
        See "Venture to the Moon," 1956. A90

A86   "Death Strikes Surov." <u>Evening Standard</u>, 25 May, p. 17.

        Retitled "Green Fingers," 1957. A96
        See "Venture to the Moon," 1956. A90

A87   "Diamonds! . . . and then Divorce." <u>Evening Standard</u>, 26 May,
        p. 11.

        Retitled "All that Glitters," 1957. A97
        See "Venture to the Moon," A90.

A88   "Who Wrote that Message to the Stars?" . . . In Letters a
        Thousand Miles Long." <u>Evening Standard</u>, 28 May, p. 17.

Retitled "Watch This Space," 1957. A109
See "Venture to the Moon," 1956. A90

A89 "Alone on the Moon." Evening Standard, 29 May, p. 17.

Retitled "A Question of Residence," 1957. A110
See "Venture to the Moon," 1956. A90

A90 "Venture to the Moon." Evening Standard, 23-29 May. [Six
short stories: "Double-Crossed in Outer Space," 23 May,
p. 17, A84; "Saved! . . . by a Bow and Arrow," 24 May,
p. 17, A85; "Death Strikes Surov," 25 May, p. 17, A86;
"Diamonds! . . . and then Divorce," 26 May, p. 11, A87;
"Who Wrote that Message to the Stars? . . . in Letters a
Thousand Miles Long," 28 May, p. 17, A88; "Alone on the
Moon," 29 May, p. 17, A89.]

Magazine of Fantasy and Science Fiction 11 (December 1956)-
12 (February 1957). [Retitled: "The Starting Line,"
(December):100-103, A94; "Robin Hood, F.R.S.," (Decem-
ber): 103-7,A95; "Green Fingers," (January) 55-59,A96;
"All that Glitters," (January): 59-62.A97; "Watch this
Space," (February):78-82, A109; "A Question of Residence,"
(January):82-85, A110. All reprints of entire series
observe these titles.]
In The Other Side of the Sky. A132
Anthony Boucher, ed. The Best from Fantasy and Science
Fiction, Seventh Series. Garden City, N.Y.: Doubleday,
1958.
In From the Ocean, From the Stars, 1961. A156
Hal Clement, ed. First Flights to the Moon. Garden City,
N.Y.: Doubleday, 1970. [Includes only first two of
six stories.]
In The Best of Arthur C. Clarke, 1973. A209

*A91 "The Reckless Ones." Adventure, October. [Source: ACC.]

Retitled "Big Game Hunt," 1957. A100

A92 "The Pacifist." Fantastic Universe Science Fiction 6
(October):4-12.

In Tales from the White Hart, 1957. [Minor revisions.]
A99
In Across the Sea of Stars, 1959. A142
Hans Stefan Santesson, ed. The Fantastic Universe Omnibus.
Englewood Cliffs, N.J.: Prentice-Hall, 1960.
Clifton Fadiman, ed. The Mathematical Magpie. New York:
Simon & Schuster, 1962.

A93 "The Reluctant Orchid." Satellite Science Fiction 1

(December):114–22.

Retitled "An Orchid for Auntie," 1975. A218
In Tales from the White Hart, 1957. A99
In Across the Sea of Stars, 1959. A142
In The Nine Billion Names of God, 1967. A186
In Of Time and Stars, 1972. A206
Edmund J. Farrell et al., eds. Science Fact/Fiction.
    Glenview, Ill.: Scott, Foresman, 1974, paper.
Frederik Pohl, Martin Harry Greenberg, and Joseph D.
    Olander, eds. The Great Science Fiction Series. New
    York: Harper & Row, 1980.

A94 "The Starting Line." Magazine of Fantasy and Science Fiction
    11 (December):100–103.

Originally "Double-Crossed in Outer Space," 1956. A84
See "Venture to the Moon," 1956. A90
Hal Clement, ed. First Flights to the Moon. Garden City,
    N.Y.: Doubleday, 1970.

A95 "Robin Hood, F.R.S." Magazine of Fantasy and Science Fiction
    11 (December):103–07.

Originally "Saved! . . . by a Bow and Arrow," 1956. A85
Retitled "Robin Hood on the Moon," 1975. A217
See "Venture to the Moon," 1956. A90
Science World 5 (10 March 1959):24–26.
Hal Clement, ed. First Flights to the Moon. Garden City,
    N.Y.: Doubleday, 1970.
In Of Time and Stars, 1972. A206

1957

A96 "Green Fingers." Magazine of Fantasy and Science Fiction 12
    (January):55–59.

Originally "Death Strikes Surov," 1956. A86
See "Venture to the Moon," 1956. A90
Hans Stefan Santesson, ed. The Days After Tomorrow.
    Boston: Little, Brown, 1971.
In Of Time and Stars, 1972. A206
Speed and Power, no. 43 (10–17 January 1975), pp. 26–28.

A97 "All that Glitters." Magazine of Fantasy and Science Fiction
    12 (January):59–62.

Originally "Diamonds! . . . and then Divorce," 1956. A87
See "Venture to the Moon," 1956. A90

A98 "Royal Prerogative." <u>New Worlds Science Fiction</u> 19 (January):
      41–51.

        Originally "?" [contest story], 1955. A77
        Retitled "The Earth of Majesty," 1956. A80
        Retitled "Refugee," 1958. A133

A99 <u>Tales from the White Hart</u>. New York: Ballantine, paper.
      ["Preface," C236; "Silence Please," A39; "Big Game Hunt,"
      A100; "Patent Pending," A101; "Armaments Race," A70;
      Critical Mass," A27; "The Ultimate Melody," A102; "The
      Pacifist," A92; "The Next Tenants," A103; "Moving Spirit,"
      A104; "The Man Who Ploughed the Sea," A105; "The Reluctant
      Orchid," A93; "Cold War," A106; "What Goes Up," A79;
      "Sleeping Beauty," A107; "The Defenestration of Ermintrude
      Inch," A108; "About Arthur C. Clarke," C187.]

        New York: Harcourt Brace Jovanovich, 1970. ["Preface"
          slightly revised.]
        London: Sidgwick & Jackson, 1972. [Includes revised
          "Preface."]
        New York: Ballantine, 1976, paper. [As <u>Tales from the</u>
          "<u>White Hart</u>."]

A100 "Big Game Hunt." In <u>Tales from the White Hart</u>, pp. 13–19.
      A99

        Originally "The Reckless Ones," 1956. A91
        In <u>Prelude to Mars</u>, 1965. A180
        Stuart David Schiff, ed. <u>Mad Scientists</u>. Garden City,
          N.Y.: Doubleday, 1980.

A101 "Patent Pending." In <u>Tales from the White Hart</u>, pp. 19–30.
      A99

        Originally "The Invention," 1954. A75
        <u>Escapade</u> 3 (December 1957):35–36, 40–41.
        Christopher Cerf, ed. <u>The Vintage Anthology of Science</u>
          <u>Fantasy</u>. New York: Vintage, 1966, paper.
        In <u>The Nine Billion Names of God</u>, 1967. A186
        Rich Jones, and Richard L. Roe, eds. <u>Valence and Vision:</u>
          <u>A Reader in Psychology</u>. San Francisco: Rinehart, 1974.
        Martin Harry Greenberg, and Joseph Olander, eds. <u>Tomorrow,</u>
          <u>Inc.: Science Fiction Stories about Big Business</u>. New
          York: Taplinger, 1976.

A102 "The Ultimate Melody." In <u>Tales from the White Hart</u>, pp. 45–
      52. A99

        Retitled "The Strange Sound of Dying," 1957. A111
        <u>If</u> 7 (February 1957):70–75. [Minor revisions, no "The" in
          title.

      In Prelude to Mars, 1965. A180
      Roger Elwood, and Sam Moskowitz, eds. Alien Earth and
         Other Stories. New York: Macfadden, 1969, paper. [No
         "The" in title.]
      Thomas F. Monteleone, ed. The Arts and Beyond: Visions
         of Man's Aesthetic Future. Garden City, N.Y.: Double-
         day, 1977. [No "The in title.]

A103 "The Next Tenants." In Tales from the White Hart, pp. 63–
      73. A99

      Satellite Science Fiction 1 (February 1957):103–11.
      In Across the Sea of Stars, 1959. A142
      *H.E.L.P., no. 5 (December 1959), pp. 40–58. [Source:
        ACC.]

A104 "Moving Spirit." In Tales from the White Hart, pp. 73–83.
      A99

      In Prelude to Mars, 1965. A180

A105 "The Man Who Ploughed the Sea." In Tales from the White Hart,
      pp. 86–103. A99

      Satellite Science Fiction 1 (June 1957):104–19.
      In Prelude to Mars, 1965. A180
      Sam Moskowitz, and Roger Elwood, eds. The Human Zero and
         Other Science Fiction Masterpieces. New York: Tower
         Books, 1967, paper.

A106 "Cold War." In Tales from the White Hart, pp. 113–120. A99

      Satellite Science Fiction 1 (April 1957):86–92.
      In Prelude to Mars, 1965. A180

A107 "Sleeping Beauty." In Tales from the White Hart, pp. 131–41.
      A99

      Retitled "The Case of the Snoring Heir," 1957. A113

A108 "The Defenestration of Ermintrude Inch." In Tales from the
      White Hart, pp. 142–48. A99

A109 "Watch this Space." Magazine of Fantasy and Science Fiction
      12 (February):78–82.

      Originally "Who Wrote that Message to the Stars? . . . in
         Letters a Thousand Miles Long," 1956. A88
      See "Venture to the Moon," 1956. A90

A110   "A Question of Residence." <u>Magazine of Fantasy and Science</u>
<u>Fiction</u> 12 (February):82-85.

   Originally "Alone on the Moon," 1956.   A89
   See "Venture to the Moon," 1956.   A90

A111   "The Strange Sound of Dying." <u>Adventure</u>, February, pp. 33-34,
85-87.

   Originally "The Ultimate Melody."   A102

A112   <u>The Deep Range</u>. New York: Harcourt, Brace.   [Includes
"Author's Note," C239.]

   Expanded from "The Deep Range," 1954.   A69
   London: Frederick Muller, 1957.
   New York: New American Library, 1958, paper.
   London: Pan, 1970, paper.
   In <u>From the Ocean, From the Stars</u>, 1962.   A156
   In <u>Four Great SF Novels</u>, 1978.   A221

A113   "The Case of the Snoring Heir." <u>Infinity Science Fiction</u> 2
(April):26-38.   [Minor revisions.]

   Originally "Sleeping Beauty," 1957.   A107

A114   "Security Check." <u>Magazine of Fantasy and Science Fiction</u> 12
(June):114-17.

   Retitled "The Intruders," 1958.   A129
   In <u>The Other Side of the Sky</u>, 1958.   A132
   <u>Ceylon Observer</u>, 5 June 1960, p. 9.
   Richard Curtis, ed.   <u>Future Tense</u>.   New York: Dell, 1968,
      paper.
   In <u>Of Time and Stars</u>, 1972.   A206

A115   "Special Delivery." <u>Infinity Science Fiction</u> 2 (September):
6-9.

   Retitled "The First Battle Begins in Outer Space," 1957.
      A123
   Retitled "The Other Side of the Sky."   A172
   See "The Other Side of the Sky."   A122
   <u>Speed and Power</u>, no. 44 (17-24 January 1975), pp. 26-28.

A116   "Feathered Friend." <u>Infinity Science Fiction</u> 2 (September):
10-13.

   Retitled "Claribel Saves the Space Station," 1957.   A124
   See "The Other Side of the Sky," 1957.   A122
   In <u>Of Time and Stars</u>, 1972.   A206

Speed and Power, no. 45 (24-31 January 1975), pp. 26-28.

A117 "Take a Deep Breath." Infinity Science Fiction 2 (September):
      14-17.

        Retitled "S.O.S. . . . Adrift in Outer Space," 1957. A125
        See "The Other Side of the Sky," 1957. A122
        Arthur C. Clarke, ed. Time Probe: The Sciences in Science
            Fiction. New York: Delacorte, 1966. A182
        Speed and Power, no. 47 (7-14 February 1975), pp. 26-28.
        Isaac Asimov, Martin Harry Greenberg, and Joseph D.
            Olander, eds. Microcosmic Tales: 100 Wondrous Science
            Fiction Short-Short Stories. New York: Taplinger, 1980.

A118 "Dazzled to Death." Dundee Sunday Telegraph, 5 September.
      [No country or page on clipping.]

        Retitled "Let There Be Light," 1958. A130

A119 "Freedom of Space." Infinity Science Fiction 2 (October):56-
      59.

        Retitled "So Long, Earth," 1957. A126
        See "The Other Side of the Sky," 1957. A122

A120 "Passer-by." Infinity Science Fiction 2 (October):59-62.

        Retitled "Half a Second to Solve a Mystery," 1957. A127
        Retitled "A Rocket for Romeo," 1964. A173
        See "The Other Side of the Sky." 1957. A122
        Speed and Power, no. 46 (31 January-7 February 1975), pp.
        26-28.

A121 "The Call of the Stars." Infinity Science Fiction 2 (October):
      63-66.

        Retitled "All Aboard for Mars," 1957. A128
        See "The Other Side of the Sky," 1957. A122
        In The Nine Billion Names of God, 1967. A186

A122 "The Other Side of the Sky." Infinity Science Fiction 2
      (September-October). [Six short-short stories: "Special
      Delivery," (September):6-9, A115; "Feathered Friend,"
      (September):10-13, A116; "Take a Deep Breath," (September):
      14-17, A117; "Freedom of Space," (October):56-59, A119;
      "Passer-by," (October):59-62, A120; "The Call of the
      Stars," (October):63-66, A121; Introductory material,
      (September):4-5 and (October):55. All reprints of the en-
      tire series observe these titles, except in Evening
      Standard.]

        Evening Standard, 14-21 October 1957. [Retitled: "The
            First Battle Begins in Outer Space," 14 October, p. 15,

A123; "Claribel Saves the Space Station," 15 October,
p. 15, A124; "S.O.S. . . . Adrift in Outer Space," 16
October, p. 17, A125; "So Long, Earth," 17 October,
p. 15, A126; "Half a Second to Solve a Mystery," 18
October, p. 15, A127; "All Aboard for Mars," 21 October,
p. 21, A128.]
In The Other Side of the Sky, 1958. A132
Anthony Boucher, ed. A Treasury of Great Science Fiction.
Vol. 2. Garden City, N.Y.: Doubleday, 1959.
In From the Ocean, From the Stars, 1961. A156

A123 "The First Battle Begins in Outer Space." Evening Standard,
14 October, p. 15.

Originally "Special Delivery," 1957. A115
Retitled "The Other Side of the Sky," 1964. A172
See "The Other Side of the Sky," 1957. A122

A124 "Claribel Saves the Space Station." Evening Standard, 15
October, p. 15.

Originally "Feathered Friend," 1957. A116
See "The Other Side of the Sky," 1957. A122

A125 "S.O.S. . . . Adrift in Outer Space." Evening Standard, 16
October, p. 17.

Originally "Take a Deep Breath," 1957. A117
See "The Other Side of the sky," 1957. A122

A126 "So Long, Earth." Evening Standard, 17 October, p. 15.

Originally "Freedom of Space," 1957. A119
See "The Other Side of the Sky," 1957. A122

A127 "Half a Second to Solve a Mystery." Evening Standard, 18
October, p. 15.

Originally "Passer-by," 1957. A120
Retitled "A Rocket for Romeo," 1964. A173
See "The Other Side of the Sky," 1957. A122

A128 "All Aboard for Mars." Evening Standard, 21 October, p. 21.

Originally "The Call of the Stars," 1957. A121
See "The Other Side of the Sky," 1957. A122

1958

A129 "The Intruders." This Week, 5 January, pp. 16-18.

Originally "Security Check," 1957. A114

A130 "Let There Be Light." Playboy 5 (February):51, 54, 70.

Originally "Dazzled to Death," 1957. A118
In Tales of Ten Worlds, 1962. A159
Editors of Playboy. Transit of Earth. Chicago: Playboy
     Press, 1971, paper.

A131 "Out from the Sun." If 8 (February):77-81, 112-13.

Retitled "Out of the Sun," 1958. A135

A132 The Other Side of the Sky. New York: Harcourt, Brace &
     World. ["The Nine Billion Names of God," A57; "Refugee,"
     A133; "The Other Side of the Sky," A122; "The Wall of
     Darkness," A31; "Security Check," A114; "No Morning After,"
     A71; "Venture to the Moon," A90; "Publicity Campaign," A62;
     "All the Time in the World," A53; "Cosmic Casanova," A134;
     "The Star," A78; "Out of the Sun," A135; "Transience," A29;
     "The Songs of Distant Earth," A136; "Bibliographical Note,"
     C263.]

New York: New American Library, 1959, paper.
London: Victor Gollancz, 1961.
In From the Ocean, From the Stars, 1962. [Omits "Biblio-
     graphical Note."] A156
London: Corgi, 1963, paper.

A133 "Refugee." In The Other Side of the Sky, pp. 15-30. A132

Originally "?" [contest story], 1955. A77
Retitled "This Earth of Majesty," 1956. A80
Retitled "Royal Prerogative," 1957. A98
In From the Ocean, From the Stars, 1961. A156
I.O. Evans, ed. Science Fiction Through the Ages. Vol. 2.
     London: Panther, 1966, paper.
In The Best of Arthur C. Clarke, 1973. A209

A134 "Cosmic Casanova." In The Other Side of the Sky, pp. 165-73.
     1958. A132

Venture Science Fiction 2 (May 1958):23-29.
Ceylon Observer, 29 May 1960, p. 9.
In From the Ocean, From the Stars, 1962. A156

A135 "Out of the Sun." In The Other Side of the Sky, pp. 185-94.
     A132

Originally "Out from the Sun," 1958. A131
In From the Ocean, From the Stars, 1962. A156

Robert Silverberg, ed. Earthmen and Strangers. New York:
    Duell, Sloane & Pearce, 1966.
In The Nine Billion Names of God, 1967. A186
Speed and Power, no. 21 (9–16 August 1974), pp. 26–28 (pt.
    1); no. 22 (16–23 August 1974), pp. 26–28 (pt. 2).

A136 "The Songs of Distant Earth." In The Other Side of the Sky,
      pp. 207–45. A132

      If 8 (June 1958):6–29.
      Science Fantasy 12 (June 1959):99–128.
      Ceylon Observer, 26 June 1960, p. 21 (pt. 1); 3 July 1960,
          p. 9 (pt. 2); 10 July 1960, p. 9 (pt. 3); 17 July 1960,
          p. 9 (pt. 4).
      In From the Ocean, From the Stars, 1962. A156

A137 "The Haunted Spacesuit." This Week, 11 May, pp. 18, 20–21.

      Retitled "Who's There?" 1958. A139
      World Digest, February 1959, pp. 3–6. [Condensed.]
      *Read 9 (1 September 1959):3–6. [Condensed.] [Source:
          ACC.]
      Star Weekly Magazine, 3 October 1959, pp. 36–37.
      *Summertime 7 (12 August 1960):12–14. [Source: ACC.]
      Isaac Asimov, and Groff Conklin, eds. Fifty Short Science
          Fiction Tales. New York: Collier, 1963, paper.

A138 "The Stroke of the Sun." Galaxy Magazine 16 (September):71–
      77.

      Retitled "A Case of Sunstroke," 1959. A140
      Retitled "A Slight Case of Sunstroke," 1962. A165

A139 "Who's There?" New Worlds Science Fiction 26 (November):91–
      95.

      Originally "The Haunted Spacesuit," 1958. A137
      In Tales of Ten Worlds, 1962. A159
      Amabel Williams-Ellis, and Mably Owen, eds. Out of this
          World 3. London: Blackie & Son, 1962.
      In The Nine Billion Names of God, 1967. A186
      Ernest H. Winter, ed. Happenings. [Ontario, Canada]:
          Thomas Nelson, 1969, paper.
      In Of Time and Stars, 1972. A206
      Jay Cline, Russell Hill, and Violet Tallman, eds. Voices
          in Literature, Language, and Composition. Lexington,
          Mass.: Ginn & Co., 1972.
      Alan Cattell, and Stan Hill, eds. Storymakers 2. [Bylined
          by A.C. Clark.] London: Harrap, 1974.
      Edmund J. Farrell et al., eds. Science Fact/Fiction.
          Glenview, Ill.: Scott Foresman, 1974, paper.

Isaac Asimov, Martin Harry Greenberg, and Joseph Olander,
    eds. The Future in Question. New York: Fawcett, 1980,
    paper.

1959

A140 "A Case of Sunstroke." Argosy 20 (February):7-14.

      Originally "The Stroke of the Sun," 1958. A138
      Retitled "A Slight Case of Sunstroke," 1962. A165

*A141 "Out of the Cradle." Dude, March. [Source: ACC.]

      Retitled "Out of the Cradle, Endlessly Orbiting," 1962.
      A161

A142 Across the Sea of Stars. New York: Harcourt, Brace & World.
      ["Introduction" by Clifton Fadiman, D19; I. "Stories from
      Expedition to Earth" (A66): "The Sentinel," A68; "In-
      heritance," A23; "Encounter at Dawn," A143; "Superiority,"
      A44; "Hide and Seek," A32; "History Lesson," A28; "'If I
      Forget Thee, Oh Earth. . . ,'" A49; "Breaking Strain,"
      A55; II. "Stories from Tales from the White Hart" (A99):
      "Silence Please," A39; "Armaments Race," A70; "The Pacifist,"
      A92; "The Next Tenants," A103; "The Reluctant Orchid," A93;
      III: "Stories from Reach for Tomorrow" (A82): "Rescue
      Party," A19; "Technical Error," A20; "The Fires Within,"
      A22; "Time's Arrow," A37; "Jupiter Five," A59; IV.
      Childhood's End, A64; V. Earthlight, A76.]

A143 "Encounter at Dawn." In Across the Sea of Stars, pp. 20-31.
      A142

      Originally "Encounter in the Dawn," 1953. A60
      Retitled "Expedition to Earth," 1953. A67
      In The Nine Billion Names of God, 1967. A186
      In Of Time and Stars, 1972. A206
      Speed and Power, no. 41 (27 December 1974-3 January 1975),
         pp. 26-28 (pt. 1); no. 42 (3-10 January 1975), pp. 26-
         28 (pt. 2).

1960

A144 "I Remember Babylon." Playboy 7 (May):73, 94-100.

      Judith Merril, ed. The Year's Best S-F: 6th Annual Edi-
         tion. New York: Simon & Schuster, 1961.
      In Tales of Ten Worlds, 1962. A159
      Editors of Playboy. The Playboy Book of Science Fiction

and Fantasy. Chicago: Playboy Press, 1966, paper.
In The Nine Billion Names of God, 1967. A186
Editors of Playboy. The Fiend. Chicago: Playboy Press,
1971.

A145 "Crime on Mars." Ellery Queen's Mystery Magazine 36 (July):
107-11.

Retitled "Trouble with Time," 1962. A164
Magazine of Fantasy and Science Fiction 20 (June 1961):30-
34.
Arthur H. Liebman, ed. Quickie Thrillers: 25 Mini-
Mysteries. New York: Washington Square Press, 1975,
paper.

A146 "Inside the Comet." Magazine of Fantasy and Science Fiction
19 (October):30-38, 46.

Retitled "Into the Comet," 1962. A163
Amabel Williams-Ellis, and Mably Owen, eds. Out of this
World 4. London: Blackie & Son, 1964.

A147 "The Hottest Piece of Real Estate in the Solar System."
Vogue 136 (November):54-55.

Retitled "Summertime on Icarus," 1962. A160
Retitled "Incident on Icarus," 1974. A210

1961

A148 "Saturn Rising." Magazine of Fantasy and Science Fiction 20
(March):44-53.

In Tales of Ten Worlds, 1962. A159
Speed and Power, no. 85 (31 October-7 November 1975), pp.
26-28 (pt. 1); no. 86 (7-14 November 1975), pp. 26-28
pt. 2).
Isaac Asimov, Martin Harry Greenberg, and Charles G. Waugh,
eds. The Science Fictional Solar System. New York:
Harper & Row, 1979.
Phyllis R. Fenner, ed. Wide-angle Lens: Stories of Space
and Time. New York: William Morrow, 1980.

A149 "Death and the Senator." Astounding Science Fiction 67 (May):
33-50.

In Tales of Ten Worlds, 1962. A159
Groff Conklin, ed. Worlds of When. New York: Pyramid,
1962, paper.
In The Nine Billion Names of God, 1967. A186

In <u>The Best of Arthur C. Clarke</u>, 1973. A209
Martin Harry Greenberg, and Patricia S. Warrick, eds.
   <u>Political Science Fiction: An Introductory Reader</u>.
   Englewood Cliffs, N.J.: Prentice-Hall, 1974.

A150 "Before Eden." <u>Amazing Stories</u> 35 (June):36-46, 66.

Retitled "The Clouds of Venus," 1974. A214
In <u>Tales of Ten Worlds</u>, 1962. A159
Brian W. Aldiss, ed. <u>Yet More Penguin Science Fiction</u>.
   Harmondsworth: Penguin Books, 1964, paper.
   Included in <u>The Penguin Science Fiction Omnibus</u>.
      Harmondsworth: Penguin, 1973, paper.
Sam Moskowitz, ed. <u>Modern Masterpieces of Science Fiction</u>.
   Cleveland and New York: World, 1965.
   Partially reprinted as <u>Doorway into Time and Other</u>
      <u>Stories from Modern Masterpieces of Science Fiction</u>.
      New York: Mcfadden-Bartell, 1966, paper.
In <u>The Nine Billion Names of God</u>, 1967. A186
Roger Mansfield, ed. <u>The Starlit Corridor</u>. Oxford:
   Pergamon, 1967, paper.
Brian W. Aldiss, ed., assisted by Harry Harrison. <u>Farewell,</u>
   <u>Fantastic Venus! A History of the Planet Venus in Fact</u>
   <u>and Fiction</u>. London: MacDonald & Co., 1968.
   Abridged as <u>All About Venus</u>. New York: Dell, 1968,
      paper.
<u>Science Fiction Greats</u>, Summer 1969, pp. 4-15.
Robert Silverberg, ed. <u>Tomorrow's Worlds</u>. New York:
   Meredith Press, 1969.
L. Sprague de Camp, and Catherine Crook de Camp, eds. <u>3000</u>
   <u>Years of Fantasy and Science Fiction</u>. New York:
   Lothrop, Lee & Shepard, 1972.
Patricia Warrick, Martin Harry Greenberg, and Joseph
   Olander, eds. <u>Science Fiction: Contemporary Mythology</u>.
   New York: Harper & Row, 1978, paper.

A151 "Buried Alive on the Moon." <u>Star Weekly Novel</u>, 12 August
      1961, 12 pp. [Condensed.]

Retitled <u>A Fall of Moondust</u>, 1961. A152

A152 <u>A Fall of Moondust</u>. <u>Evening Standard</u>: 4 September, p. 17
      (pt. 1); 5 September, p. 10 (pt. 2); 6 September, p. 8
      (pt. 3); 7 September, p. 8 (pt. 4); 8 September, p. 8 (pt.
      5); 11 September, p. 10 (pt. 6); 12 September, p. 17 (pt.
      7); 13 September, p. 8 (pt. 8); 14 September, p. 21 (pt.
      9); 15 September, p. 10 (pt. 10). [Condensed.]

Originally "Buried Alive on the Moon," 1961. A151
New York: Harcourt,Brace, 1961. [First unabridged edition.]

London: Victor Gollancz, 1961.
Reader's Digest Condensed Books. No. 4: Autumn. New
    York, 1961. [Condensed.]
Reader's Digest Condensed Books. No. 32: Summer. London,
    1962. [Condensed, includes introduction, "Tomorrow:
    The Moon," C369.]
New York: Dell, 1963, paper.
London: Pan, 1964, paper.
London: University of London Press, 1964. [Abridgement
    "approved by the author."]
London: Thomas Nelson, 1967. [Freely adapted (simplified
    for young or slow readers) by S.D. Kneebone, illustrated
    by R. Micklewright, with study exercises.]
London: Victor Gollancz, 1967. [Includes "Author's Note,"
    C478.]
In An Arthur C. Clarke Second Omnibus, 1968. [Includes
    "Author's Note," C478.]   A190
In Four Great SF Novels, 1978. A221
[Of the shorter editions, only the Reader's Digest condensa-
    tions have identical texts.]

A153 "At the End of the Orbit." If 11 (November):84-99.   Second
    "the" omitted on title page.

    Retitled "Hate," 1962. A162
    Frederik Pohl, ed. The Expert Dreamers. Garden City,
        N.Y.: Doubleday, 1962.

*A154 "Love that Universe." Escapade. [Source: ACC.]

    In The Wind from the Sun, 1972. A201

A155 Master of Space. New York: Lancer, paper.   Includes "Fore-
    word," C348.

    Originally Prelude to Space, 1951. A41
    Retitled The Space Dreamers, 1969. A193

                            1962

A156 From the Ocean, From the Stars. New York: Harcourt, Brace
    & World. ["Introduction," C353; The Deep Range, A112;
    The Other Side of the Sky, A132; The City and the Stars,
    A81.]

A157 "Moondog." Galaxy Science Fiction 20 (April):188-94.

    Retitled "Dog Star," 1962. A166

A158 "An Ape About the House." Dude 6 (May):37-39, 62.

    In Tales of Ten Worlds, 1962. A159

Argosy 24 (March 1963):66-72. [Omits "An" in title.]
In Of Time and Stars, 1972. A206

A159   Tales of Ten Worlds. New York: Harcourt, Brace & World.
       ["I Remember Babylon," A144; "Summertime on Icarus," A160;
       "Out of the Cradle, Endlessly Orbiting," A161; "Who's
       There?" A139; "Hate," A162; "Into the Comet," A163; "An
       Ape About the House," A158; "Saturn Rising," A148; "Let
       There Be Light," A130; "Death and the Senator," A149;
       "Trouble with Time," A164; "Before Eden," A150; "A Slight
       Case of Sunstroke," A165; "Dog Star," A166; "The Road to
       the Sea," A167.]

       London: Gollancz, 1963.
       New York: Dell, 1964, paper.
       London: Pan, 1965, paper.

A160   "Summertime on Icarus." In Tale of Ten Worlds, pp. 15-29.
       A159

       Originally "The Hottest Piece of Real Estate in the Solar
          System," 1960. A147
       Retitled "Incident on Icarus," 1974. A210
       Groff Conklin, ed. Great Science Fiction by Scientists.
          New York: Collier, 1962, paper.
       Alan Frank Barter, and Raymond Wilson, eds. Untravelled
          Worlds. London: Macmillan, 1966.
       In The Nine Billion Names of God, 1967. A186
       In The Best of Arthur C. Clarke, 1973. A209
       Sylvia Z. Brodkin, and Elizabeth J. Pearson, eds. Science
          Fiction. Evanston, Ill.: McDougal, Littell & Co.,
          1973, paper.

A161   "Out of the Cradle, Endlessly Orbiting. . . ." In Tales of
       Ten Worlds, pp. 31-38. A159

       Originally "Out of the Cradle," 1959. A141
       Groff Conklin, and Noah D. Fabricant, eds. Great Science
          Fiction About Doctors. New York: Collier, 1963, paper.
       [Ellipsis marks omitted from title.]

A162   "Hate." In Tales of Ten Worlds, pp. 47-66. A159

       Originally "At the End of the Orbit," 1961. A153
       In The Best of Arthur C. Clarke, 1973. A209

A163   "Into the Comet." "In Tales of Ten Worlds, pp. 67-80. A159

       Originally "Inside the Comet," 1960. A146
       In Of Time and Stars, 1972. A206
       In The Best of Arthur C. Clarke, 1973. A209
       Speed and Power, no. 3 (5-12 April 1974), pp. 26-28 (pt.

1); no. 4 (12-19 April 1974), pp. 26-28 (pt. 2).

A164   "Trouble with Time." In <u>Tales of Ten Worlds</u>, pp. 141-48.
       A159

       Originally "Crime on Mars," 1960. A145
       Brian W. Aldiss, ed. <u>Introducing Science Fiction</u>. London:
          Faber & Faber, 1964.
       In <u>The Nine Billion Names of God</u>, 1967. A186

A165   "A Slight Case of Sunstroke." In <u>Tales of Ten Worlds</u>, pp.
       165-75. A159

       Originally "The Stroke of the Sun," 1958. A138
       Retitled "A Case of Sunstroke," 1959. A140

A166   "Dog Star." In <u>Tales of Ten Worlds</u>, pp. 175-84. A159

       Originally "Moondog," 1962. A157
       In <u>The Nine Billion Names of God</u>, 1967. A186
       Frederik Pohl, ed. <u>The Science Fiction Roll of Honor</u>.
          New York: Random House, 1975.

A167   "The Road to the Sea." In <u>Tales of Ten Worlds</u>, pp. 185-245.
       A159

       Originally "Seeker of the Sphinx," 1951. A43
       Robert Silverberg, and Martin Harry Greenberg, eds. <u>The
          Arbor House Treasury of Great Science Fiction Short
          Novels</u>. New York: Arbor House, 1980.

                                1963

A168   "People of the Sea." <u>Worlds of Tomorrow</u> 1 (April):6-56 (pt.
       1); (June):114-62 (pt. 2).

       Retitled <u>Dolphin Island: A Story of the People of the
          Sea</u>, 1963. A169

A169   <u>Dolphin Island: A Story of the People of the Sea</u>. New York:
          Holt, Rinehart. [Includes "A Note from the Author," C415;
          "About the Author," D32.]

       Originally "People of the Sea," 1963. A168
       London: Victor Gollancz, 1963.
       New York: Berkley, 1968, paper.
       London: Atlantic, 1968, paper.
       Excerpt [chapter 4] retitled "Rescue!" 1971. A198
       New York: Holt, Rinehart & Winston, 1973. [Abridged.]
       London: Pan (Piccolo Science Fiction), 1976, paper.
          [Illustrated.]

Kuala Lumpur, Malaysia: Oxford University Press, 1976.
[Simplified text.]

A170 "The Secret of the Men in the Moon." This Week, 11 August,
pp. 8-11.

Retitled "The Secret," 1972. A203

A171 Glide Path. New York: Harcourt, Brace & World.

New York: Dell, 1965, paper.
London: Sidgwick & Jackson, 1969.
London: Sphere, 1970, paper.

1964

A172 "The Other Side of the Sky." Reveille, 13 February, pp. 26-
27.

Originally "Special Delivery," 1957. A115
Retitled "The First Battle Begins in Outer Space," 1957.
A123
See "The Other Side of the Sky." A122

A173 "A Rocket for Romeo." Reveille, 27 February, pp. 26-27.

Originally "Passer-by," 1957. A120
Retitled "Half a Second to Solve a Mystery," 1957. A127
See "The Other Side of the Sky," 1957. A121

A174 "The Sunjammer." Boy's Life 54 (March):15-18, 67-70. [Re-
prints omit "The."]

Retitled "The Wind from the Sun," 1972. A202
Argosy 26 (January 1965):70-88.
New Worlds Science Fiction 48 (March 1965):26-46.
Amazing Stories 40 (February 1966):6-25.
G.D. Doherty, ed. Stories from Science Fiction. London:
Thomas Nelson & Sons, 1966.
Donald A. Wollheim, and Terry Carr, eds. World's Best
Science Fiction: 1966. New York: Ace, 1966, paper.
Harry Harrison, ed. Worlds of Wonder. Garden City, N.Y.:
Doubleday, 1969.
William F. Nolan, ed. A Wilderness of Stars. Los
Angeles: Sherbourne Press, 1969.
In The Best of Arthur C. Clarke, 1973. A209
Roger Elwood, and Vic Ghidalia, eds. Androids, Time
Machines, and Blue Giraffes. Chicago: Follett, 1973.
Harry Harrison, and Carol Pugner, eds. A Science Fiction

Reader. New York: Charles Scribner's Sons, 1973, paper.

Speed and Power, no. 16 (5-12 July 1974), pp. 26-28 (pt. 1); no. 17 (12-19 July 1974), pp. 26-28 (pt. 2); no. 18 (19-26 July 1974), pp. 26-29 (pt. 3).

Roger Elwood, ed. Visions of Tomorrow. New York: Pocket, 1976, paper.

Terry Carr, ed. The Infinite Arena. Nashville, Tenn.: Thomas Nelson, 1977.

Thomas Durwood, and Armand Eisen, eds. Masterpieces of Science Fiction, New York: Ballantine, 1978, paper.

A175 "The Food of the Gods." Playboy 11 (May):113-14.

Editors of Playboy. Last Train to Limbo. Chicago: Playboy Press, 1971, paper.

In The Wind from the Sun, 1972. A201

"Supplementary Materials T262 4, Man-made Futures: Design and Technology." Milton Keynes, England: Open University, 1975, pp. 5-6.

A176 "The Shining Ones." Playboy 11 (August):100-101, 108-11, 113-14.

Argosy 25 (December 1964):77-91.

Judith Merril, ed. The Year's Best S-F: 10th Annual Edition. New York: Delacorte, 1965.

In The Wind from the Sun, 1972. A201

Speed and Power, no. 59 (2-9 May 1975), pp. 26-28 (pt. 1); no. 60 (9-16 May 1975), pp. 26-28 (pt. 2); no. 61 (16-23 May 1975), pp. 26-28 (pt. 3).

A177 "Dial 'F.' for Frankenstein." Playboy 12 (January):148-49, 215-16.

Editors of Playboy. The Playboy Book of Science Fiction and Fantasy. Chicago: Playboy Press, 1966, paper.

Editors of Playboy. Last Train to Limbo. Chicago: Playboy Press, 1971, paper.

In The Wind from the Sun, 1972. [Omits internal quotation marks.] A201

1965

A178 An Arthur Clarke Omnibus. London: Sidgwick & Jackson. [Childhood's End, A64; Prelude to Space, A41; Expedition to Earth, A66 (U.K. contents).]

A179 "Maelstrom II." Playboy 12 (April):84, 90, 178, 180.

Retitled "Moon Maelstrom," 1975. A219
Argosy 26 (August 1965):40-54.
Judith Merril, ed. *The Year's Best S-F: 11th Annual Edi-*
    tion. New York: Delacorte, 1966.
Editors of *Playboy*. *The Dead Astronaut*. Chicago: Playboy
    Press, 1971, paper.
In *The Wind from the Sun*, 1972. A201
Leo P. Kelley, ed. *Themes in Science Fiction*. New York:
    McGraw-Hill, 1972, paper.

A180 *Prelude to Mars*. New York: Harcourt, Brace & World. [I.
    "Foreword," C348; *Prelude to Space*, A41; II. "On the
    Light Side": "Big Game Hunt," A100; "Critical Mass," A27;
    "The Ultimate Melody," A102; "Moving Spirit," A104; "The
    Man Who Ploughed the Sea," A105; "Cold War," A106; "What
    Goes Up," A79; "Trouble with the Natives," A83; III. "On
    the Serious Side": "A Walk in the Dark," A38; "The For-
    gotten Enemy," A26; "The Parasite," A58; "The Curse," A65;
    "The Possessed," A56; "The Awakening," A52; "Exile of the
    Eons," A34; "Second Dawn," A47; IV. *The Sands of Mars*,
    A51.]

A181 "The Last Command." *Bizarre Mystery Magazine* 1 (November):
    29-31.

    In *The Wind from the Sun*, 1972. A201

                              1966

A182 *Time Probe: The Sciences in Science Fiction* [anthology].
    New York: Delacorte. [Includes "Introduction: Science
    and Science Fiction," C466, and "Take a Deep Breath,"
    A117.]

    London: Victor Gollancz, 1967.
    New York: Dell, 1967, paper.

A183 "The Light of Darkness." *Playboy* 13 (June):113, 174-76.

    In *The Wind from the Sun*, 1972. A201

A184 "A Recursion in Metastories." *Galaxy Science Fiction* 25
    (October):78-79.

    Retitled "The Longest Science Fiction Story Ever Told,"
        1972. A204

A185 "Playback." *Playboy* 13 (December):220-27.

    In *The Wind from the Sun*, 1972. A201

1967

A186   The Nine Billion Names of God: The Best Short Stories of
          Arthur C. Clarke. New York: Harcourt, Brace & World.
          ["Introduction," C471; "The Nine Billion Names of God,"
          A77; "I Remember Babylon," A144; "Trouble with Time,"
          A164; "Rescue Party," A19; "The Curse," A65; "Summertime
          on Icarus," A160; "Dog Star," A166; "Hide and Seek," A32;
          "Out of the Sun," A135; "The Wall of Darkness," A30; "No
          Morning After," A71; "The Possessed," A56; "Death and the
          Senator," A149; "Who's There?" A139; "Before Eden," A150;
          "Superiority," A48; "A Walk in the Dark," A38; "The Call
          of the Stars," A121; "The Reluctant Orchid," A93; "En-
          counter at Dawn," A143; "If I Forget Thee, Oh Earth. . . ,"
          A49; "Patent Pending," A101; "The Sentinel," A68; "Tran-
          sience," A29; "The Star," A78.]

          New York: Harbrace Paperbound Library, 1971.

A187   "The Cruel Sky." Boy's Life 57 (July):22-23, 49 (pt. 1);
          (August):46-48, 56 (pt. 2).

          In The Wind from the Sun, 1972. A201
          Speed and Power, no. 28 (27 September-4 October 1974),
          pp. 26-28 (pt. 1); no. 29 (4-11 October 1974), pp. 26-
          28 (pt. 2); no. 30 (11-18 October 1974), pp. 26-29 (pt. 3).

1968

A188   2001: A Space Odyssey. New York: New American Library.
          [Based on a screenplay by Stanley Kubrick and Arthur C.
          Clarke. Includes "Foreword," C492.]

          London: Hutchinson, 1968.
          New York: New American Library, 1968, paper.
          London: Arrow, 1968, paper.
          Munich: Max Hueber, 1972, paper. [Abridged by H.G.
             Stenzel.]
          Excerpts [chapters 29 and 33] retitled "Alone in Space,"
             1978. A222
          See also cancelled chapters and commentary, The Lost
             Worlds of 2001, 1972. A200

*A189   "Peak of Promise." Summertime 15 (24 June):12-13 (pt. 1);
          (1 July):1-3 (pt. 2). [Source: ACC.]

          Originally "Sentinel of Eternity," 1951. A44
          Retitled "The Sentinel," 1954. A68

A190   An Arthur C. Clarke Second Omnibus. London: Sidgwick &

Jackson. [A Fall of Moondust, A152; Earthlight, A76; The Sands of Mars, A51 ("The" omitted on dust jacket and fly-leaf, included on pages of text).]

A191 The Lion of Comarre and Against the Fall of Night. New York: Harcourt, Brace & World. ["Introduction," C499; "The Lion of Comarre," A31; Against the Fall of Night, A63.]

       London: Victor Gollancz, 1970.
       London: Corgi, 1972, paper.

A192 "Crusade." In The Farthest Reaches. Edited by Joseph Elder. New York: Trident, pp. 103–108.

       In The Wind from the Sun, 1972. A201

1969

A193 The Space Dreamers. New York: Lancer, paper. [Includes "Foreword," C348.]

A194 "Neutron Tide." Galaxy Science Fiction 30 (May):82–85.

       In The Wind from the Sun, 1972. A201

A195 "Coming Distractions." Penthouse 7 (July):36, 38. [Reviews of nonexistent books.]

       Worm-Runner's Digest 14 (December 1972):56–59.

1971

A196 "Reunion." In Infinity Two. Edited by Robert Hoskins. New York: Lancer, pp. 231–32, paper.

       In The Wind from the Sun, 1972. A201

A197 "Transit of Earth." Playboy 18 (January):109–11, 210, 272–74.

       Editors of Playboy. Transit of Earth. Chicago: Playboy Press, 1971, paper.
       In The Wind from the Sun, 1972. A201
       Donald A. Wollheim, ed. The 1972 Annual World's Best SF. New York: DAW Books, 1972, paper.
       Speed and Power, no. 26 (13–20 September 1974), pp. 26–29 (pt. 1); no. 27 (20–27 September 1974), pp. 26–29 (pt. 2).
       Hugh M. Hefner, ed. Twentieth Anniversary Playboy Reader. [Chicago]: Playboy Press, 1974.
       Mike Ashley, ed. The Best of British SF 2. London: Futura, 1977, paper.

Joseph D. Olander, and Martin Harry Greenberg, eds. <u>Time of Passage</u>. New York: Taplinger, 1978.

A198 "Rescue!" In <u>Time for New Magic</u>. Edited by May Hill Arbuthnot and Mark Taylor. Glenview, Ill.: Scott, Foresman, pp. 232-35.

May Hill Arbuthnot et al., eds. <u>The Arbuthnot Anthology of Children's Literature</u>. 3d ed. Glenview, Ill: Scott, Foresman, 1971.
Excerpt [chapter 4] from <u>Dolphin Island</u>, 1963. A169

A199 "A Meeting with Medusa." <u>Playboy</u> 18 (December):160-64, 270-72, 274-76, 278-80.

Retitled "A Day to Remember" (parts 1-3), A211, and "Journey to Jupiter" (parts 1-4, 7-8 [sic]), A212, 1974.
In <u>The Wind from the Sun</u>, 1972. A201
Terry Carr, ed. <u>The Best Science Fiction of the Year</u>. New York: Ballantine, 1972.
Harry Harrison, and Brian W. Aldiss, eds. <u>The Year's Best Science Fiction #5</u>. London: Sphere, 1972, paper. Slightly revised as <u>Best SF: 1971</u>. New York: G.P. Putnam's Sons, 1972.
In <u>The Best of Arthur C. Clarke</u>, 1973. A209
Isaac Asimov, ed. <u>Nebula Award Stories 8</u>. New York: Harper & Row, 1973.
Frederik Pohl, and Carol Pohl, eds. <u>Jupiter</u>. New York: Ballantine, 1973, paper.
Ben Bova, ed. <u>Aliens</u>. New York: St. Martin's, 1977.

1972

A200 <u>The Lost Worlds of 2001</u>. New York: New American Library, paper. [Includes "The Sentinel," A68; cancelled chapters for <u>2001: A Space Odyssey</u>, A188; nonfictional material, C556-64.]

London: Sidgwick & Jackson, 1972.
London: Sidgwick & Jackson, 1976, paper.
Boston: Gregg Press, 1979. [Includes "Introduction" by Foster Hirsch, D246.]
In <u>The Lost Worlds of 2001/Expedition to Earth</u>, 1980. A226

A201 <u>The Wind from the Sun: Stories of the Space Age</u>. New York: Harcourt Brace Jovanovich. ["Preface," C576; "The Food of the Gods," A175; "Maelstrom II," A179; "The Shining Ones," A176; "The Wind from the Sun," A202; "The Secret," A203; "The Last Command," A181; "Dial F for Frankenstein," A177; "Reunion," A196; "Playback," A185; "The Light of Darkness,"

A184; "The Longest Science-Fiction Story Ever Told," A204;
"Herbert George Morley Roberts Wells, Esq.," C476; "Love
That Universe," A154; "Crusade," A192; "The Cruel Sky,"
A186; "Neutron Tide," A194; "Transit of Earth," A197; "A
Meeting with Medusa," A199.]

London: Victor Gollancz, 1972.
New York: New American Library, 1973, paper.
London: Corgi, 1974, paper.

A202   "The Wind from the Sun." In The Wind from the Sun, pp. 43–
       64. A201

       Originally "The Sunjammer," 1964. A174
       Malcolm Edwards, ed. Constellations. London: Victor
           Gollancz, 1980.

A203   "The Secret." In The Wind from the Sun, pp. 65–70. A201

       Originally "The Secret of the Men in the Moon," 1963. A170
       Arthur Acklye, ed. Far Out. London: Nelson, 1974.

A204   "The Longest Science-Fiction Story Ever Told." In The Wind
       from the Sun, p. 95. A201

       Originally "A Recursion in Metastories," 1966. A184

A205   "When the Twerms Came" [comic strip]. Playboy 19 (May):120–
       21. With Skip Williamson.

       In The View from Serendip, 1977. [Without drawings.]
           C638

A206   Of Time and Stars: The Worlds of Arthur C. Clarke. London:
       Victor Gollancz. ["Introduction" by J.B. Priestley, D133;
       "Foreword" by Clarke, C579; "The Nine Billion Names of
       God," A57; "An Ape about the House," A158; "Green Fingers,"
       A96; "Trouble with the Natives," A83; "Into the Comet,"
       A163; "No Morning After," A71; "If I Forget Thee, Oh
       Earth. . .," A49; "Who's There," A139; "All the Time in
       the World," A53; "Hide and Seek," A32; "Robin Hood, F.R.S.,"
       A95; "The Fires Within," A22; "The Forgotten Enemy," A26;
       "The Reluctant Orchid," A93; "Encounter at Dawn," A143;
       "Security Check," A114; "Feathered Friend," A116; "The
       Sentinel," A68; "Bibliogrpahy," D123.]

       Harmondsworth: Puffin, 1974, paper.

1973

A207   Rendezvous with Rama.   London: Victor Gollancz.

        New York: Harcourt Brace Jovanovich, 1973.
        Galaxy Science Fiction 34 (September 1973):4–75 (pt. 1);
            (October 1973):107–75 (pt. 2).
        Kenneth Bulmer, ed. New Writings in Science Fiction 22.
            London: Sidgwick & Jackson, 1973. [Excerpt, chapter 1.]
        London: Pan, 1974, paper.
        New York: Ballantine, 1974, paper. [Includes "About the
            Author," C603.]
        In Four Great SF Novels, 1978. A221
        London: Oxford University Press, 1979, paper. [Adapted
            by David Fickling.]

*A208   "Twilight in Tibet."   Summertime 20 (2 July):10–12. [Source:
        ACC.]

        Originally "The Nine Billion Names of God," 1953. A57

A209   The Best of Arthur C. Clarke. Edited by Angus Wells. London:
        Sidgwick & Jackson. ["1933: A Science Fiction Odyssey,"
        (listed as "Introduction" on contents page), C597; "Travel
        by Wire!" A8; "Retreat from Earth," A10; "The Awakening,"
        A16; "Whacky," A17; "Castaway," A21; "History Lesson," A28;
        "Hide and Seek," A32; "Second Dawn," A47; "The Sentinel,"
        A68; "The Star," A78; "Refugee," A132; "Venture to the
        Moon," A90; "Into the Comet," A163; "Summertime on Icarus,"
        A160; "Death and the Senator," A149; "Hate," A162; "Sun-
        jammer," A174; "A Meeting with Medusa," A199; "The Science
        Fiction Books of Arthur C. Clarke" by Gerald Bishop, D141.]

        London: Sidgwick & Jackson, 1976–1977, paper. 2 Vols.:
            The Best of Arthur C. Clarke, 1937–1955 (1976). [In-
                cludes "1933: A Science Fiction Odyssey," C597,
                listed as "Preface" on contents page; bibliography
                D141 updated to 1977.]
            The Best of Arthur C. Clarke, 1955–1972 (1977). [In-
                cludes a new "Preface," C657; bibliography, D141,
                updated to 1977.]
        London: Sidgwick & Jackson, 1977. [2 vols; hardbound;
            dust jacket of volume 1 says "1932–1955."]

1974

A210   "Incident on Icarus."   Speed and Power, no. 1 (22–29 March),
        pp. 26–29 (pt. 1); no. 2 (29 March–5 April), pp. 26–29
        (pt. 2).

Originally "The Hottest Piece of Real Estate in the Solar
System," 1960. A147
Retitled "Summertime on Icarus," 1962. A160

A211 "A Day to Remember." Speed and Power, no. 5 (19–26 April),
pp. 26–28 (pt. 1); no. 6 (26 April–3 May), pp. 26–28 (pt.
2); no. 7 (3–10 May), pp. 26–28 (pt. 3).

Originally "A Meeting with Medusa" (sections 1–2), 1971.
A199

A212 "Journey to Jupiter." Speed and Power: "The World of the
Gods," no. 8 (10–17 May), pp. 26–28 (pt. 1); "Voices of
the Deep," no. 9 (17–24 May), pp. 26–28 (pt. 2); "Wheels
of Poseidon," no. 10 (24–31 May), pp. 26–29 (pt. 3);
"Meeting with Medusa," no. 11 (31 May–7 June), pp. 26–28
(pt. 4); "Prime Directive," no. 12 (7–14 June), pp. 26–28
(pt. 7) [sic]; "Between Two Worlds," no. 13 (14–21 June),
pp. 26–27 (pt. 8). [Error in numbering is the magazine's.]

Originally "A Meeting with Medusa", (sections 3–8), 1971.
A199

A213 "Secret of the Sphere." Speed and Power, no. 15 (28 June–5
July), pp. 26–28.

Originally "Retreat from Earth," 1938. [Second half, subtitled.] A10

A214 "The Clouds of Venus." Speed and Power, no. 19 (26 July–2
August), pp. 26–28 (pt. 1); no. 20 (2–9 August), pp. 26–
28 (pt. 2).

Originally "Before Eden," 1961. A150

A215 "Exiles from Earth." Speed and Power, no. 35 (15–22 November),
pp. 26–28.

Originally "If I Forget Thee, Oh Earth. . . ," 1951. A49

1975

A216 Imperial Earth: A Fantasy of Love and Discord. London:
Victor Gollancz. [Includes "Acknowledgements and Notes,"
C620.]

New York: Harcourt Brace Jovanovich, 1976. [Subtitle
deleted, five chapters added, others expanded; "Acknowledgements and Notes," C620, expanded.]
New York: Ballantine, 1976, paper. [Includes "Additional

Note," C629.
London: Pan, 1977, paper.

A217 "Robin Hood on the Moon." Speed and Power, no. 54 (28 March-
4 April), pp. 26-28.

Originally "Saved! . . . by a Bow and Arrow," 1956. A85
Retitled "Robin Hood, F.R.S.," 1956. A95
See "Venture to the Moon," 1956. A90

A218 "An Orchid for Auntie." Speed and Power, no. 52 (14-21 March),
pp. 26-28 (pt. 1); no. 53 (21-28 March), pp. 26-28 (pt. 2).

Originally "The Reluctant Orchid," 1956. A93

A219 "Moon Maelstrom." Speed and Power, no. 23 (23-30 August),
pp. 26-28 (pt. 1); no. 24 (30 August-6 September), pp. 26-
28 (pt. 2); no. 25 (6-13 September), pp. 26-28 (pt. 3).

Originally "Maelstrom II," 1964. A179

1977

A220 "Quarantine." Isaac Asimov's Science Fiction Magazine 1
(Spring):49-50.

George Scithers, ed. Asimov's Choice: Astronauts and
Androids. New York: Davis Publications, 1977, paper.
George Scithers, ed. Isaac Asimov's Masters of Science
Fiction. New York: Dial, 1978.
Same as Isaac Asimov's Science Fiction Anthology. Vol.
1. New York: Dell, 1978, paper.

1978

A221 Four Great SF Novels. London: Victor Gollancz. [The City
and the Stars, A81; The Deep Range, A112; A Fall of Moondust, A152; Rendezvous with Rama, A207.]

A222 "Alone in Space." In Alone. Edited by Francesca Greenoak.
London: Ward Lock Educational, pp. 25-27, paper.

Excerpt [chapters 29 and 33] from 2001: A Space Odyssey,
1968. A188

1979

A223 "The Fountains of Paradise." Playboy 26 (January):146-48,
150, 168, 228, 230, 359-60, 362, 365-66, 368-70 (pt. 1);

(February):116-17, 124, 178, 180-87 (pt. 2).

Excerpt [chapters 2, 4-5, 7, 9-10, 13, 15, 17-18, 43-47, 49, 51-57] from The Fountains of Paradise, A224.

A224   The Fountains of Paradise. London: Victor Gollancz. [Includes "Foreword," C677, and "Sources and Acknowledgements," C678.]

New York: Harcourt Brace Jovanovich, 1979. ["Foreword," C677, retitled "Preface," C679.]
London: Pan, 1980, paper.
New York: Ballantine, 1980, paper.
Excerpt, 1979. A223

1980

A225   The Sands of Mars/Prelude to Space. London: New English Library, paper. [The Sands of Mars, A51; Prelude to Space, A41.]

A226   The Lost Worlds of 2001/Expedition to Earth. London: New English Library, paper. [The Lost Worlds of 2001, A200; Expedition to Earth, A66 (U.K. contents, omits contents page).]

Part B: Miscellaneous Media

1934

B1 "Jule Gets His." [Clericus, pseud.]. Huish Magazine 23
    (Summer):41-43. Filmscript.

1935

B2 "The Magic Potion." [DIL, pseud.; partly by Clarke.] Huish
    Magazine 24 (Autumn):46-51. Play.

1938

B3 "Prelude to the Conquest of Space." [Bylined Arthur
    ("Ego") Clarke.] Novae Terrae [fanzine] 2 (April):20.
    Poem.

1939

*B4 "The Twilight of the Sun." Fantast 1 (April): page unknown.
    Poem. [Source: SM.]

1951

*B5 "All the Time in the World," Tales of Tomorrow. Foley-Gordon
    Productions (13 June, ABC Television Network). [Clarke
    script based on A52. Source: ACC, industry sources;
    actual script or video version not seen.]

1960

B6 Beneath the Seas of Ceylon. Colombo, Ceylon: [Clarke-
    Wilson Associates]. Documentary film for National Tea
    Board of Ceylon.

1963

*B7   Profiles of the Future. TB00153 (6 discs, narrated by Robert
       Donley), recorded and distributed by American Foundation
       for the Blind (New York). [Source: LC.]

1964

*B8   The Treasure of the Great Reef. TB00550 (5 discs, narrated by
       Michael Horgan), recorded and distributed by the American
       Foundation for the Blind (New York). [Source: LC.]

1965

*B9   Prelude to Mars. TB00986 (15 discs, narrated by Robert Donley
       and Robert Readick), recorded and distributed by American
       Foundation for the Blind (New York). [Source: LC.]

B10   "2001: A Space Odyssey." 251-page filmscript by Stanley
       Kubrick and Arthur C. Clarke. [Copy at Theater Arts
       Library, University of California, Los Angeles, has pages
       dated 4 October to 14 December 1965; stamped "received" by
       Metro-Goldwyn-Mayer, 3 January 1966.]

1966

*B11 "The Shining Ones." In The Year's Best Science Fiction 1966.
       Edited by Judith Merril. TB012114 (10 discs, narrated by
       Robert Donley, Alan Hewitt, Rose Norman, Kermit Murdock,
       Guy Sorel, and Eugenia Rawls), recorded and distributed
       by the American Foundation for the Blind (New York).
       [Source: LC.]

B12   "2001: A Space Odyssey." 71-page filmscript ("cutting con-
       tinuity") by Stanley Kubrick and Arthur C. Clarke. [Un-
       dated copy at Margaret Herrick Library of the Academy of
       Motion Picture Arts and Sciences, Beverly Hills, Calif.]

*B13 2001: A Space Odyssey. New York: Tom Craven Film Corpora-
       tion. Documentary film for Metro-Goldwyn-Mayer on the
       making of the feature film (B19). [Source: TC.]

*B14 Voices from the Sky. TB01118 (6 discs, narrated by Robert
       Donley), recorded and distributed by the American Founda-
       tion for the Blind (New York). [Source: LC.]

1967

B15   "Dial 'F' for Frankenstein" and "I Remember Babylon." In The
       Playboy Book of Fantasy and Science Fiction. TB01524 (9
       discs, narrated by Staats Cotsworth), recorded and dis-
       tributed by the American Foundation for the Blind (New
       York).

1968

*B16 Interview by Dick Strout. Recorded for Metro-Goldwyn-Mayer
       film promotion. [Source: 2001: A Space Odyssey Ex-
       hibitors' Campaign Book (MGM, 1969).]

*B17 The Promise of Space. New York: Tom Craven Film Corporation.
       60-minute documentary film for Spaceward Corporation.
       [Source: TC.]

 B18 "The Songs of Distant Earth." 57-page screenplay by Robert
       Temple. [Copy at home of Fred Clarke, Bishop's Lydeard,
       Taunton, Somerset, England.]

 B19 2001: A Space Odyssey. Culver City, Calif.: Metro-Goldwyn-
       Mayer [shot in England]. 160-minute feature film by
       Stanley Kubrick, based on screenplay by Stanley Kubrick
       and Arthur C. Clarke.

B19a 2001 . . . And Even Beyond (interview). Los Angeles: Pacifica
       Tape Library. BB2020, 32-minute audio cassette (taped
       20 May 1968 for broadcast over Pacifica Radio Network).
       Interviewer: Poul Anderson.

1969

*B20 "Apollo." 34-page screenplay. [Copy at Mugar Memorial
       Library, Boston University.] [Source: ML.]

*B21 Space: Communications. New York: Tom Craven Film Corpora-
       tion. 30-minute documentary for Spaceward Corporation.
       [Source: TC.]

*B22 Space: Earth Resources. New York: Tom Craven Film Corpora-
       tion. 30-minute documentary film for Spaceward Corporation.
       [Source: TC.]

*B23 Space: Education. New York: Tom Craven Film Corporation.

30-minute documentary film for Spaceward Corporation.
[Source: TC.]

1970

B24 2001 Revisited: Interview with Arthur C. Clarke. North
     Hollywood, Calif.: Center for Cassette Studies. CBC956,
     60-minute audio cassette. Interviewer: Stephen Banker.

B25 The Unexplained.(introduction). New York: Encyclopedia
     Britannica Films. 56-minute documentary film.

1971

*B26 "The Nine Billion Names of God." In The Science Fiction Hall
      of Fame. [Vol. 1.] Edited by Robert Silverberg. TB03713
      (20 discs, narrated by Robert Donley), recorded and dis-
      tributed by the American Foundation for the Blind (New
      York). [Source: LC.]

*B27 The Other Side of the Sky. CB00295 (5 cassettes, narrated by
      Viviette Rifki), recorded by Johanna Bureau for the Blind
      and Physically Handicapped (Chicago), distributed by
      Certron Corporation (Anaheim, Calif.). [Source: LC.]

*B28 "The Star." In Science Fiction for People Who Hate Science
      Fiction. Edited by Terry Carr. CB00200 (1 cassette,
      narrated by Phyllis Dorflinger), recorded by Houston Taping
      for the Blind, distributed by the American Foundation for
      the Blind (New York). [Source: LC.]

      Re-recorded in June 1979 by Halvorson Associates (Washing-
      ton, D.C.), RC14669.

*B29 Tales of Ten Worlds. CB00458 (6 cassettes, narrated by Carl
      Hess), recorded by Houston Taping for the Blind [mailed to
      Library of Congress 23 December], distributed by Certron
      Corporation (Anaheim, Calif.). [Source: LC.]

1972

*B30 Arthur C. Clarke: The 2001 Ideas of the Prophet of the Space
      Age. Leeds, England: Yorkshire Television. Documentary
      film for television by Michael Deakin. [Source: FC.]

*B31 Indian Ocean Adventure. TB04536 (2 discs, narrated by Lou
      Harpenau), recorded and distributed by the American Print-
      ing House for the Blind (Louisville, Ky.). [Source: LC.]

1973

*B32   Childhood's End. CB00835 (6 cassettes, narrated by Hazel
          Kiley), recorded by Houston Taping for the Blind [mailed
          to Library of Congress, 27 February], distributed by the
          American Printing House for the Blind (Louisville, Ky.).
          [Source: LC.]

 B33   The City and the Stars. RD06725 (4 discs, narrated by Buckley
          Kozlow), recorded [September] and distributed by the Amer-
          ican Foundation for the Blind (New York).

 B34   Earthlight. RD06393 (2 discs, narrated by Tom Martin), re-
          corded [May] and distributed by the American Foundation
          for the Blind (New York).

 B35   A Fall of Moondust. RD06232 (3 discs, narrated by Robert
          Donley), recorded and distributed by the American Founda-
          tion for the Blind (New York).

 B36   "A Fall of Moondust." 379-page screenplay, based on A151, by
          Robert Temple. 2 vols. [Copy at home of Fred Clarke,
          Bishop's Lydeard, Taunton, Somerset, England.]

 B37   Rendezvous With Rama. RD06813 (3 discs, narrated by Earle
          Hyman), recorded [December] and distributed by the American
          Foundation for the Blind (New York).

*B38   Report on Planet Three. CBA00675 (3 cassettes, narrated by
          Jo Moritz), recorded by Dallas Taping for the Blind, dis-
          tributed by Halvorson Associates (Washington, D.C.).
          [Source: LC.]

          Re-recorded in 1973 [mailed to Library of Congress 19
             November] for the Division for the Blind and Physically
             Handicapped, Library of Congress, RC09395.

1974

 B39   "Introducing Isaac Asimov." In Edited Highlights of a Lecture
          Given by Isaac Asimov at the Commonwealth Hall (London,
          June 14, 1974). BMO-1 (audiocassette) recorded and dis-
          tributed by British Mensa (Wolverhampton, England).

          Magazine of Fantasy and Science Fiction 48 (January 1975):
             113-16. C613
          In The View from Serendip, 1977. C638

1975

B40 The Lost Worlds of 2001. RC07786 (3 cassettes, narrated by
       Peter Griffin Case), recorded for the Division of the
       Blind and Physically Handicapped, Library of Congress,
       distributed by Cartridge Control Corporation (Atlanta, Ga.).

1976

B41 Arthur C. Clarke Reads from His "2001: A Space Odyssey."
       [Chapters 37-47.] TC1504 (disc), CDL1504 (cassette), re-
       corded and distributed by Caedmon (New York). [Liner notes
       from "Christmas, Shepperton, 1972 (C558).]

B42 Arthur Clarke [sic]. New York: Tom Craven Film Corporation.
       Program introduction and conclusion, 10-second introduc-
       tions to six commercials, American Telephone and Telegraph
       presentation of The Man in the Iron Mask. Three-minute
       spot incorporated into B47.

B43 Imperial Earth. RC09949 (2 cassettes, narrated by Roger
       Brown), recorded [November] by the American Foundation for
       the Blind (New York), distributed by Magnetix (Winter
       Garden, Fla.).

B44 Reach for Tomorrow. RC10817 (1 cassette, narrated by Billie
       Shepard), recorded [November] by Dallas Taping for the
       Blind, distributed by Ampex (Redwood City, Calif.).

B45 2001: A Space Odyssey. New York: Marvel Comics. Comic
       book adaptation by Jack Kirby.

B46 2001: A Space Odyssey.. New York: Marvel Comics. Comic
       book series (10 issues, 1976-1977, primarily concerned
       with film's characters from prehistoric times).

1977

*B47 The Making of 2076. New York: Tom Craven Film Corporation.
       Documentary film about making Arthur Clarke (B42).
       [Source: TC.]

*B48 Rescue Party. Santa Monica, Calif.: BFA Educational Media.
       Film (16 mm.) and videocassette, based on A18. [Source:
       BFA.]

B49 "The Sentinel." In Space Odysseys: A New Look at Yester-
       day's Futures. Edited by Brian W. Aldiss. RD10233 (4
       discs, narrated by John Polk, recorded [September] and

distributed by the American Printing House for the Blind
(Louisville, Ky.).

1978

B50   "Transit of Earth"--"The Nine Billion Names of God" and "The
      Star" Read by the Author, Arthur C. Clarke. TC1566 (disc),
      CDL1566 (cassette), recorded and distributed by Caedmon
      (New York). [Liner notes by Clarke (C672), Ward Botsford
      (D223).]

1979

B51   "Childhood's End" Excerpts Read by the Author, Arthur C.
      Clarke. [Chapters 1, 4-5, 8, 14, 16, 18, 20, 21, 24.]
      TC1614 (disc), CDL1614 (cassette), recorded and distributed
      by Caedmon (New York). [Liner notes by Ward Botsford
      (D223, uncredited), Isaac Asimov (D243).]

B52   Childhood's End. 8 cassettes, narrated by Dan Lazar, recorded
      and distributed by Books on Tape (Newport Beach, Calif.).

B53   Earthlight. 6 cassettes, narrated by Dan Lazar, recorded and
      distributed by Books on Tape (Newport Beach, Calif.).

B54   The Fountains of Paradise. RC12962 (2 cassettes, narrated by
      Patrick Horgan), recorded [June] and distributed by the
      American Foundation for the Blind (New York).

B55   "Fountains of Paradise" [sic] Read by the Author, Arthur C.
      Clarke. [Chapters 1, 4, 8, 10, 13, 26, 47, 50-52, 57.]
      TC1606 (disc), CDL1606 (cassette), recorded and distributed
      by Caedmon (New York). [Liner notes by Ward Botsford
      (D223, uncredited), Buckminster Fuller (D246).]

B56   "A Meeting with Medusa." In Aliens: Three Novellas. Edited
      by Ben Bova. RC12633 (1 cassette, narrated by Robert
      Donley), recorded [April] and distributed by the American
      Foundation for the Blind (New York).

*B57 Rendezvous With Rama. 3 cassettes, narrated by Paul Knight,
      recorded and distributed by the Connecticut State Library
      for the Blind and Physically Handicapped (Hartford).
      [Source: OCLC.]

B58   "Transit of Earth." In Time of Passage. Edited by Joseph D.
      Olander and Martin Harry Greenberg. RD13159 (4 discs, nar-
      rated by Roy Ayers), recorded [July] and distributed by

55

the American Printing House for the Blind (Louisville, Ky.).

*B59   2001: A Space Odyssey. 3 cassettes, narrated by William
        Barry, recorded and distributed by the Connecticut State
        Library for the Blind and Physically Handicapped (Hartford).
        [Source: OCLC.]

                                1980

B60   Across the Sea of Stars. 8 cassettes, narrated by Dan Lazar,
       recorded and distributed by Books on Tape (Newport Beach,
       Calif.).

B61   Arthur C. Clarke Reads the Arthur C. Clarke Soundbook. No.
       121 (4 discs or cassettes [B41, B50, B51, B55]), recorded
       and distributed by Caedmon (New York).

B62   Arthur C. Clarke's Mysterious World. Leeds, England: York-
       shire Television. 13 one-hour television programs, intro-
       ductions and afterwords. [Source: FC.]

B63   The Deep Range. Eight cassettes, narrated by Dan Lazar,
       recorded and distributed by Books on Tape (Newport Beach,
       Calif.).

B64   The Other Side of the Sky. RC14532 (1 cassette, narrated by
       Johnathan Farwell), recorded [January] and distributed by
       American Foundation for the Blind (New York).

B65   Rendezvous With Rama. 8 cassettes, narrated by Dan Lazar,
       recorded and distributed by Books on Tape (Newport Beach,
       Calif.).

*B66   Sri Lanka: Past, Present and People (introduction). New
       York: Tom Craven Film Corporation. Documentary film for
       the United Nations Family Planning Agency. [Source: TC.]

                              Undated

B67   "The Road Between the Worlds." 50-page filmscript. [Copy at
       home of Fred Clarke, Bishop's Lydeard, Taunton, Somerset,
       England.]

Part C: Nonfiction

1932

C1 Editorial Committee. <u>Huish Magazine</u> 21, no. 3 (Autumn 1932)-
    25, no. 2 (Summer 1936). Sub-Editor, 24, no. 3 (Autumn
    1935)-25, no. 2 (Summer 1936).

1933

C2 "The Jon Bloc Soc." [Clericus, pseud.]. <u>Huish Magazine</u> 22
    (Christmas):41-42. [Burlesques regular report of John
    Locke Society, school intellectual forum.]

1934

C3 "Octogenarian Observations." [Clericus, pseud.]. <u>Huish Maga-
    zine</u> 23 (Spring):22-23. [Probably fictitious interview
    with old-timers concerning lapsed school traditions.]

C4 "Interviews with Celebrities, VI." <u>Huish Magazine</u> 24 (Spring):
    32-34. [Interview of Clarke (alias Professor "Archie"
    Larke, M.D., A.S.S.) by AGER, pseud. for Richard H. Mead.]

C5 "Answers to Correspondents." [Clericus, pseud.]. <u>Huish Maga-
    zine</u> 23 (Summer):44-45. [Column of replies to probably
    fictitious letters of inquiry regarding moustaches, ink-
    stains, matrimony, and antiquity.]

C6 "French Without Tears." [Clericus, pseud.]. <u>Huish Magazine</u>
    23 (Summer):47-48.

C7 "Letters to the Editor." [Batsin Belphry, pseud.]. <u>Huish
    Magazine</u> 23 (Autumn):29.

C8 "Musical Interlude." [Clericus, pseud.]. <u>Huish Magazine</u> 23
    (Autumn):33-34.

C9   "The Technical Institute." [Clericus, pseud.]. Huish Maga-
     zine 23 (Autumn):33-34.

     Huish Magazine 52 (Summer 1967):23-25.

                              1935

C10 "Brendon House." Bylined A.C. Clarke. ["House Notes" sec-
     tion]. Huish Magazine 24 (Spring):3. With R.W. Small.

C11 "Brendon House." Bylined A.C. Clarke. ["House Notes" sec-
     tion]. Huish Magazine 24 (Summer):4. With R.W. Small.

C12 "Mars." IDA and Victoria Magazine 21 (July):147-52. [For
     circulation among the employees of F.B. & Co.]

C13 "Brendon House." Bylined A.C. Clarke. ["House Notes" sec-
     tion]. Huish Magazine 24 (Autumn):5-6. With R.B. Canever.

C14 "Huish and Hollywood." [Clericus, pseud.]. Huish Magazine
     24 (Autumn):32-34.

C15 "Our Noble Heritage." [ARCH, pseud.]. Huish Magazine 24
     (Autumn):39-41.

                              1936

C16 "The Ciné Club." Huish Magazine 25 (Spring):4.

C17 "Brendon." Bylined A.C. Clarke. ["House Notes" section].
     Huish Magazine 25 (Spring):11. With R.B. Canever.

C18 "Further Exploits of Huish Films, Inc." [Clericus, pseud.].
     Huish Magazine 25 (Spring):46-47.

C19 "Interviews with Notorieties--No. 1." [Ego, pseud.]. Huish
     Magazine 25 (Spring):47-50.

C20 "In Darkest Somerset." [Clericus, pseud.]. Huish Magazine
     25 (Summer):41-43.

                              1937

*C21 Associate [Editor]. Novae Terrae [fanzine], 1937-1939
     [precise issues undetermined, 2:12 (June 1938) verified].

C22 "Science Fiction--Past, Present, and Future." Novae Terrae
     [fanzine] 2 (June Supplement):9-12.

C23 "Zero to Eighty." British Scientifiction Fantasy Review [fan-
     zine] 1 (October):5.

     Review of Zero to Eighty by Akkad Pseudoman [E.F. Northrup].

C24 "Into Space." Checquer Board [The Gazette of the Exchecquer
     and Audit Department Association] 13 (October):17-19.

C25 "Science Fiction v. Mr. Youd." Novae Terrae [fanzine] 2
     (November):13-15.

C26 "Technicalities." Journal of the British Interplanetary
     Society 4 (December):8-15. [Report of the Technical com-
     mittee, bylined by R.A. Smith, A. Janser, E. Ross, H.
     Bramhill and A.C. Clarke, under the direction of J.H.
     Edwards.] See also C33 and C40.

C27 Introduction to "Astronautics at the 'Palais de la Découverte,'"
     by Robert Lencement. Journal of the British Interplanetary
     Society 4 (December):20.

                              1938

C28 "Science Fiction for Beginners." British Scientifiction
     Fantasy Review [fanzine] 1 (January):4, 6.

C29 "The Fantastic Muse." Novae Terrae [fanzine] 2 (May):18-20.

C30 "Arthur C. Clarke." Novae Terrae [fanzine] 2 (June):14-17.
     [Interview by William F. Temple, 3d in series, "The British
     Fan in his Natural Habitat."]

C31 "Man's Empire of Tomorrow." Tales of Wonder and Super-
     Science 5 (Winter):74-79.

                              1939

C32 Editor. Bulletin of the British Interplanetary Society 3
     (1939).

C33 "The B.I.S. Technical Report." [Unsigned.] Journal of the
     British Interplanetary Society 5 (January)17-21. See also
     C26 and C40.

C34 "An Elementary Mathematical Approach to Astronautics." Jour-
     nal of the British Interplanetary Society 5 (January):26-28.

C35 "The British Fan, #7, William F. Temple." Novae Terrae [fan-
     zine] 3 (January):19-21.

Cosmag [fanzine] 3 (September 1952):7-8.

C36 Associate [Editor]. New Worlds [fanzine] 1, nos. 2-3 (April,
     May). Assistant [Editor]. 1, no. 4 (August).

C37 "The Interplanetary Approach." Bulletin of the British Inter-
     planetary Society 3 (April):3-5.

C38 "Trade Follows the Rocket." [Unsigned.] Bulletin of the
     British Interplanetary Society 3 (April):6-9. [Text of
     April 1938 lecture.]

C39 "We Can Rocket to the Moon--Now!" Tales of Wonder, no. 7
     (Summer), pp. 84-88.

C40 "Report of the Technical Committee." [Unsigned.] Journal of
     the British Interplanetary Society 5 (July):17-20. See
     also C26 and C33.

C41 "Reverie." New Worlds [fanzine] 1 (Autumn):10-11.

                               1940

C42 "How to Build a Spaceship." Futurian [fanzine] 3 (Winter):
     2-5.

C43 "Letters to the Secretary of an Interplanetary Society."
     [Bylined Arthur Ego Clarke.] Fantast [fanzine] 2 (March):
     17.

                               1941

C44 "Disney on the Screen." Urania [Journal of the Junior
     Astronomical Association], November, pp. 4-6. [Review of
     the "Rite of Spring" segment of the film Fantasia by Walt
     Disney.]

                               1942

C45 "Bicarbonate for Eric." Fantast [fanzine] 3 (April):6-7.

C46 "More Television Waveforms." Electronic Engineering 15
     (November):245-47.

1944

C47 "Linearity Circuits." Wireless Engineer 21 (June):256-66.

C48 "Dunsany--Lord of Fantasy." Futurian War Digest [fanzine] 4
(December):[2-4. (Originally written 19 July 1942; 1944
epilogue added.)]

C49 "Rockets: The Future of Travel Beyond the Stratosphere."
Futurian War Digest [fanzine] 4 (December):[7-8]. [Review
of Rockets: The Future of Travel Beyond the Stratosphere
by Willy Ley.]

1945

C50 "The Ideal Astronautical Society." [Bylined Arthur Clark.]
Spacewards [Official Journal of the Combined British
Astronautical Societies] 6 (January):2-5.

C51 "V2 for Ionospheric Research?" Wireless World 52 (February):
58. [Letter, first mention in print of "stationary"
satellites.]

C52 "The Coming Age of Rocket Power." [Bylined Arthur Clarke.]
Spacewards 6 (April-July):7-8. [Review of The Coming Age
of Rocket Power by G. Edward Pendray.]

C53 "The Astronomer's New Weapons: Electronic Aids to Navigation."
Journal of the British Astronomical Association 55
(August):143-47 (discussion, p. 137).

C54 "Extra-Terrestrial Relays." Wireless World 51 (October):305-8.

In Voices from the Sky, 1965. [As Appendix, omits hyphen
in title.] C446
Offprint distributed at speaking engagements, no date indicated.

1946

C55 "Radar Echoes from the Moon." [Bylined A.C. Clarke.]
Journal of the British Astronomical Association 56 (March):
57.

C56 "The Rocket and the Future of Warfare." RAF Quarterly and
Empire Forces Journal 17 (March):61-69. [Prize-winning
essay.]

C57 "Radar and Astronomy." Bulletin of the British Interplanetary
Society [n.s.] 1 (July):6-7.

C58   "Approach by Ground Control." [Unsigned.] Flight 50 (11
        July):47–49.

C59   "Luminous Tube Lighting." [Bylined A.C. Clarke.] Chemistry
        and Industry 24 (28 September):359. [Review of Luminous
        Tube Lighting by H(enry) A(rthur) Miller.]

C60   "Electron Optics and the Electron Microscope." [Bylined
        A.C. Clarke.] Chemistry and Industry 24 (5 October):366.
        [Review of Electron Optics and the Electron Microscope by
        V(ladimir) K(osma) Zworykin et al.]

C61   "Radio Propagation and the Sun." Journal of the British
        Astronomical Association 56 (October):149.

C62   "Astronomical Radar: Some Future Possibilities." Wireless
        World 52 (October):321–23.

C63   "By Rocket to the Moon." Star, 18 October, p. 9.

C64   "The Challenge of the Spaceship." Journal of the British
        Interplanetary Society 6 (December):66–78 (discussion, pp.
        79–81).

        Retitled "Space Travel and Human Affairs," 1961. [Ex-
            cerpt.] C339
        Retitled "Spaceships," 1979. [Condensed.] C681
        Impact of Science on Society 4 (Spring 1953):15–28. [Re-
            vised.]
        UNESCO Courier 10 (November 1957):22–26. [Revised text.]
        In The Challenge of the Spaceship, 1959. [Revised text.]
            C302
        UNESCO Courier 22 (August 1969):25–28. [Revised text.]

                                1947

C65   "Rockets and Orbits." Bulletin of the British Interplanetary
        Society 2 (January):14.

C66   "Out of this World." Everywoman 9 (January):27.

C67   "Principles of Rocket Flight." Aeroplane 72: "The Laws of
        Rocket Motion," (3 January):14–16 (pt. 1); "Rocket Flight
        in Space," (10 January):48–50 (pt. 2).

C68   "First Men on the Moon." Star, 30 January, p. 6.

        English Digest 24 (June 1947):66–67. [Condensed.]

C69   "Into Space." Air Mail [The Official Organ of the RAFA],
        February, pp. 19, 21.

C70   "Astronautics and Poetry." <u>Bulletin of the British Inter-</u>
       <u>planetary Society</u> 2 (February):21-24.

       In <u>The Coming of the Space Age</u>, 1967.   C473

C71   "Moon Rocket." [Bylined A.C. Clarke.] <u>Bulletin of the</u>
       <u>British Interplanetary Society</u> 2 (February):38. [Review
       of <u>Moon Rocket</u> by Arthur Wilcox.]

C72   "Astronautics for the Millions." <u>Fantasy Review</u> [fanzine] 1
       (February-March):14. [Review of <u>Moon Rocket</u> by Arthur
       Wilcox and <u>Dawn of the Space Age</u> by Harry Harper.]

C73   Untitled brief questions, comments, discussion on various
       papers and talks at association meetings, 1947-1959. <u>Jour-</u>
       <u>nal of the British Astronomical Association</u> 57 (April):164-
       65; 58 (April 1948):90-91; (May 1949):119; (August 1948):
       203-4; 59 (February 1949):106; (April 1949):144-45; (May
       1949):172; (July 1949):198; (October 1949):244; 60 (January
       1950):46; (February 1950):70, 76; (May 1950):161; (July
       1950):186; 61 (January 1951):38; (February 1951):68;
       (March 1951):93, 96, 99; (April 1951):124; (July 1951):176,
       178, 184; 62 (February 1952):98-99, 122; (March 1952):134;
       (April 1952):166-67; 63 (December 1952):32; (February 1953):
       101; (March 1953):136, 139; (April 1953):175; 64 (December
       1953):21; (January 1954):61-62; (February 1954):113;
       (March 1954):154; 69 (October 1959):258.

C74   "Champion of Space-Flight." <u>Fantasy Review</u> [fanzine] 1
       (April-May):7. [Interview by Thomas Sheridan (pseud. for
       Walter Gillings).]

C75   "Atomic Whodunit." <u>Fantasy Review</u> [fanzine] 1 (April-May):10.
       [Review of <u>The Murder of the U.S.A.</u> by Will F. Jenkins.]

C76   "A Universal Escape-Velocity Mass-Ratio Chart." <u>Bulletin of</u>
       <u>the British Interplanetary Society</u> 2 (May):72-73.

C77   "Rockets and Space Travel." [Bylined A.C. Clarke.]
       <u>Bulletin of the British Interplanetary Society</u> 2 (May):77-
       78. [Review of <u>Rockets and Space Travel: The Future of</u>
       <u>Travel Beyond the Stratosphere</u> by Willy Ley.]

C78   "Rockets ,and Space Travel." [Bylined A.C.C.] <u>Aeroplane</u>
       72(23 May):549. [Review of <u>Rockets and Space Travel:</u>
       <u>The Future of Travel Beyond the Stratosphere</u> by Willy Ley.]

C79   "Chairman's Address." <u>Annual Report of the British Inter-</u>
       <u>planetary Society</u> (1946-1947), pp. 4-7. [Pagination dis-
       tinct, bound with the <u>Journal</u> and <u>Bulletin</u> of the B.I.S.,
       issued in September.]

C80 "Exploration of Moon and Planets." London Calling [Journal of
     the British Broadcasting Corporation], no. 419 (2 October),
     p. 12. [Text of a broadcast, no. 5 in series, "The World
     Has Wings."]

C81 "Stationary Orbits." [Bylined A.C. Clarke.] Journal of
     the British Astronomical Association 57 (December):232-37
     (discussion, pp. 220-21).

                              1948

C82 "The Interplanetary Project." [Bylined A.C. Clarke, formal
     response.] Journal of the British Interplanetary Society 7
     (January):36-37. [Review of "The Interplanetary Project"
     by A. V(alentine) Cleaver, Journal of the British Inter-
     planetary Society 7 (January):21-28.]

C83 "A Walk on the Moon." Everywoman 9 (March):13.

C84 "Electronics and Space-Flight." Journal of the British Inter-
     planetary Society 7 (March):49-69.

C85 "Rocket Exploration." Endeavour 7 (April):70-74.

     Retitled "Rocket to the Moon," 1948. [Condensed.] C90

C86 "A Link with Jeffries: Unpublished Letters Written When He
     Was Engaged on 'Red Deer.'" Field 191 (May):494.

C87 "The Coming Age of Rocket Power." [Bylined A.C.C.]
     Journal of the British Interplanetary Society 7 (May):130-
     31. [Review of The Coming Age of Rocket Power (rev. ed.)
     by G. Edward Pendray.]

C88 "The Problem of Dr. Campbell." [Bylined A.C. Clarke.]
     Journal of the British Interplanetary Society 7 (September):
     195-97.

C89 "Astronomie." Journal of the British Interplanetary Society
     7 (November):249-50. [Review of Astronomie by Lucien
     Rudaux and G. de Vaucouleurs.]

*C90 "Rocket to the Moon." Thinker's Digest, Winter, pp. 19-22.
     [Condensed.] [Source: ACC.]

     Originally "Rocket Exploration," 1948. C85

1949

C91   Assistant Editor. <u>Science Abstracts</u> 52 (1949). [Listed as
      Abstractor for volumes 53 (1950) and 54 (1951), but no
      specific abstracts credited.]

C92   "Infared Image Tubes." <u>Journal of the British Astronomical
      Association</u> 59 (February):106.

C93   "Morphological Astronomy." [Bylined A.C. Clarke.] <u>Journal
      of the British Astronomical Association</u> 59 (February):110-
      11. [Review of "Morphological Astronomy" (lecture) by
      Fritz Zwicky from <u>Observatory</u> 8 (August 1948):121-43.]

C94   "The Lackeys of Wall Street." <u>Fantasy Review</u> [fanzine] 3
      (February-March):2-3. [Defense of science fiction against
      Victor Bulkhovitinov and Vassilij Zakhartchenko. "The
      World of Nightmare Fantasies." <u>Literaturnaya Gazyeta</u>.
      Condensed as "Science Fiction--The World's Nightmare."
      <u>Fantasy Review</u> [fanzine] 2 (December 1948-January 1949):
      2-4.

C95   "The Danger of Damage by Meteors." [Bylined A.C.C.]
      <u>Journal of the British Astronomical Association</u> 59 (March):
      134-35. [Review of "Probability that a Meteor will Hit or
      Penetrate a Body Situated in the Vicinity of the Earth" by
      George Grimm(ing)er, <u>Journal of Applied Physics</u> 19 (October
      1948):947-56. Title given by Clarke as "The Probability
      that a Meteor Will Hit or Penetrate a Body in the Vicinity
      of Earth."]

C96   "Diurnal Variations of Meteor Trails." [Bylined A.C.C.]
      <u>Journal of the British Astronomical Association</u> 59 (March):
      135. [Review of "Diurnal Variations of Meteors Trails"
      (letter) by Charles A. Little, <u>Physical Review</u> 74 (15
      December 1948):1875-76.]

C97   "The Dynamics of Space-Flight." <u>Journal of the British Inter-
      planetary Society</u> 8 (March):71-84.

      <u>Journal of the Institute of Navigation</u> [Royal Geographic
         Society] 3 (October 1950):357-64. [Revised.]
      <u>Rosicrucian Digest</u> 29 (May 1951):166-68 (pt. 1); (June
         1951):207-10 (pt. 2). [Revised text.]
      L[eonard] J[ames] Carter, ed. <u>Realities of Space Travel:
      Selected Papers of the British Interplanetary Society</u>.
      London: Putnam's, 1957

C98   "The Radio Telescope." [Bylined A.C. Clarke.] <u>Journal of

the British Astronomical Association 59 (April):156–59
(discussion, pp. 146–48).

C99   "The Shape of Ships to Come." New Worlds 2 (April):40–42.

C100 "Principles and Methods of Telemetering." [Bylined A.C.C.]
      Journal of the British Interplanetary Society 8 (May):130.
      [Review of Principles and Methods of Telemetering by Perry
      A. Borden and Gustave M. Thyness.]

C101 "Radio Transmission from the Moon." [Bylined A.C. Clarke.]
      Journal of the British Astronomical Association 59 (July):
      175 [includes discussion].

C102 "The Correlation of Radar and Visual Observation of Meteors."
      [Bylined A.C. Clarke.] Journal of the British Astronomi-
      cal Association 59 (July):206. [Review of "Three-Station
      Radar and Visual Triangulation of Meteors" by Peter M.
      Millman and D.W.R. McKinley, Sky and Telescope 8 (March
      1949):114–16. (Clarke's citation incomplete.)]

C103 "Meteors as a Danger to Space Flight." Journal of the British
      Interplanetary Society 8 (July):157–62.

C104 "Voyages to the Moon." [Bylined A.C.C.] Journal of the
      British Interplanetary Society 8 (September)207–9. [Re-
      view of Voyages to the Moon by Marjorie Hope Nicolson.]

      Fantasy Advertiser [fanzine], January 1950, pp. 14–15.

C105 "You're on the Glide Path––I Think." [Bylined A.C.C.]
      Aeroplane 77 (23 September):441–42.

      IEEE Transactions on Aerospace and Navigational Electronics
      vol. ANE–10 (June 1963):90–93.

C106 "The Existence of a Lunar Atmosphere." Journal of the British
      Astronomical Association 59 (October):244. [Review of
      Y.N. Lipski, "The Existence of a Lunar Atmosphere."
      Doklady of the U.S.S.R. Academy of Science 65 (April 1949):
      465–68.]

C107 "The Conquest of Space." Journal of the British Astronomical
      Association 60 (December):39. [Review of The Conquest of
      Space by Willy Ley and Chesley Bonestell.]

C108 "Guided Missiles." [Bylined A.C.C.] Aeroplane 77 (16
      December):825. [Review of Guided Missiles by A(lfred)
      R(ichard) Weyl.]

C109 "Twelve Months Reviewed." [Unsigned.] Aeroplane 77 (30
      December):862

C110 "Rockets." [Unsigned.] <u>Everyman's Encyclopedia</u>. 3d ed.
      London: J.M. Dent, 1949-1950; 11:191.

                          1950

C111 "The Conquest of Space." [Bylined A.C. Clarke.] <u>Journal
      of the British Astronomical Association</u> 60 (January):48.
      [Oral review of <u>The Conquest of Space</u> by Willy Ley and
      Chesley Bonestell.]

C112 "The Determination of Meteor Orbits by Radar." <u>Journal of the
      British Astronomical Association</u> 60 (January):62-63. [Re-
      view of D.W.R. McKinley and P(eter) M. Millman, "Determina-
      tion of the Elements of Meteor Paths from Radar Observa-
      tions," <u>Canadian Journal of Research</u> 27 (May 1949):53-67.]

C113 "Astronomy and Astronautics." [Bylined A.C.C.] <u>Journal
      of the British Astronomical Association</u> 60 (January):64.
      [Review of "Astronomy and Astronautics" (lecture) by
      Michael W. Ovenden, <u>Journal of the British Interplanetary
      Society</u> (8) (September 1949):(180-93).]

C114 "The Conquest of Space." [Bylined A.C. Clarke.] <u>Journal
      of the British Interplanetary Society</u> 9 (January):41-42.
      [Review of <u>The Conquest of Space</u> by Willy Ley and Chesley
      Bonestell.]

C115 "The Conquest of Space." [Bylined A.C.C.] <u>Aeroplane</u> 78
      (6 January):25. [Review of <u>The Conquest of Space</u> by Willy
      Ley and Chesley Bonestell.]

C116 "Recent Measurement of Lunar Temperature." [Bylined A.C.
      Clarke.] <u>Journal of the British Astronomical Association</u>
      60 (March):98-99. [Review of "Microwave Thermal Radiation
      from the Moon" by J.H. Piddington and H.C. Minett,
      <u>Australian Journal of Scientific Research</u> 2 (March 1949):
      63-77; response by (Michael W.) Ovenden. Clarke's cita-
      tion incomplete.]

C117 "Observations of Markings on Ganymede." [Bylined A.C.
      Clarke.] <u>Journal of the British Astronomical Association</u>
      60 (March):101-2. [Review of "Four Independent Simulta-
      neous Drawings of Ganymede" by Walter Hass, <u>Sky and Tele-
      scope</u> 9 (January 1950):59. Clarke's citation incomplete.]

C118 "Rockets and Jets." [Bylined A.C.C.] <u>Aeroplane</u> 78 (17
      February):198. [Review of <u>Rockets and Jets</u> by R(obert)
      Bernard (<u>sic</u>, Barnard) Way and Noel Greene.]

C119 "Conquest of Space." <u>Fortnightly</u> 173 (March):161-67.

Retitled "Rocket Tours to Mars," 1950. [Condensed.] C127

C120 "Weltraumfahrt--Utopie." [Bylined A.C.C.] Journal of the
      British Interplanetary Society 9 (March):85. [Review of
      Weltraumfahrt--Utopie by Kurt Pervesler et al.]

C121 "New Worlds by Rocket." Public Opinion 177 (17 March):9.

C122 "Arthur C. Clarke Examines the Spaceships of Fiction." Science
      Fantasy Review [fanzine] 4 (Spring):10-13. [1 April lec-
      ture described.] See also C134, C179.

C123 "Astronautics." [Bylined A.C.C.] Chambers' Encyclopedia.
      London: George Newnes, 11:741-42. [Subtitle under
      "Rockets."]

C124 "To the Moon in 100 Hours." Star, 22 May, p. 9.

C125 "According to Hoyle." Public Opinion 177 (26 May):14-15.
      [Review of The Nature of the Universe by Fred Hoyle.]

C126 Interplanetary Flight: An Introduction to Astronautics.
      London: Temple.

      New York: Harper, 1951.
      London: Temple, 1960. [Revised by J.G. Strong.]
      New York: Harper, 1960. [Revised edition.]

C127 "Rocket Tours to Mars." English Digest 33 (June):80-83.
      [Condensed.]

      Originally "Conquest of Space," 1950. C119

C128 "Mind of the Machine." Public Opinion 177 (9 June):10.

C129 "Flying Saucers--Ours or Theirs?" Answers, 10 June, p. 15.

C130 "Kleine Raketenkunde." [Bylined A.C.C.] Journal of the
      British Interplanetary Society 9 (July):206. [Review of
      Kleine Raketenkunde by Hans K. Kaiser.]

C131 "L'Astronautique." [Bylined A.C.C.] Journal of the British
      Interplanetary Society 9 (July):209. [Review of
      L'Astronautique by Lionel Laming.]

C132 "Short-Wave Radio and the Ionosphere." Journal of the British
      Interplanetary Society 9 (July):211. [Review of Short-
      Wave Radio and the Ionosphere by T.W. Bennington.]

C133 "Islands in the Sky." Lilliput 27 (July):31-43. No con-
      nection with A54.

C134 "Space-Travel in Fact and Fiction." Journal of the British
      Interplanetary Society 9 (September):213-30.

          Fantasy Advertiser [fanzine] 4 (February 1951):10-14 (pt.
          1); 5 (21 April):15-19 (pt. 2). See also C122, C179.

C135 "Interplanetary Politics." Public Opinion 178 (1 September):
      10-11.

C136 "The Stars Out of Step." Public Opinion 178 (15 September):
      10-11.

C137 "Artificial Satellites." [Bylined A.C. Clarke.] Journal of
      the British Astronomical Association 60 (October):236-37.
      [Talk.]

C138 "Destination Moon." [Bylined A.C. Clarke.] Journal of the
      British Astronomical Association 60 (October):258-59.
      [Review of the film Destination Moon by George Pal.]

C139 "Electromagnetic Launching as a Major Contribution to Space
      Flight." Journal of the British Interplanetary Society 9
      (November):261-67.

C140 "Beyond the Mountains of the Moon." [Bylined Arthur Clarke.]
      Public Opinion 178 (3 November):15. [Review of The Conquest
      of Space by Willy Ley and Chesley Bonestell.]

                              1951

C141 "The Computation of Orbits." [Bylined A.C.C.] Journal of
      the British Interplanetary Society 10 (January):45. [Re-
      view of The Computation of Orbits by Paul Herget.]

C142 "Warfare by Rockets." Public Opinion 179 (26 January):13-14.

C143 "Signals from the Stars." Radar Bulletin [Official Journal of
      the Radar Association] 2 (Spring):14.

C144 "Science Without Trimmings." Public Opinion 179 (20 April):
      19-20. [Review of Profile of Science by Ritchie Calder.]

C145 "Worlds of Tomorrow." Sunday Chronicle: "First Man on the
      Moon: The Greatest Adventure Story of the Ages," 22 April,
      p. 2 (pt. 1); "Adrift in Space 500 Miles Up," 29 April,
      p. 2 (pt. 2); "Falling Through Space to a Moon Landing,"
      6 May, p. 2 (pt. 3); "Man Builds the First City on the
      Moon," 13 May, p. 2 (pt. 4); "Life in a Luxury Hotel Built
      in the Sky," 20 May, p. 2 (pt. 5).

C146　"Spacesuits Will Be Worn." New Worlds 4 (Summer):56-58.

C147　"Astronautics--The Dawn of Space-Flight." Programme of the
　　　　Daily Express "50 Years of Flying" Exhibition and Display
　　　　(Hendon, England:　19-21 July), pp. 65, 69.

C148　"To the Moon by 1980." Sunday Times, 16 September, p. 4.

C149　"Chairman's Address." Journal of the British Interplanetary
　　　　Society 10:310-15.　[Annual Report bound and paginated with
　　　　Journal, issued in September.]

C150　The Exploration of Space. London:　Temple.

　　　　　　New York:　Harper, 1952.
　　　　　　Baltimore Sun, 9 November-5 December 1952 (9 November =
　　　　　　　　Baltimore Sunday Sun; all others = Baltimore Evening
　　　　　　　　Sun):　"The Exploration of Space," 9 November, sec. A,
　　　　　　　　p. 1 (pt. 1); "Model Focusses Space Distance to Help
　　　　　　　　Humans' Imagination," 10 November, p. 21 (pt. 2);
　　　　　　　　"Rocket History Provides Striking Instance of Weapon's
　　　　　　　　Comeback," 11 November, p. 19 (pt. 3); "Departure Time
　　　　　　　　Must Be Exact for Journey Between Planets," 12 November,
　　　　　　　　p. 39 (pt. 4); "'Orbital Refueling' Held Key to Inter-
　　　　　　　　planetary Journeys," 13 November, p. 33 (pt. 5); "Earth's
　　　　　　　　Atmosphere to Aid in Planet-Ship Return," 14 November,
　　　　　　　　p. 33 (pt. 6); "Exploration of Space" [14 November pre-
　　　　　　　　view title:　"'Deep Space' Ships with Atomic Engines"],
　　　　　　　　15 November, p. 4 (pt. 7); "Exploration of Space" [pre-
　　　　　　　　view title:　"Spaceflight Cargoes of Pure Oxygen"], 17
　　　　　　　　November, p. 23 (pt. 8); "Exploration of Space" [pre-
　　　　　　　　view title:　"A Trip to the Moon"], 18 November, p. 21
　　　　　　　　(pt. 9); "Exploration of Space" [preview title:　"Naviga-
　　　　　　　　tion in Space"], 19 November, p. 41 (pt. 10); "Explora-
　　　　　　　　tion of Space" [preview title:　"Life in a Spaceship"],
　　　　　　　　20 November, p. 35 (pt. 11); "Exploration of Space"
　　　　　　　　[preview title:　"Producing Artificial Gravity"], 21
　　　　　　　　November, p. 31 (pt. 12); "The Problem:　Man on the
　　　　　　　　Moon," 22 November, p. 4 (pt. 13); "Building a City on
　　　　　　　　the Moon," 24 November, p. 29 (pt. 14); "Investigation
　　　　　　　　of Other Planets," 25 November, p. 17 (pt. 15); "Life
　　　　　　　　on Mars:　Probably Uncomfortable," 26 November, p. 13
　　　　　　　　(pt. 16); "What and Where Are the Outer Planets?"
　　　　　　　　27 November, p. 41 (pt. 17); "Life Adaptable on Outer
　　　　　　　　Planets," 28 November, p. 33 (pt. 18); "The Problem of
　　　　　　　　Living on a Planet," 29 November, p. 4 (pt. 19); "The
　　　　　　　　Importance of a Space Station," 1 December, p. 23 (pt.
　　　　　　　　20); "Building Living Areas in Space," 2 December, p.
　　　　　　　　25 (pt. 21); "What Makes Up the Universe?" 3 December,
　　　　　　　　p. 37 (pt. 22); "It Takes a Lifetime to Reach a Star,"
　　　　　　　　4 December, p. 33;(pt. 23); "Man May Solve the Riddle

of the Universe," 5 December, p. 35 (pt. 24).
New York: Pocket Books, 1954, paper. [Revised preface.]
Harmondsworth: Penguin, 1958, paper.
New York: Harper, 1959. [Revised, preface revised again.]
London: Temple, 1959. [Revised text and preface.]
Excerpt, "Means and Ends in the Space Age," 1959. C320

C151 "No Apologies for Science Fiction." Smith's Trade Circular,
no. 1 (3 November), p. 43.

C152 "Interplanetary Navigation." [Bylined A.C. Clarke.] Journal
of the British Astronomical Association 62 (December):41-
43. [Response by (Martin) Davidson, pp. 43-44.]

*C153 "Professor Brittain." Eagle [Features on submarines, tele-
phony, barometers, and atomic structure in weekly comic
paper, U.K., with some annual volumes.] [Source: DH.]

*C154 Work on "Dan Dare" comic strips for Adventure (1951-1953).
[Weekly comic paper, U.K., presumably represented in occasional book publications.] [Source: DH.]

1952

C155 "When Worlds Collide." [Bylined A.C. Clarke.] Journal of
the British Interplanetary Society 11 (January):1-3. [Re-
view of the film When Worlds Collide by George Pal.]

C156 "200 Miles Up." [Bylined A.C.C.] Journal of the British
Interplanetary Society 11 (March):94-95. [Review of 200
Miles Up by J. Gordon Vaeth.]

C157 "Liner to Mars." Picture Post, 1 March, pp. 24-25, 57.

C158 "What Will We Do With the Moon?" Popular Science 160 (April):
164-67, 264, 266.

C159 "Radio Astronomy." [Bylined A.C.C.] Journal of the British
Interplanetary Society 11 (May):140. [Review of Radio
Astronomy by B(ernard) Lovell and J(ohn) A(therton) Clegg.]

C160 "Journey into Space." Illustrated, 5 July, pp. 20-23 (pt. 1);
"The First Landing on the Moon," 12 July, pp. 20-21, 37-38
(pt. 2); "What Will We Find on Mars?" 19 July, pp. 32-33,
42 (pt. 3); "Pioneers in Space Suits," 26 July, pp. 39, 41
(pt. 4).

Excerpt retitled "Rocket Ship to a Space Station," 1952.
[Condensed.] C168

C161 "Cities in Space." In <u>Islands in the Sky</u>. Philadelphia:
        Winston, pp. vii-ix. [Extensive revision, 1958, C265a.]

C162 "We Are on the Way." <u>Collins Magazine</u> 5 (August):11.

C163 "Discoverer of Radium: The Story of Marie Curie." In <u>The
        "Girl" Book of Modern Adventurers</u>. London: Hulton, pp.
        97-110.

C164 "Chairman's Address." <u>Journal of the British Interplanetary
        Society</u> 11:306-11. [<u>Annual Report</u> bound and paginated
        with <u>Journal</u>, issued in September.]

C165 "The Shape of Things to Come." [Baltimore] <u>Sunday Sun Maga-
        zine</u>, 2 November, pp. 9, 30. [Interview by Frank Henry,
        preview of <u>Sun</u> serialization of <u>The Exploration of Space</u>
        C150.]

C166 "Introduction." In <u>No Place Like Earth</u>. Edited by John
        Carnell. London and New York: T.V. Boardman, pp. 7-9.

C167 "Sinbad in a Spaceship." <u>New York Times Book Review</u>, 26
        November, p. 6.

C168 "Rocket Ship to a Space Station." <u>English Digest</u> 41 (Decem-
        ber):27-30. [Condensed.]

        Excerpt from "Journey into Space," 1952. C160

C169 "The Rocket and the Future of Astronomy." <u>Occasional Notes
        of the Royal Astronomical Society</u> 2 (December):127-36.

        <u>Hunting Group Review: Shipping, Oil, Aviation</u>, Winter
            1952, pp. 4-8.

C170 "The Conquest of Space Has Already Begun." <u>Daily Telegraph</u>,
        5 December, p. 8. [Review of <u>Across the Space Frontier</u>
        ed. Cornelius Ryan.]

C171 "Introduction to the Temple Memoirs." <u>Slant</u> [fanzine], no.
        7 (Winter 1952-1953), p. 31.

                              1953

C172 "'Ego' Visits America." <u>A.S.F.O.</u> [fanzine; newsletter of the
        Atlanta (Ga.) Science Fiction Organization.] 1 (January):
        13-15.

C173 "Arthur C. Clarke in Baltimore." <u>A.S.F.O.</u> [fanzine] 1 (Jan-
        uary). Unnumbered two-page insert. [Report by I. Allen
        Newton, Jr. on 6 June 1952 lecture.]

C174 "Is There Too Much?" <u>Authentic Science Fiction Monthly</u>, no. 29 (January), p. 30.

C175 Untitled talk on American tour. [Bylined A.C. Clarke.] <u>Journal of the British Astronomical Association</u> 63 (January): 66-69.

C176 "Man on the Moon." [Bylined A.C.C.] <u>Journal of the British Interplanetary Society</u> 12 (January):65-66. [Review of <u>Collier's Magazine</u> symposium (18-25 October 1952). Symposium published in book form as <u>Conquest of the Moon</u>, ed. Cornelius Ryan, 1953.]

C177 "Across the Space Frontier." <u>New Worlds</u> 7 (January):94. [Review of <u>Across the Space Frontier</u>, ed. Cornelius Ryan.]

C178 "The Road to the Planets." In <u>Astronomy for Everyman</u>. Edited by Martin Davidson. London: J.M. Dent, pp. 480-85.

C179 "Science Fiction: Preparation for the Age of Space." In <u>Modern Science Fiction: Its Meaning and Its Future</u>. Edited by Reginald Bretnor. New York: Coward-McCann, pp. 197-220. See also C122, 134.

C180 "A Journey to Mars." <u>Holiday</u> 13 (March):98-100, 121-22, 124, 126-30.

   Retitled "So You're Going to Mars," 1959. C306

C181 "The Sky and Its Mysteries." [Bylined A.C. Clarke.] <u>Journal of the British Interplanetary Society</u> 12 (March):96. [Review of <u>The Sky and Its Mysteries</u> by E. Agar Beet.]

C182 "About Ray Bradbury." <u>Science Fiction News</u> [flyer of the Science Fiction Book Club, U.K.] 1 (March-April):4-5.

C183 "Will We Ever Reach the Stars?" <u>Science Digest</u> 33 (April):31-36.

C184 "Flying Saucers." [Bylined A.C. Clarke.] <u>Journal of the British Interplanetary Society</u> 12 (May):97-100.

C185 "The Mystery of Other Worlds Revealed." [Bylined A.C. Clarke.] <u>Journal of the British Interplanetary Society</u> 12 (May):141-42. [Review of <u>The Mystery of Other Worlds Revealed</u>, ed. Lloyd Mallan.]

C186 "To Quote: Arthur C. Clarke." <u>Amazing Stories</u> 27 (June-July):2.

C187 "About Arthur C. Clarke." <u>Childhood's End</u>. 1st printing.
        New York: Ballantine, pp. 215-17, paper. [Anonymous com-
        mentary followed by autobiographical statement.] A64

            In <u>Expedition to Earth</u>. 1st printing. New York:
                Ballantine, 1953, pp. [167-68]., paper. [Commentary re-
                vised.] A66
            In <u>Prelude to Space</u>. 1st printing. New York: Ballantine,
                1954, pp. 167-69, paper. [Commentary revised.] A41
            In <u>Tales from the White Hart</u>. 1st printing. New York:
                Ballantine, 1955, pp. 149-51, paper. [Commentary re-
                vised.] A99
            Text revised November, 1966, appearing as follows:
                In <u>Childhood's End</u>. 7th printing. New York:
                    Ballantine, 1967, pp. 219-22, paper.
                In <u>Expedition to Earth</u>. 3d printing. New York:
                    Ballantine, 1967, pp. [166-67], paper.
                In <u>Tales from the White Hart</u>. 4th printing. New York:
                    Ballantine, 1970, pp. 149-50, paper.
            Retitled "Arthur C. Clarke," 1961. [Revised.] C336
            Retitled "About the Author," 1974. [Revised.] C603
            Retitled "Arthur C. Clarke," 1976. [Revised.] C625

C188 "Chairman's Address." <u>Journal of the British Interplanetary
        Society</u> 12:298-302. [<u>Annual Report</u> bound and paginated
        with <u>Journal</u>, issued in September.]

C189 "Space Flight." <u>Star</u>: "Men on the Moon in Thirty Years,"
        15 September, p. 5 (pt. 1); "Moon-Based Men Land on Mars,"
        16 September, p. 9 (pt. 2); "Light Rocket Reaches Saturn's
        Moons," 17 September, p. 11 (pt. 3); "Man's Fantastic
        Cities on Mars," 18 September, p. 5 (pt. 4); "Shall We
        Find Life on Other Worlds?" 21 September, p. 9 (pt. 5);
        "The Flying Gasworks," 22 September, p. 11 (pt. 6);
        "Millions of Worlds Like Ours," 23 September, p. 9 (pt. 7).

C190 "If Earth is Left Behind." <u>New York Times Book Review</u>, 25
        October, p. 36. [Review of <u>Flight Into Space: The Facts,
        Fancies, and Philosophy</u> by Jonathan N. Leonard.]

C191 "Outer-Space Vacation." <u>Holiday</u> 14 (November):72-73, 75-78,
        97-98.

            Retitled "Hotel in Space," 1954. [Condensed.] C194
            Retitled "Vacation in Vacuum," 1959. [Revised.] C304

C192 "50 Men in the Moon." <u>Daily Telegraph</u>, 8 November. [Review
        of <u>Man on the Moon</u> by Wernher von Braun.]

1954

C193 "Flying Saucers Have Landed." Journal of the British Interplanetary Society 13 (March):119-22. [Review of Flying
Saucers Have Landed by D. Leslie and G. Adamski.]

C194 "Hotel in Space." [Bylined Arthur Clarke.] Everybody's, 27
March, pp. 33-35. [Condensed.]

  Originally "Outer-Space Vacation," 1953. C191
  Retitled "Vacation in Vacuum," 1959. [Revised.] C304

C195 "Pioneering Space Flights Coming in this Century." Roanoke
[Va.] Times, 25 April. [Interview by Rochelle Gibson.]
Youngstown [Ohio] Vindicator, 25. April.
Ottawa [Ontario] Citizen, 26 April.
Erie [Pa.] Times, 9 May.

C196 "Treasure Hunting on the Sea Floor." New York Times, 16 May,
p. 6. [Review of 4000 Years Under the Sea by Philippe
Diolé, tr. Gerard Hopkins.]

C197 "Undersea Holiday." Holiday 16 (August):52-54, 80-81.

  Retitled "Underwater Holiday." C700
  In The Challenge of the Sea, 1960. [Revised, retitled
  "The Submarine Playground."] C330

C198 "Where Do We Go From Here?" Seventeen 13 (September):52-54.
["A Look at the Future" series; not explicitly so stated.]

C199 The Exploration of the Moon. London: Frederick Muller.
With R.A. Smith.

  Retitled "Conquest of the Moon," 1954. [Condensed.] C204
  New York: Harper, 1955.

C200 The Young Traveller in Space. London: Phoenix House.

  Retitled Going Into Space, 1954. C201
  Retitled The Scottie Book of Space Travel, 1957, paper.
  C258
  Retitled Into Space, 1971. [Revised.] C553

C201 Going Into Space. New York: Harper.

  Originally The Young Traveller in Space, 1954. C200
  Retitled The Scottie Book of Space Travel, 1957, paper.
  C258
  Retitled Into Space, 1971. [Revised.] C553
  Los Angeles: Trend Books, 1957, paper.
  Excerpt, "Why the Moon Doesn't Fall Down," 1955. C212

Excerpt [chapter 8], "Flight to the Moon," 1956.   C228

C202   "Observations Made above Hudson Bay."   [Bylined A.C. Clarke.]
       Journal of the British Astronomical Association 64 (October):
       366-68.   [Photographs of 1954 solar eclipse.]

C203   "Frontier in the Sky."   Seventeen 13 (October):50, 52.   ["A
       Look at the Future" series.]

C204   "Conquest of the Moon."   Everybody's: 9 October, pp. 27-30
       (pt. 1); "Man Lands on the Moon," 16 October, pp. 25-28
       (pt. 2); "Man Colonises the Moon," 23 October, pp. 25-27
       (pt. 3). [Condensed.] With R.A. Smith.

       Adapted from The Exploration of the Moon, 1954.   C199

C205   "Astronautical Fallacies."   Journal of the British Inter-
       planetary Society 13 (November):324-28.

C206   "Dawn of the Space Age."   Seventeen 13 (November):18, 21.
       ["A Look at the Future" series.]

C207   "What Was the Star of Bethlehem?"   Holiday 16 (December):95-
       99, 101-2.

       Retitled "Does the Star of Bethlehem Still Shine?" 1955.
          [Condensed.]   C211
       Retitled "The Star of the Magi," 1959.   [Footnote, post-
          script added.]   C308
       Retitled "What Star Was This?" 1976.   [Abridged, longer
          than C211.]   C631

C208   "Before the Tourists Get There."   Men Only 19 (December):127-
       28, 131-32, 135.

C209   "The Challenge of the Planets."   Seventeen 13 (December):16,
       21.   ["A Look at the Future" series.]

C210   "Science Fiction and Space Flight."   In The Authentic Book of
       Space. Edited by H.J. Campbell. London: Authentic Sci-
       ence Fiction, n.d., p. 6. [Pages photocopied by PC, date
       verified by British Library.]

                                1955

C211   "Does the Star of Bethlehem Still Shine?"   Reader's Digest 66
       (January):121-23. [Condensed.]

       Originally "What Was the Star of Bethlehem?" 1954.   C207
       Retitled "The Star of the Magi," 1959. [Footnote, post-
          script added.]   C308

Retitled "What Star Was This?" 1976. [Abridged, longer than C211.] C631
Our Amazing World of Nature: Its Marvels and Its Mysteries. Pleasantville, N.Y.: Reader's Digest, 1969.

C212 "Why the Moon Doesn't Fall Down." Science Digest 37 (January): 75-78.

Excerpt from Going into Space, 1954. C201

C213 "Weekend on the Moon." Holiday 17 (February):35-36, 117-20.

Retitled "Journey by Earthlight," 1959. [Minor revisions.] C305

C214 "The Age of Expendability." Seventeen 14 (February):48, 50. ["A Look at the Future" series.]

C215 "Man vs. Machine." Seventeen 14 (March):38-39. ["A Look at the Future" series.]

C216 "Love and Electronics." Seventeen 14 (April):13-14. ["A Look at the Future" series.]

C217 "The Perfect Pet." Seventeen 14 (May):62. ["A Look at the Future" series.]

C218 "Greatest Show Off Earth." Holiday 17 (June):74, 76, 127-28, 130-31, 133.

C219 "Into the Abyss." Seventeen 14 (July):16. ["A Look at the Future" series.]

C220 "Bread from the Waters." Seventeen 14 (August):110-11. ["A Look at the Future" series.]

C221 "Devil on the Reef." Natural History 64 (Ocotber):410-13.

Excerpt [chapter 12, condensed] from The Coast of Coral, 1956. C230

C222 "The Great Barrier Reef." Holiday 18 (November):98-101, 117-18.

Excerpt [chapters 1, 8-10, condensed] from The Coast of Coral, 1956. C230

C223 "The Planets Are Not Enough." Saturday Review 38 (26 November):11-12, 34-36.

Retitled "Space Flight to the Stars," 1956. [Condensed.]
    C226
Magazine of Fantasy and Science Fiction 10 (June 1956):39–
    45.
In The Challenge of the Spaceship, 1959. [Minor revisions.]
    C302
In Report on Planet Three, 1972. [Revised text.] C565

1956

C224 "Preface." In The City and the Stars. New York: Harcourt,
      Brace, pp. vii–viii. A81

C225 Untitled talk on Australian tour. [Bylined A.C. Clarke.]
      Journal of the British Astronomical Association 66 (Feb-
      ruary):93–95.

C226 "Space Flight to the Stars." Science Digest 39 (March):37–42.
      [Condensed.]

      Originally "The Planets Are Not Enough," 1955. C223

C227 "Preface." In Reach for Tomorrow. New York: Ballantine,
      pp. v–vi. A82

      Revised, 1970. C535

C228 "Flight to the Moon." Scholastic Summertime, 15 July, pp. 8–
      9.

      Excerpt [chapter 8] from Going into Space, 1954. C201

C229 "Ugliest Fish in the World." Science Digest 40 (August):72–76.

      Excerpt [chapter 14 condensed] from The Coast of Coral,
          1956. C230

C230 The Coast of Coral. New York: Harper & Row. With Mike
      Wilson.

      London: Frederick Muller, 1956. [Omits chapter 2, "Fair
          Dinkum, Etc.," later chapters moved up one number each.]
      New York: Harper Perennial Library, 1965, paper. [Omits
          last chapter, "Postscript: For Photographers Only,"
          includes "About the Author," D39.]
      New York: Avon Camelot, 1968, paper. [Omits postscript
          and "About the Author," includes untitled brief vita,
          D50.]
      Excerpt [chapter 12 condensed], "Devil on the Reef," 1955.
          C221

Excerpt [chapters 1, 8-10 condensed], "The Great Barrier
Reef," 1955. C222
Excerpt [chapter 14 condensed], "Ugliest Fish in the
World," 1956. C229

C231 "They Take a Dim View of Mars." Daily Mail, 6 September, p. 6.

C232 "The Report on Unidentified Flying Objects." [Bylined A.C.
Clarke.] Journal of the British Interplanetary Society 15
(September–October):289-90. [Review of The Report on Un-
identified Flying Objects by Edward J. Ruppelt.]

C233 "The Exploration of Mars." [Bylined A.C. Clarke.] Journal of
the British Interplanetary Society 15 (September-October):
290-92. [Review of The Exploration of Mars by Willy Ley
and Wernher von Braun.]

C234 "Space Ships Will Change Your Life." Everybody's, 27 October,
pp. 14, 30.

C235 "The Beautiful and Deadly." Natural History 65 (December):
548-51.

Excerpt [chapter 13 condensed] from The Reefs of
Taprobane, 1957. C240

1957

C236 "Preface." In Tales from the White Hart. New York:
Ballantine, pp. v-vi, paper. A99

New York: Harcourt Brace Jovanovich, 1970. [Minor revisions.]
Retitled "The White Hart Series," 1980. C695

C237 "The Secret of the Sun." Holiday 21 (March):94-95, 178-92.

Retitled "Secrets of the Sun," 1957. [Condensed.] C249
Retitled "The Sun," 1959. C309
Reader's Digest 71 (August 1957):206-8. [Condensed.]

*C238 "Springboard to Space." Lion, March. [Source: ACC, con-
firmed by, but unavailable from, Lions International.]

C239 "Author's Note." In The Deep Range. New York: Harcourt,
Brace, n.p. [2 pages before p. 1]. A112

C240 The Reefs of Taprobane: Underwater Adventures Around Ceylon.
New York: Harper & Brothers. With Mike Wilson.

London: Frederick Muller, 1957.
Excerpt, "The Beautiful and Deadly," 1956. [Chapter 14,
    condensed.] C235

C241 "Man-Made Weather." Holiday 21 (May):74-75, 188-90, 193.

Retitled "What Can We Do About the Weather?" 1959. C310

C242 "Introduction." [Bylined A.C. Clarke.] In Space Research and
    Exploration. Edited by D[avid] R[obert] Bates. London:
    Eyre and Spottiswood, pp. 13-25.

C243 "Visit to Vanguard." Spaceflight 1 (July):127-29.

C244 The Making of a Moon. New York: Harper & Brothers.

London: Frederick Muller, 1957.
New York: Harper & Brothers, 1958. [Revised.]
Excerpt, "There's Nothing New About Sputniks," 1957. C257
Excerpt, "Transition--from Fantasy to Science," 1958. C276
Excerpt, "Stairway to the Stars," 1958. C279

C245 "Beneath the Seas of Ceylon." Ceylon Today 6 (August):14-19.

C246 "Fire-Streaks from Outer Space." Holiday 22 (August):11-12,
    14, 16, 20-22.

Retitled "Meteors," 1959. C307

C247 "Housekeeping Without Gravity." Seventeen 16 (August):112.

C248 "London to the Moon by 1980?" Everybody's, 3 August, pp. 14-
    15, 29.

C249 "Secrets of the Sun." Reader's Digest [U.K.] 71 (September):
    70-72. [Condensed.]

Originally "The Secret of the Sun," 1957. C237
Retitled "The Sun," 1959. C309

C250 "Why Let the Moon Slip from Our Grasp?" Evening Standard,
    23 September, p. 21.

C251 "Any Minute Now . . . This Rocket Will Be 4000 Miles Up."
    Daily Mail, 1 October, p. 6.

C252 "On the Morality of Space." Saturday Review 40 (5 October):
    8-10, 35-36.

C253 "Where's Everybody?" Harper's 215 (November):73-77.

In The Challenge of the Spaceship, 1959. C302

C254 "A New Moon is Born." Holiday 22 (November):60-61, 104-6.

C255 "The First Space Man Will Not Be a Superman." Daily Mail, 6
      November, p. 6.

C256 "The Conquest of Gravity." Holiday 22 (December):62.

C257 "There's Nothing New About Sputniks." Everybody's, 7 Decem-
      ber, pp. 26-27.

      Adapted from The Making of a Moon, 1957. C244

C258 The Scottie Book of Space Travel. London: Transworld Pub-
      lishers, paper.

      Originally The Young Traveller in Space, 1954. C200
      Retitled Going Into Space, 1954. C201
      Retitled Into Space, 1971. [Revised.] C553

C259 "Visions for a New Year . . . and a New Era." This Week, 29
      December, p. 2. ["Words to Live By" column.]

      Congressional Record, 14 January 1958, Appendix, p. A248.

                              1958

C260 "Opening the Doors of Memory." Holiday 23 (January):27.

      Everybody's, 10 January 1959, p. 6.

C261 "Our Dumb Colleagues." Harper's 216 (February):32-22.

C262 "Gone Today, Here Tomorrow." Holiday 23 (February):28.

      Everybody's, 23 January 1959, p. 6.

C263 "Bibliographical Note." In The Other Side of the Sky. New
      York: Harcourt, Brace & World, pp. vii-viii. A132

C264 "When Life Becomes a Dream." Holiday 23 (March):34.

      Retitled "After Hollywood--What?" 1958. C285

C265 "Standing Room Only." Harper's 216 (April):54-57.

C265a "Cities in Space." In Islands in the Sky. 5th printing.
      Philadelphia: Winston, pp. vii-ix. [New essay, post-
      Sputnik, replaces C161.]

C266   "Getting Ready for Space Travel." Holiday 23 (May):64-65, 126,
        128-29.

        Retitled "Which Way Is Up?" 1959. C312

C267   "A World Beyond Aladdin's Dreams." Holiday 23 (June):42.

        Retitled "You Name It and It's Yours," 1959. C290

C268   "Coming: the Mechanical Man." Holiday 24 (July):22.

        Retitled "Change Your Body, Sir?" 1959. C289

C269   "First Step--The Moon." Think, 24 July, 14-16.

C270   "Transition--From Fantasy to Science." In SF '58: The Year's
        Greatest Science-Fiction and Fantasy. Edited by Judith
        Merril. Hicksville, N.Y.: Gnome Press, pp. 226-31.

        Excerpt from The Making of a Moon, 1957. C244

C271   "Man's Fate in Space." Coronet 44 (August):88-90. [Con-
        densed.]

        Retitled "Across the Sea of Stars," 1959. C311

C272   "Gateway to the Animal Mind." Holiday 24 (August):25.

C273   Voice Across the Sea. New York: Harper.

            London: Frederick Muller, 1958.
            London: William Luscombe, 1974. [Revised.]
            New York: Harper & Row, 1975. [Revised text.]
            Excerpt, "I'll Put a Girdle Round the Earth in Forty
                Minutes," 1958. C276
            Excerpt [chapter 26, rev. ed.], "Star of India," 1974.
                C609

C274   "Robots in the Nursery." Holiday 24 (September):19.

C275   "The Navy's Eye in the Sky." This Week, 21 September, pp.
        10, 35.

C276   "I'll Put a Girdle Round the Earth in Forty Minutes." American
        Heritage 9 (October):40-44, 85-96.

        Excerpt from Voice Across the Sea, 1958. C273

C277   "U.S.A.: A Spaceman Rides the Lecture Circuit." Holiday 24
        (October):28, 30-32.

        Retitled "Question Time," 1959. C314

C278 "Of Mind and Matter." <u>Magazine of Fantasy and Science Fiction</u> 15 (October):20-26.

    In <u>The Challenge of the Spaceship</u>, 1959. C302

C279 "Stairway to the Stars." <u>Everybody's</u>, 25 October, pp. 6-7.

    Excerpt from <u>The Making of a Moon</u>, 1957. C244

C280 "A Shortcut Through Space." <u>Holiday</u> 24 (November):48.

C281 <u>Boy Beneath the Sea</u>. New York: Harper. With Mike Wilson.

C282 "First Man on the Moon—A Profile: Not too Young, Stable, Intelligent." <u>Chicago Sun-Times</u>, 16 November, sec. 2, pp. 1-2.

C283 "Messages from the Invisible Universe." <u>New York Times Magazine</u>, 30 November, pp. 29-30, 32.

    Retitled "The Radio Universe," 1959. C316
    <u>Space Digest</u> 2 (January 1959):66-69.

C284 "Sleep No More." <u>Holiday</u> 24 (December):40.

    Retitled "The End of Night," 1959. C288

C285 "After Hollywood—What?" <u>Everybody's</u>, 27 December, p. 10.

    Originally "When Life Becomes a Dream," 1958. C264.

1959

C286 "Space and the Spirit of Man." <u>Horizon</u> 1 (January):27-30, 122-23.

    Retitled "Outer Space: What Is Out There?" 1959. [Condensed.] C292
    Retitled "Outer Space: Worlds Without End," 1959. [Condensed.] C295
    Retitled "Of Space and the Spirit," 1959. [Minor expansions.] C317

C287 "Recent Astronomical Observations in Ceylon." <u>Journal of the British Astronomical Association</u> 69 (January):20-21.

C288 "The End of Night." <u>Everybody's</u>, 17 January, p. 8.

    Originally "Sleep No More," 1958. C284

C289 "Change Your Body, Sir?" Everybody's, 24 January, pp. 5-6.

    Originally "Coming: The Mechanical Man," 1958. C268

C290 "You Name It, and It's Yours." Everybody's, 31 January, p. 8.

    Originally "A World Beyond Aladdin's Dreams," 1958. C267

C291 "Men on the Moon." Holiday 25 (February):48-49, 153-55.

    In The Challenge of the Spaceship, 1959. [Revised, titled
    "The Men on the Moon."] C302
    In Report on Planet Three, 1972. [Prologue added, titled
    "The Men on the Moon."] C565

C292 "Outer Space: Waht Is Out There?" Reader's Digest 74 (Feb-
    ruary):123-25. [Condensed.]

    Originally "Space and the Spirit of Man," 1959. C286
    Retitled "Outer Space: Worlds Without End," 1959. [Con-
    densed.] C295
    Retitled "Of Space and the Spirit," 1959. C317
    Our Amazing World of Nature: Its Marvels and Its Mys-
    teries. Pleasantville, N.Y.: Reader's Digest, 1969.

C293 "Beating the Clock." Everybody's, 14 February, pp. 12-13.

C294 "What's Up There?" Holiday 25 (March):32, 34-37, 39-40.

    Retitled "Things in the Sky," 1959. C315

C295 "Outer Space: Worlds Without Ends." Reader's Digest [U.K.]
    74 (March):143-46. [Condensed.]

    Originally "Space and the Spirit of Man," 1959. C286
    Retitled "Outer Space: What Is Out There?" 1959. [Con-
    densed.] C292
    Retitled "Of Space and the Spirit," 1959. C317

C296 "Way Stations in Space: The Planets." New York Times Maga-
    zine, 8 March, pp. 30, 37-38, 40.

C297 "Booty at the Bottom of the Sea." Saturday Review 42 (21
    March):50. [Review of Sea Diver: A Quest for History
    Under the Sea by Marion Clayton Link.]

C298 "From Mars--: A Report on Earth." Holiday 25 (May):39-43.

    Retitled "Report on Planet Three," 1959. [Minor revisions.]
    C313

C299 Untitled excerpt from testimony. <u>The Next Ten Years in Space,</u>
      <u>1959-1969: Staff Report of the Select Committee on Astro-</u>
      <u>nautics and Space Exploration.</u> Washington: Government
      Printing Office [H.R. Document #115, 86th Congress, 1st
      Session], p. 32.

C300 "Introduction." In <u>Journey to the Center of the Earth</u> by
      Jules Verne. New York: Dodd, Mead, pp. v-viii.

C301 "Oh For the Wings. . . ," <u>Holiday</u> 25 (June):51-52.

      In <u>The Challenge of the Spaceship</u>, 1959. [Revised.]   C302

C302 <u>The Challenge of the Spaceship: Previews of Tomorrow's World.</u>
      New York: Harper. ["Introduction," C303; "The Challenge
      of the Spaceship," C64; "Vacation in Vacuum," C304; "Jour-
      ney by Earthlight," C305; "So You're Going to Mars," C306;
      "The Planets Are Not Enough," C223; "Meteors," C307; "The
      Star of the Magi," C308; "Where's Everybody?" C253; "The
      Sun," C309; "What Can We Do About the Weather?" C310; "Oh,
      For the Wings. . . ," C301; "Across the Sea of Stars,"
      C311; "Of Mind and Matter," C278; "Which Way Is Up?" C312;
      "Report on Planet Three," C313; "Question Time," C314;
      "Things in the Sky," C315; "The Men on the Moon," C291;
      "The Radio Universe," C316; "Of Space and the Spirit,"
      C317; "Envoi," C318.]

      New York: Ballantine, 1961, paper. [Omits subtitle and
         "Introduction," includes "Revised Preface," C335, and
         "Arthur C. Clarke," C336.]

C303 "Introduction." In <u>The Challenge of the Spaceship</u>, p. vii.
      C302

C304 "Vacation in Vacuum." In <u>The Challenge of the Spaceship</u>, pp.
      17-28. C302

      Originally "Outer-Space Vacation," 1953. C191
      Retitled "Hotel in Space," 1954. C194
      In <u>Report on Planet Three</u>, 1972. C565

C305 "Journey by Earthlight." The <u>Challenge of the Spaceship</u>, pp.
      29-41. C302

      Originally "Weekend on the Moon," 1955. C213

C306 "So You're Going to Mars?" In <u>The Challenge of the Spaceship</u>,
      pp. 42-53. C302

      Originally "A Journey to Mars," 1953. C180
      <u>Reader's Digest</u> 86 (January 1965):131-35. [Condensed.]

Our Amazing World of Nature: Its Marvels and Its Mys-
   teries. Pleasantville, N.Y.: Reader's Digest, 1969.
   [Condensed.]
In Report on Planet Three, 1972. C565

C307 "Meteors." In The Challenge of the Spaceship, pp. 66-76.
      C302

      Originally "Fire-Streaks from Outer-Space," 1957. C246
      In Report on Planet Three, 1972. [New postscript.] C565

C308 "The Star of the Magi." In The Challenge of the Spaceship,
      pp. 77-86. [Footnote, postscript added.] C302

      Originally "What Was the Star of Bethlehem?" 1954. C207
      Retitled "Does the Star of Bethlehem Still Shine?" 1955.
         [Condensed.] C211
      Retitled "What Star Was This?" 1976. [Abridged, longer
         than C211.] C631
      In Report on Planet Three, 1972. [Footnote incorporated.]
         C565

C309 "The Sun." In The Challenge of the Spaceship, pp. 98-107.
      C302

      Originally "The Secret of the Sun," 1957. C237
      Retitled "Secrets of the Sun," 1957. C249

C310 "What Can We Do About the Weather?" In The Challenge of the
      Spaceship, pp. 108-17. C302

      Originally "Man-Made Weather," 1957. C241

C311 "Across the Sea of Stars." In The Challenge of the Spaceship,
      pp. 124-30. C302

      Originally "Man's Fate in Space," 1958. C271
      In Report on Planet Three, 1972. C565

C312 "Which Way Is Up?" In The Challenge of the Spaceship, pp.
      140-50. C302

      Originally "Getting Ready for Space Travel," 1958. C266
      In Report on Planet Three, 1972. [Postscript added.] C565

C313 "Report on Planet Three." In The Challenge of the Spaceship,
      pp. 151-58. C302

      Originally "From Mars--: A Report on Earth," 1959. C298
      In Report on Planet Three, 1972. C565

C314 "Question Time." In The Challenge of the Spaceship, pp. 159-68. C302

   Originally "U.S.A.: A Spaceman Rides the Lecture Circuit," 1958. C277

C315 "Things in the Sky." In The Challenge of the Spaceship, pp. 169-81. [With new postscript.] C302

   Originally "What's Up There?" 1959. 294
   In Report on Planet Three, 1972. [Adds second new post-script.] C565

C316 "The Radio Universe." In The Challenge of the Spaceship, pp. 194-200. C302

   Orginally "Messages from the Invisible Universe," 1958. C283

C317 "Of Space and the Spirit." In The Challenge of the Spaceship, pp. 201-12. C302

   Originally "Space and the Spirit of Man," 1959. C286
   Retitled "Outer Space: What Is Out There?" 1959. [Condensed.] C292
   Retitled "Outer Space: Worlds Without End," 1959. [Condensed.] C295.

C318 "Envoi." In The Challenge of the Spaceship, p. 213. C302

C319 "Faces from the Sky." Holiday 26 (September):48-49, 109-11.

   Retitled "Voices from the Sky." 1962. [Minor revisions.] C398.

C320 "Means and Ends in the Space Age." Space Digest 2 (November): 74-76.

   Excerpt from The Exploration of Space, 1951. C150

1960

C321 "Shaw and the Sound Barrier." Virginia Quarterly Review 36 (Winter):72-77.

   Shaw Society Newsletter 3 (March 1960):1, 3-4.

C322 "Of Whales and Perfume: Secrets of the Sea." Holiday 27 (February):36.

C323   The First Five Fathoms: A Guide to Underwater Adventure.
          New York: Harper. With Mike Wilson.

C324   "Shaver's Regress." D.A.C. News [Detroit Athletic Club] 45
          (April):39-40.

C325   "Riding on Air." Holiday 27 (May):24, 26-30.

          In Profiles of the Future, 1962. C384

C326   "We'll Never Conquer Space." Science Digest 47 (June):53-58.
          [Condensed.]

          Retitled "Space, the Unconquerable," 1962. C392
          Edmund Farrell et al., eds., Science Fact/Fiction. Glen-
             view, Ill.: Scott, Foresman, 1974.

C327   "A New Look at Space." Amazing Science Fiction Stories 34
          (July):76-79.

          Thrilling Science Fiction, April 1974, pp. 4, 113-15.

C328   "Rocket to the Renaissance." Playboy 7 (July):34, 38, 48, 83-
          84. [Condensed.]

          In Profiles of the Future, 1962. C384
          Hugh M. Hefner, ed. The Bedside Playboy. Chicago: Play-
             boy Press, 1963. [Condensed.]

C329   "Off the Moon Talk III." The Paper: A Chicago Weekly 1 (3
          September):[3]. [Interview by Lois Solomon.]

C330   The Challenge of the Sea. New York: Holt, Rinehart, Winston.
          [Includes "Introduction" by Wernher von Braun, D23.]

          London: Frederick Muller, 1961
          Excerpt [chapter 12], "Undersea Holiday," 1954. C197
          Excerpt [chapter 12], "Underwater Holiday," undated. C700
          Excerpt [chapter 8 condensed], "Will a Hungry World Raise
             Fish for Food?" 1960. C331
          Excerpt [chapter 5 condensed and revised], "Loud Voices in
             the Deep," 1961. C321
          Excerpt [chapter 1 adapted], "The World of Water," 1972.
             C585

C331   "Will a Hungry World Raise Fish for Food?" Popular Science
          177 (November):74-76, 216.

          Excerpt [chapter 8 condensed] from The Challenge of the
             Sea. C330

*C332   "Science in Ceylon." Ceylon Observer, 17 December, p. 6.
         [Source: ACC, confirmed by publisher.]

                               1961

C333   "Eclipses of the Sun." Ceylon Daily News, 15 February, p. 6.

C334   "Two Leagues Under the Sea." Saturday Review 44 (25 March):
        26-27. [Review of Seven Miles Down: The Story of the
        Bathyscaph Trieste by Jeacques Piccard and Robert S. Dietz.]

C335   "Revised Preface." In The Challenge of the Spaceship, pp. 7-
        8, C302

C336   "Arthur C. Clarke." In The Challenge of the Spaceship, pp.
        187-89, paper. C302

        In Childhood's End. 17th printing. New York: Ballantine,
           1967, pp. 219-22, paper. [Revised.] A64
        See also "About Arthur C. Clarke," 1953. C187

C337   "Loud Voices in the Deep." Holiday 29 (May):16. [Condensed
        and revised.]

        Excerpt from The Challenge of the Sea, 1960. [Chapter 5.]
           C330

C338   "The Gulf Stream." Holiday 29 (June):80-81.

C339   "Space Travel and Human Affairs." Vidja [Ceylon Association
        for the Advancement of Science] 2 (June):1-2.

        Excerpt from "The Challenge of the Spaceship," 1946. C64

C340   "Machina Ex Deux." Playboy 8 (July):45-66, 70, 100-2. [Con-
        densed.]

        Retitled "The Evolutionary Cycle from Man to Machine,"
           1961. C334
        Retitled "The Obsolescence of Man," 1962. C400

C341   "Lights Under the Sea." D.A.C. News [Detroit Athletic Club]
        46 (September):55-56.

C342   "Space Flight and the Spirit of Man." Astronautics 6 (Oc-
        tober):62-63, 90, 92, 94.

        Retitled "Not Yet Space-Minded," 1962. [Condensed.] C350
        Reader's Digest 80 (February):73-76. [Condensed.]
        In Voices from the Sky, 1965. C446
        Our Amazing World of Nature: Its Marvels and Its Mysteries.
           Pleasantville, N.Y.: Reader's Digest, 1969. [Con-
           densed.]

C343   Indian Ocean Adventure. New York: Harper. With Mike Wilson.

     London: Arthur Barker, 1962.

C344   "Ceylon's Fortress in the Sky." Holiday 30 (November):160-62,
     190.

     Retitled "Sigiri--Fortress in the Sky," 1962. C408

C345   "The Evolutionary Cycle from Man to Machine." Industrial Re-
     search 3 (November):30-35. [Condensed.]

     Originally "Machina Ex Deux," 1961. C340
     Retitled "The Obsolescence of Man," 1962. C400

C346   "Down to Earth Survey of Space." New York Times Magazine, 5
     November, pp. 32, 40, 42.

C347   "The Uses of the Moon." Harper's 223 (December):55-62.

     In Voices from the Sky, 1965. C446
     In Space the Unconquerable, 1970. C547

C348   "Foreword." In Master of Space. New York: Lancer, pp. 5-7,
     paper. A155

     Retitled "Foreword to the 1962 [sic] Edition," 1970. C539
     In Prelude to Mars, 1965. A180

1962

C349   "The Social Consequences of the Communications Satellites."
     Horizon 4 (January):16-21.

     In Voices from the Sky, 1965. [Omits one paragraph,
       second "the" in title on contents page, first "the" in
       running titles.] C446

C350   "Not Yet Space-Minded." Space Digest 5 (January):55-58.
     [Condensed.]

     Originally "Space Flight and the Spirit of Man," 1961.
       C342

C351   "Half a Million Laxapanas from Our Noon-day Sun." [Bylined
     Arthur Clarke.] Ceylon Observer, 7 January, p. 3.

C352   "The Planets in February." Sunday Times of Ceylon, 7 January,
     p. 9.

C353   "Introduction." In From the Ocean, From the Stars. New York:
       Harcourt, Brace & World, pp. ix-xi. A156

C354   "Commonsense and the Planets." Sunday Times of Ceylon, 28
       January, p. 8.

       Retitled "The Stars in Their Courses," 1977. C642

C355   "Did the Whale Really Swallow Jonah?" Holiday 31 (March):
       178-80.

C356   "Arthur C. Clarke." Skin Diver 11 (March):33, 52. [Inter-
       view by Connie Johnson.]

C357   "The Hazards of Prophecy." Playboy 9 (March):51, 56, 102, 104.

       Retitled "Hazards of Prophecy: The Failure of Nerve,"
           C386; "Hazards of Prophecy: The Failure of Imagination,"
           C387; "Invisible Men, and Other Prodigies," C396; 1962.
           [All greatly expanded.]

C358   "Worlds Beyond Belief." This Week, 18 March, p. 2. ["Words
       to Live By" column.]

C359   "You Can't Get There From Here." Playboy 9 (April):87-88,
       124-26.

       In Profiles of the Future, 1962. [Minor revisions.] C384
       J. Richard Suchman, and Lawrence McCombs, eds. Readings
           for Geological Inquiry. Chicago: Science Research
           Associates, 1968.

C360   "Their Skin Diving Paid Off." This Week, 29 April, pp. 9-10.

       Retitled "The Scent of Treasure," 1977. [Revised.] C641
       Adapted from The Treasure of the Great Reef, 1964. C429

C361   "Ships for the Stars." Rotarian 100-01 (May):12-15, 65-66,
       68.

       In Voices from the Sky, 1965. C446

C362   "The Planets: Facts and Fancies." Think 28 (May):22-25.

C363   "The Servant Problem--Oriental Style." D.A.C. News [Detroit
       Athletic Club] 47 (June):99-100, 102, 104, 106.

       In The View from Serendip, 1977. [As "Servant Problem--
           Oriental Style."] C638

C364   "The Playing Fields of Space." Holiday 31 (June):87-89, 92.

In <u>Voices from the Sky</u>, 1965. C446

C365 "From Lilliput to Brobdingnag." <u>Playboy</u> 9 (June):102, 116–19.

Retitled "The Road to Lilliput," 1962. [Minor revisions.]
C397

C366 "The Tyranny of Time." <u>Horizon</u> 4 (July):80–88. [Condensed.]

Retitled "About Time," 1962. C393

C367 "Blacking Out the Sun: The Risks are Slight." <u>Ceylon Observer</u>, 15 July, p. 8.

C368 "Sunken Treasure Off the Coast of Ceylon." <u>Ceylon Observer</u>, 15 July, p. 9.

Adaptation, <u>The Treasure of the Great Reef</u>, 1964. C429

C369 "Tomorrow: the Moon." Preface to <u>A Fall of Moondust</u>.
<u>Reader's Digest Condensed Books</u>, no. 32. London: Reader's Digest, pp. 9–11. A152

C370 "World Without Distance." <u>Playboy</u> 9 (August):69–70, 94–97.

Retitled "The Future of Transport," C388; "The Quest for Speed," C390; "World Without Distance," C391; 1962. [All greatly expanded.]

C371 "This is Only the Start." <u>Evening News</u>, 13 August, pp. 1–2.

C372 "Introduction." In <u>The Invisible Man and the War of the Worlds</u> by H.G. Wells. New York: Washington Square Press, pp. xi–xix, paper.

Retitled "H.G. Wells and Science Fiction," 1965. C461

C373 "Potentials in Power." <u>D.A.C. News</u> [Detroit Athletic Club] 47 (October):69–70, 72.

Retitled "Ages of Plenty" [first part], 1962. C394

C374 "A Star to Steer To." <u>Elks Magazine</u> 41 (October):6–7, 48–50.

C375 "Mind Beyond Matter." <u>Playboy</u> 9 (October):105–6, 144–45. [Condensed.]

Retitled "Brain and Body," 1962. C399

C376 "Telstar on Broadway." <u>Playbill</u> New York 6 (8 October):5, 7, 9, 32.

Retitled "Broadway and the Satellites," 1965. C455

C377 "The Kalinga Award." New Worlds 42 (November):2-3, 117-18.
[Lacks conclusion; guest editorial.]

Originally "In Defense of Science Fiction," 1962. [Lacks
introduction.] C379
Retitled "Inspirational Value of Science Fiction," 1963.
[Excerpts.] C410
Retitled "Kalinga Award Speech," 1965. C457

*C378 "How I Lost a Billion Dollars in My Spare Time by Inventing
Telstar." Rogue (November). [Source: ACC, SM.]

Retitled "A Short Pre-History of Comsats, or: How I Lost
a Billion Dollars in My Spare Time," 1965. C454

C379 "In Defense of Science Fiction." UNESCO Courier 15 (November):
14-17. [Lacks introduction.]

Retitled "The Kalinga Award," 1962. [Lacks conclusion.]
C377
Retitled "Inspirational Value of Science Fiction," 1963.
[Excerpts.] C410
Retitled "Kalinga Award Speech," 1965. C457

C380 "The Robot Space Explorers." Ceylon Daily News, 3 November,
p. 6.

C381 "Spacecrews Will Fly to the Stars in Deep-Freeze." Sunday
Citizen, 4 November, p. 8. ["This is Your Future" series.]

Excerpt from Profiles of the Future, 1962. [From "Space,
the Unconquerable," C392.]

C382 "Tomorrow's Ocean Ports Will Be Inland." Sunday Citizen, 11
November, p. 8. ["This is Your Future" series.]

Excerpt from Profiles of the Future, 1962. [From "The
Future of Transport," C388.]

C383 "Dial World--Via a Radio Station on Your Wrist." Sunday
Citizen, 18 November, p. 8. ["This is Your Future" series.]

Excerpt from Profiles of the Future, 1962. [From "Voices
from the Sky," C398.]

C384 Profiles of the Future: An Enquiry into the Limits of the
Possible. London: Victor Gollancz. ["Introduction,"
C385; "Hazards of Prophecy: The Failure of Nerve," C386;
"Hazards of Prophecy: The Failure of Imagination," C387;

"The Future of Transport," C388; "Riding on Air," C325;
"Beyond Gravity," C389; "The Quest for Speed," C390;
"World Without Distance," C391; "Rocket to the Renaissance,"
C328; "You Can't Get There From Here," C359; "Space, the
Unconquerable," C392; "About Time," C393; "Ages of Plenty,"
C394; "Aladdin's Lamp," C395; "Invisible Men, and Other
Prodigies," C396; "The Road to Lilliput," C397; "Voices
from the Sky," C398; "Brain and Body," C399; "The Ob-
solescence of Man," C400; "The Long Twilight," C401; "Chart
of the Future," C402.]

New York: Harper & Row, 1963. ["Inquiry" in subtitle.]
London: Pan, 1964, paper.
New York: Bantam, 1967, paper. ["Inquiry" in subtitle.]
New York: Harper & Row, 1973. [Minor revisions.]
London: Pan, 1973, paper. [Revised text; "Inquiry" in
    subtitle; includes "Preface to the Second Edition, 1973.]
    C473
London: Victor Gollancz, 1974. [Same as Pan, 1973.]
Excerpt, "Spacecrews Will Fly to the Stars in Deep-Freeze,"
    1962. [From "Space, the Unconquerable," C392.] C381
Excerpt, "Tomorrow's Ocean Ports Will Be Inland," 1962.
    [From "The Future of Transport," C388.] C382
Excerpt, "Dial World—Via a Radio Station on Your Wrist,"
    1962. [From "Voices from the Sky," C398.] C383
Excerpt, "Just Dial—for Your Heart's Desire," 1962.
    [From "Aladdin's Lamp," C395.] C404
*Adaptation, "List of Expected Includes Sheer Fantasy,"
    1968. [From "Hazards of Prophecy: The Failure of
    Nerve," C386, and "Hazards of Prophecy: The Failure of
    Imagination," C387.] C494

C385 "Introduction." In Profiles of the Future, pp. 9-12. C384

C386 "Hazards of Prophecy: The Failure of Nerve." In Profiles of
      the Future, pp. 13-22. C384

          Originally "The Hazards of Prophecy" [first part], 1962.
          C357.
          *Adaptation, "List of Expected Includes Sheer Fantasy,"
          1968. C494

C387 "Hazards of Prophecy: The Failure of Imagination." In Pro-
      files of the Future, pp. 23-31. C384.

          Originally "The Hazards of Prophecy" [second part], 1962.
          C357.
          *Adaptation, "List of Expected Includes Sheer Fantasy,"
          1968. C494

C388 "The Future of Transport." In Profiles of the Future, pp. 32-
      45. C384

> Originally "World Without Distance" [first part], 1962.
>   C370
> Excerpt, "Tomorrow's Ocean Ports Will Be Inland," 1962.
>   C382

C389 "Beyond Gravity." In Profiles of the Future, pp. 54-66. C384

>   *Playboy* 10 (February 1963):71, 80, 112, 114. [Condensed.]

C390 "The Quest for Speed." In Profiles of the Future, pp. 67-74.
      C384

> Originally "World Without Distance" [second part], 1962.
>   C370

C391 "World Without Distance." In Profiles of the Future, pp. 75-
      85. C384

> Originally "World Without Distance" [third part], 1962.
>   C370

C392 "Space, the Unconquerable." In Profiles of the Future, pp.
      113-20. C384

> Originally "We'll Never Conquer Space," 1960. C326
> Excerpt, "Spacecrews Will Fly to the Stars in Deep-Freeze,"
>   1962. C381
> In Space the Unconquerable, 1970. C547

C393 "About Time." In Profiles of the Future, pp. 121-36. C384

> Originally "The Tyranny of Time," 1962. C366

C394 "Ages of Plenty." In Profiles of the Future, pp. 137-50.
      C384

> First part originally "Potentials in Power," 1962. C373
> Second part retitled "Mining the Universe," 1963. C409
> In Space the Unconquerable, 1970. C547

C395 "Aladdin's Lamp." In Profiles of the Future, pp. 151-56.
      C384

> Excerpt, "Just Dial--for Your Heart's Desire," 1962. C404

C396 "Invisible Men, and Other Prodigies." In Profiles of the
      Future, pp. 157-67. [Comma omitted in U.S. editions.]
      C384

         Originally "The Hazards of Prophecy" [third part], 1962.
            C357

C397 "The Road to Lilliput." In Profiles of the Future, pp. 168-77.
         C384

         Originally "From Lilliput to Brobdingnag," 1962. C365

C398 "Voices from the Sky." In Profiles of the Future, pp. 178-87.
         C384

         Originally "Faces from the Sky," 1959. C319
         Radio-Electronics, August 1963, pp. 25, 42, 46. [Condensed.]
         Excerpt, "Dial World--Via a Radio Station on Your Wrist,"
            1962. C383
         No connection with C446, 483, or 583.

C399 "Brain and Body." In Profiles of the Future, pp. 188-201.
         C384

         Originally "Mind Beyond Matter," 1962. C375
         Excerpt, Joseph F. Doherty,,and William C. Stephenson, eds.
         The Inward Journey. New York: Harcourt Brace
         Jovanovich, 1973.

C400 "The Obsolescence of Man." In Profiles of the Future, pp.
         202-16. C384

         Originally "Machina Ex Deux," 1961. C340
         Retitled "The Evolutionary Cycle from Man to Machine,"
            1961. C334

C401 "The Long Twilight." In Profiles of the Future, pp. 217-20.
         C384

C402 "Chart of the Future." In Profiles of the Future, pp. [221-
         23]. C384

         Retitled "Next 100 Years," 1975. C619

C403 "The Popularisation of Science." Ceylon Daily News, 22
         November, pp. 6, 9.

C404 "Just Dial--for Your Heart's Desire." Sunday Citizen, 25
         November, p. 6. ["This is Your Future" series.]

         Excerpt from Profiles of the Future, 1962. [From "Aladdin's
         Lamp," C395.]

C405 "Introduction." In From the Earth to the Moon and Around the
         Moon by Jules Verne. New York: Dodd, Mead, pp. v-viii.

C406 "Spark of the Second Industrial Revolution." New York Times
      Magazine, 9 December, p. 32.

         Retitled "The Electronic Revolution," 1965. C460
         Retitled "Epilogue," 1972. C584

C407 "A Critical Evaluation of the Space Race." In Space Flight
      Report to the Nation. Edited by Jerry and Vivian Grey.
      New York: Basic Books, pp. 163-94. [Panel discussion
      moderated by Clarke.]

C408 "Sigiri--Fortress in the Sky." Times of Ceylon Annual, pp.
      [29-35].

         Originally "Ceylon's Fortress in the Sky," 1961. C344

                              1963

C409 "Mining the Universe." Rotarian, 102-3 (January):21-23, 54,
      56-57.

         Originally "Ages of Plenty" [second part], 1962. C394

C410 "Inspirational Value of Science Fiction." Science Digest 53
      (March):34. [Excerpts.]

         Originally "In Defense of Science Fiction," 1962. [Lacks
            introduction.] C379
         Retitled "The Kalinga Award," 1962. [Lacks conclusion.]
            C377
         Retitled "Kalinga Award Speech," 1965. C457

C411 "Class of '00." Tartan [in-house magazine of 3M Co.]
      [Spring], pp. 25-27.

         In Voices from the Sky, 1965. C446

C412 "Editorial." Worlds of Tomorrow 1 (April):4. [Condensed.]

         Retitled "A Note from the Author," 1963. C415

C413 "Trouble in Aquila, and Other Astronomical Brainstorms." In
      The Scientist Speculates: An Anthology of Partly-Baked
      Ideas. Edited by I.J. Good. New York: Basic Books, pp.
      235-38.

         Cosmic Search 1 (January 1979):22-23. [Postscript added.]

C414 "Armchair Astronauts." Holiday 33 (May):94-95, 175-78, 184.

Retitled "Memoirs of an Armchair Astronaut (Retired),"
1965. C458

C415 "A Note from the Author." In Dolphin Island, pp. 185-86.
A169

New York: Holt, Rinehart.
Originally, "Editorial," 1963. [Condensed.] C412

C416 "1984 and Beyond." Playboy 10 (July):25-37 (pt. 1); (August):
31-35, 108, 112, 114, 116-18 (pt. 2). [Panel with Poul
Anderson, Isaac Asimov, James Blish, Ray Bradbury, Algis
Budrys, Robert A. Heinlein, Frederik Pohl, Rod Serling,
Theodore Sturgeon, "Willian Tenn" (pseudonym for Philip
Klass), and A.E. Van Vogt.]

C417 "A Star in Space." Ceylon Observer, 4 August, no page on
clipping. [Interview by Neville Weereraine.]

C418 "In the Light of the Sun." Horizon 5 (November):48-55.

Retitled "The Light of Common Day," 1965. C449

C419 "Schoolmaster Who Foresaw Space Flights." Times of Ceylon,
26 November, p. 4.

C420 "Treasure of the Great Reef." Triton 8 (November-December):
26-29. [Précis of Clarke story "told exclusively to
Triton."]

Adapted from The Treasure of the Great Reef, 1964. C429

*C421 "Space and Ceylon." Mathematica [Journal of the Ceylon Uni-
versity Mathematics Society], December, pp. 3-5. [Source:
ACC.]

C422 "Most Wonderful Time Machine Yet Made by Man." Sunday Times
of Ceylon, 1 December, pp. 14-15. [Text of radio talk on
the National Service, 3 September.]

*C423 "Science and Spirituality." In Vivekananda: The Cosmic Con-
science. Edited [?] by Prafullo Chandra Das. Calcutta:
Cuttack, Orissa. [Source: ACC; sources in India unable
to confirm.]

In Voices from the Sky, 1965. C446

1964

C424 "The First Rocket." This Week, 5 January, p. 2. ["Words to
Live By" column, "It Can Be Done" series.]

C425 "Men Against the Sea." This Week, 12 January, p. 2. ["Words
        to Live By" column, "It Can Be Done" series.]

C426 "The Thousands He Saved." This Week, 26 January, p. 2.
        "Words to Live By" column, "It Can Be Done" series.]

C427 "The World of the Communications Satellite." Astronautics
        and Aeronautics 2 (February):45-48.

        In Voices from the Sky, 1965. C446
        UNESCO Courier 19 (November 1966):24-29. [Condensed.]

C428 "Gift of Light." This Week, 2 February, p. 2. ["Words to
        Live By" column, "It Can Be Done" series.]

C429 The Treasure of the Great Reef. London: Arthur Barker.

        New York: Harper, 1964.
        New York: Ballantine, 1974, paper. [Revised.]
        Adaptation, "Their Skin Diving Really Paid Off," 1962.
          C360
        Adaptation, "Sunken Treasure off the Coast of Ceylon,"
          1962. C368
        Adaptation, "Treasure of the Great Reef," 1963. C420
        Excerpt, "The Unforgettable Sight of Treasure," 1964. C430
        Adaptation, "Silver Reed," 1964. C435
        Saga 28 (August 1964):12-15, 58-64. [Condensed.]
        Adaptation, Indian Ocean Treasure, 1964. C438
        Excerpt, "Mogul Silver," 1969. C526

C430 "The Unforgettable Sight of Treasure." Weekly Herald (Ceylon),
        21 February, no page on clipping.

        Excerpt from The Treasure of the Great Reef, 1964. C412

C431 "The Meddlers." Playboy 11 (March):103, 168.

        *Space Intelligence Notes 5 (June 1964):13-18.
        In Voices from the Sky, 1965. [Footnotes added.] C446

C432 "Must the Satellite Race Leave Britain Grounded?" Daily
        Telegraph, 4 March, p. 7.

C433 "From Space Ships to the Buddha's Message." Ceylon Observer,
        8 March, pp. 7, 11. [Interview by Peter Van Reyk.]

C434 "Our Future in the Sea." In Sea Hunt at the New York World's
        Fair, 1964-1965, p. [16]. [Official souvenir program.]

C435   "Silver Reef." Boy's Life 54 (June):20-21, 72-73.

      Adaptation of The Treasure of the Great Reef, 1964. C429

C436   Man and Space. New York: Time. [With the editors of Life.]

C437   "The Fascinating Shark." Holiday 36 (September):116.

C438   Indian Ocean Treasure. New York: Harper. With Mike Wilson.

      London: Sidgwick & Jackson, 1972.
      Adaptation of The Treasure of the Great Reef, 1964. C429

C439   "Everybody in Instant Touch." Life 57 (25 September):118-20,
      122-24, 126-28, 131.

      In The Coming of the Space Age, 1967. C473

C440   "Fantasies of the Future." Listener and BBC Television Re-
      view 72 (15 October):573-75.

C441   "Beyond Centaurus." Playboy 11 (November):115-16, 176, 178,
      180.

      In Voices from the Sky, 1965. C446

C442   "How to Dig Space, or The Idiot's Guide to Astronautics."
      D.A.C. News [Detroit Athletic Club] 49 (December):81-82, 84.

      In The View from Serendip, 1977. [Subtitle omitted, foot-
      note added.] C638

1965

C443   "Beyond the Stars." New Yorker 41 (24 April):38-39. [Un-
      signed interview of Clarke and Stanley Kubrick by Jeremy
      Bernstein.]

      Jerome Agel, ed. The Making of Kubrick's 2001. New York:
      New American Library, 1970, paper. D95

C444   "To Prepare Man for the Extraordinary." Esquire 65 (May):117.
      [Anonymous interview of Clarke and Stanley Kubrick.]

C445   "Foreword." In The Case for Going to the Moon by Neil P.
      Ruzic. New York: G.P. Putnam's Sons, pp. xi-xiv.

C446   Voices from the Sky: Previews of the Coming Space Age. New
      York: Harper & Row. ["Preface 1," C447; "Space Flight

and the Spirit of Man," C342; "The Uses of the Moon," C347;
"To the Stars," C448; "Beyond Centaurus," C448; "The Light
of Common Day," C449; "Ships for the Stars," C361; "Seas
of Tomorrow," C450; "The Winds of Space," C451; "Time for
the Stars," C452; "The Playing Fields of Space," C364;
"Preface 2," C453; "A Short Pre-History of Comsats, or:
How I Lost a Billion Dollars in My Spare Time," C454; "The
Social Consequences of the Communications Satellites," C349;
"Broadway and the Satellites," C455; "The World of the
Communications Satellite," C427; "Preface 3," C456;
"Kalinga Award Speech," C457; "Memoirs of an Armchair
Astronaut, (Retired)," C458; "Science and Spirituality,"
C423; "Class of '00," C411; "The Meddlers," C431; "The
Lunatic Fringe," C459; "The Electronic Revolution," C460;
"H.G. Wells and Science Fiction," C461; "Dear Sir. . . ,"
C462; "Appendix: Extraterrestrial Relays," C54.]

London: Victor Gollancz, 1966.
New York: Pyramid, 1967, paper.
London: Mayflower, 1969, paper.
No connection with C398, C483, or C583.

C447   "Preface 1." In Voices from the Sky, p. 1.   C446

C448   "To the Stars." In Voices from the Sky, pp. 27–37.   C446

      In Space the Unconquerable, 1970.   C547

C449   "The Light of Common Day." In Voices from the Sky, pp. 53–63.
      C446

      Originally "In the Light of the Sun," 1963.   C418

C450   "Seas of Tomorrow." In Voices from the Sky, pp. 78–83.   C446
      [Original 1961 publication by Gilberton Co. not confirmed;
      source: ACC.]

C451   "The Winds of Space." In Voices from the Sky, pp. 84–95.
      C446

C452   "Time for the Stars." In Voices from the Sky, pp. 95–107.
      C446

C453   "Preface 2." In Voices from the Sky, pp. 117–18.   C446

C454   "A Short Pre-History of Comsats, or: How I Lost a Billion
      Dollars in My Spare Time." In Voices from the Sky, pp.
      119–28.   C446

      *Originally, "How I Lost a Billion Dollars in My Spare
      Time by Inventing Telstar," 1962.   C378

C455 "Broadway and the Satellites." In Voices from the Sky, pp.
      141-45. C446

      Originally "Telstar on Broadway," 1962. C376.

C456 "Preface 3." In Voices from the Sky, p. 159. C446

C457 "Kalinga Award Speech." In Voices from the Sky, pp. 161-66.
      C446

         Originally "In Defense of Science Fiction," 1962. [Lacks
            introduction.] C379
         Retitled "The Kalinga Award," 1962. [Lacks conclusion.]
            C377
         Retitled "Inspirational Value of Science Fiction," 1963.
            [Excerpts.] C410

C458 "Memoirs of an Armchair Astronaut (Retired)." In Voices from
      the Sky, pp. 167-80. C446

      Originally "Armchair Astronauts," 1963. C414

C459 "The Lunatic Fringe." In Voices from the Sky, pp. 197-203.
      C446

C460 "The Electronic Revolution." In Voices from the Sky, pp. 204-
      10. C446

         Originally "Spark of the Second Industrial Revolution,"
            1962. C406
         Retitled "Epilogue," 1972. C584

C461 "H.G. Wells and Science Fiction." In Voices from the Sky,
      pp. 211-19. C446

      Originally "Introduction," 1962. C372

C462 "Dear Sir. . . ." In Voices from the Sky, pp. 220-29. C446

C463 "Our World Will Never Be the Same." Life International, 26
      December, pp. 17-27.

                              1966

C464 "1965--Year of the Breakthrough." Liverpool Daily Post, 12
      January; "Mars in Close-Up," undated supplement, pp. 7-8
      [Man into Space series, no. 3].

C465 "Foreword." In Intelligence in the Universe by Roger A.
      McGowan and Frederick I. Ordway III. Englewood Cliffs,
      N.J.: Prentice-Hall, pp. v-vi.

                               102

C466 "Introduction: Science and Science Fiction." In Time Probe,
    pp. vii-ix. [Comments also on individual stories.] A182

C467 "When Television Comes Here." Ceylon Times Weekender, 26
    December, p. 5.

                    1967

C468 "Television: Medium of Mass Communication." Ceylon Radio
    Times Magazine, 9-25 January, pp. 40-41.

C469 "A Breath of Fresh Vacuum." Astronautics and Aeronautics 5
    (February):16, 21. [Letter.]

    In The View from Serendip, 1977. C638

C470 "Foreword." In The Sands of Mars. New York: Harcourt,
    Brace & World, pp. v-vi. A51

C471 "Introduction." In The Nine Billion Names of God: The Best
    Short Stories of Arthur C. Clarke. New York: Harcourt,
    Brace & World. A186

C472 "Colossus." New Yorker 43 (27 May):25-26. [Unsigned inter-
    view by Jeremy Bernstein, "Talk of the Town" column.]

C473 Editor. The Coming of the Space Age: Famous Accounts of
    Man's Probing the Universe. New York: Meredith. [Con-
    tents include: "Astronautics and Poetry," C70; "Everybody
    in Instant Touch," C439.]

    London: Victor Gollancz, 1967.
    London: Panther, 1970, paper.

C474 "A Glimpse of the Future--Near and Otherwise." AIA Journal
    49 (August):52, 56. [Adapted from a speech to the American
    Institute of Architects, 18 May 1967.]

    Retitled "Some Startling Predictions for the 21st Century,"
    1967. [Condensed.] C475
    Retitled "Technology and the Future," 1972. [Minor addi-
    tions.] C568

C475 "Some Startling Predictions for the 21st Century." Glamour
    57 (August):150, 220, 222-23, 225. [Condensed.]

    Originally "A Glimpse of the Future--Near and Otherwise,"
    1967. C474

Retitled "Technology and the Future," 1972. [Minor additions.] C568

C476 "Herbert George Morley Roberts Wells, Esq." <u>If</u> 17 (December): 4-5. ["Robert" in contents; guest editorial.]

In <u>The Wind from the Sun</u>, 1972. A201

C477 "Foreword." In <u>Venus Equilateral</u> by George O. Smith. New York: Pyramid, pp. 5-7, paper.

Retitled "Introduction," 1976. [Minor updating.] C628

C478 "Author's Note." <u>A Fall of Moondust</u>. London: Victor Gollancz, copyright page. [Not in American editions.] A152

In <u>An Arthur C. Clarke Second Omnibus</u>, 1968. A190

1968

C479 "When Earthmen and Alien Meet." <u>Playboy</u> 15 (January):118-21, 126, 210-12.

Retitled "When the Aliens Come," 1972. [Minor revisions.] C567

C480 "The Vandals--of the Past and Future." <u>Observer Magazine</u> (Ceylon), 14 January, p. 8.

C481 "Sigiriya--Some Modest Proposals." <u>Times Weekender</u> (Ceylon), 29 January, p. 3.

C482 "2001." <u>Clipper</u> [Pan Am inflight magazine], February-March, pp. 30-32. [Interview by Charles Power.]

C483 "Voices from the Sky." <u>Spaceflight</u> 10 (March):78-84.

<u>Radar and Electronics</u>, Spring 1968, pp. 15-26.
No connection with C398, 446, or 583.

C484 "The Space-Station: It's [sic] Radio Applications." <u>Spaceflight</u> 10 (March):85-86. [British Interplanetary Society memo, 25 May 1945.]

<u>Radar and Electronics</u>, Spring 1968, pp. 26-28.

C485 "Space Age Decade No. 2: A Prophecy." <u>Los Angeles Times</u>, 31 March, "Calendar" section, pp. 1, 22-23.

C486 "More than Five Senses." Boy's Life 58 (April):23-25, 52-53.

    In Report on Planet Three, 1972. [Minor revisions.] C565

C487 "Next: On Earth, the Good Life?" Vogue 151 (15 April):84-86, 142-44.

    Retitled "Speech Delivered in Columbus," 1969. [Oral
       transcription.] C529
    Retitled "2001: An Earth Odyssey," 1971. [Condensed.]
       C552
    Retitled "The World of 2001," 1977. [Expanded.] C643

C488 Slab It to 'Em, Arthur." Books 5 (May): 1, 8. [Anonymous
    interview.]

C489 "2001: A Space Odyssey." Military Life 5 (May):12, 14.

C490 "Arthur C. Clarke (Excerpts from a Conversation with the
    Author)." In Men of Space, by Shirley Thomas. Vol. 8.
    Philadelphia: Chilton, pp. 14-16.

C491 "Man of Many Worlds." Senior Scholastic 92 (9 May):21.
    [Interview by William Johnson, "Lively Arts" column.]

C492 "Foreword." In 2001: A Space Odyssey. New York: New
    American Library, p. 5. A188

C493 "Writer Discusses 'Space Odyssey.'" San Diego Union, 16 May,
    p. A15. [Interview by James Meade.]

*C494 "List of Expected Includes Sheer Fantasy." New Orleans States-
    Item, 3 June, p. 46. [Press clipping, not confirmed by
    microfilm available.]

    Adapted from Profiles of the Future, 1962. ["Hazards of
       Prophecy: The Failure of Nerve," C386, and "Hazards of
       Prophecy: The Failure of Imagination," C387.]

C495 "From the Conquest of Space, the Exciting Bonus for Man on
    Earth." Daily Mirror, 10 June, p. 14.

C496 "Portrait of a Man Reading, No. XV." Book World 2 (30 June):
    2. [Interview by Dale Gold.]

C497 "Destination: 2001--Kubrick at the Controls." [Bylined
    Arthur Clarke.] New York 1 (11 August):100-01. ["Lively
    Arts" column.]

    Retitled "Son of Dr. Strangelove: or, How I Learned to
       Stop Worrying and Love Stanley Kubrick," 1972. [Minor
       revisions.] C571

C498 "2001: the Book Behind the Movie . . . and the Man Who Wrote
      It." Scientific Research, 16 September, pp. 38-39. [Re-
      view and interview by Roger P. Smith.]

C499 "Introduction." In The Lion of Comarre and Against the Fall
      of Night. New York: Harcourt, Brace & World, pp. vii-x.
      A191

C500 "Author of Space Odyssey Unravels Some of the Mystery."
      Daily Variety, 20 March, no page on clipping. [Interview
      by Jerry Biegel.]

C501 "Idea for Space Movie Came from a Fertile Mind." Washington
      Post, 31 March, pp. G 1-2. [Interview by Victor Cohn.]

C502 "'Space Odyssey' in Science Fact." Dallas Morning News, 26
      May, p. 1 C. [Interview by William A. Payne.]

C503 "'Space Odyssey'--A Realistic Myth, Appropriate to Our Times."
      Times Weekender (Ceylon), 14 June, p. 4. [Interview by
      Deloraine Brohier.]

C504 "Homer on his 2nd Odyssey." Hindustani Times, 22 June, pp.
      7-8. [Interview by Allen Bradford.]

C505 The Promise of Space. New York: Harper & Row.

          London: Hodder & Stoughton, 1968.
          New York: Pyramid, 1970, paper.
          No connection with C572.

C506 "Speculations of a Space Man." This Week, 24 August, p. 7.
      [Interview by Alan Bradford.]

C507 "Haldane and Space." In Haldane and Modern Biology. Edited
      by K.R. Dronamraju. Baltimore: Johns Hopkins University
      Press, pp. 243-48.

          In Report on Planet Three, 1972. C565

                              1969

C508 "Possible, That's All!" Magazine of Fantasy and Science Fic-
      tion 35 (October):63-68.

          In Report on Planet Three, 1972. [Footnotes deleted,
            postscript added.] C565
          Jack Dann, and George Zebrowski, eds. Faster than Light:

An Anthology about Interstellar Travel. New York: Harper & Row, 1976. [Revised text.]

C509 "Of Metaphysics and Moonshots." International Herald-Tribune, 4 October, p. 14. [Interview by Mary Blume.]

C510 "Science Fiction--Points the Way Ahead." British Engineer 6 (November):28, 30.

C511 "The Mind of the Machine." Playboy 15 (December):116-18, 122, 293-94.

    Retitled "Are You Thinking Machines?" 1969. [Condensed.] C516
    In Report on Planet Three, 1972. C565

C512 "Electronic Library a Marvel of the Future." In "2001: A Space Odyssey" Exhibitor's Campaign Book. N.p.: Metro-Goldwyn-Mayer, p. 20. [Anonymous interview.]

C513 "Tired Businessman Can Look Forward to Six-Day Weekend." In "2001: A Space Odyssey" Exhibitor's Campaign Book. N.p.: Metro-Goldwyn-Mayer, p. 20. [Anonymous interview.]

C514 "'Survival' in a Vacuum of Space." In "2001: A Space Odyssey" Exhibitor's Campaign Book. N.p.: Metro-Goldwyn-Mayer, p. 22.

C515 "Views from Earth on the Odyssey into Space." Look 33 (4 February):72, 77. [With I.I. Rabi and C.P. Snow.]

C516 "Are You Thinking Machines?" Industrial Research 11 (March): 52-55. [Condensed.]

    Originally "The Mind of the Machine," 1968. C511

C517 "Next--the Planets." Playboy 16 (March):95-96, 100, 168.

    Horizons [United States Information Service, Manila], 20 [May] 1971, 50-55. [Condensed.]

    In Report on Planet Three, 1972. [Title ends with exclamation point, prologue added.] C565

C518 "They Wouldn't Have Made Such Fools of Themselves." Radio Times 182 (20 March):33.

C519 "The Myth of 2001." Cosmos: Science-Fiction Review [fanzine] no. 1 (April), pp. 10-11.

    In Report on Planet Three, 1972. [Postscript added.] C565

C520 "Free Press Interview: Arthur C. Clarke." Los Angeles Free
      Press 6 (25 April):42–43, 47. [Interview by Gene
      Youngblood and Ted Zatlyn.]

C521 "Author, Director All Out for Space-Age Authenticity." Los
      Angeles Times, 27 April, "Calendar" section, p. 18.
      [Interview by Wayne Warga.]

C522 "Apollo and Beyond." Look 33 (15 July):43–49.

C523 "Will Advent of Man Awaken a Sleeping Moon?" New York Times,
      17 July 1969, Special Supplement: "Apollo 11: Man and
      the Moon," p. 47.

      Retitled "Beyond the Moon's Horizon," 1969. C525
      Retitled "Time and the Times" [first part], 1977. C645

C524 "Beyond the Moon: No End." Time 94 (18 July):31. [Con-
      densed.]

      Retitled "Time and the Times" [second part], 1977. C645

C525 "Beyond the Moon's Horizon." [Bylined Arthur Clarke.] Ceylon
      Observer Magazine, 21 July, p. 11.

      Originally "Will Advent of Man Awaken a Sleeping Moon?"
          1969. C523

C526 "Mogul Silver." In Treasure and Treasure Hunters. Edited by
      R. Armstrong. London: Hamish Hamilton, 1969, pp. 50–59.

      Excerpt, The Treasure of the Great Reef, 1964. C429

C527 "Spinoff from Space." Bell Telephone Magazine 48 (September–
      October):26–32.

C528 "Beyond Babel." UNESCO Features, nos. 564–65: "The Third
      Parent and the Survival of Mankind," I/II (December):7–11
      (pt. 1); no. 566, "Tomorrow the World," I (January 1970):
      12–15 (pt. 2). [Condensed from an address to December 1969
      UNESCO Conference on Space Communications.]

      UNESCO Courier 23 (March 1970):32–37. [Condensed.]
      Excerpt, "The Great Teacher in the Sky," 1970. C540
      In Report on Planet Three, 1972. [Subtitled "The Century
          of the Communications Satellite."] C565

C529 "Speech Delivered in Columbus [Ohio]." foma [fanzine] 1
      [year not given]:12–21. [Oral transcript.]

      Originally "Next: On Earth, the Good Life?" 1968. C487
      Retitled "2001: An Earth Odyssey," 1971 [Condensed.] C552

Retitled "The World of 2001," 1977. [Expanded.] C643

C530 "Foreword." In Three for Tomorrow: Three Original Novellas
      of Science Fiction. [Edited by Robert Silverberg.] New
      York: Meredith, pp. ix-x.

      London: Sphere, 1972, paper. [Erroneously credited to
         Clarke as editor.]

C531 "God and Einstein." [Bylined Arthur C. Clarke.] Sigma [The
      Journal of the Mathematical and Astronomical Societies,
      University of Colombo, Ceylon], 1969-1971, p. 25.

      Retitled "Einstein and Science Fiction," 1980. [Expanded.]
         C697
      In Report on Planet Three, 1972. C565

C532 "The Future Isn't What It Used to Be." In SF Symposium.
      Edited by José Sanz. [Rio de Janeiro]: Instituto
      Nacional do Cinema, pp. 181-88. [Remarks at a conference
      held in March, 1969; text in English, pp. 185-86, notes,
      p. 188.]

      Retitled "From a Speech: Rio, 1969," 1974. C606

                              1970

C533 "Communications by Earth Satellite." Weekend (Ceylon), 15
      January, p. 29.

C534 "Preface." In Expedition to Earth. New York: Harcourt,
      Brace & World, pp. vii-viii. A66

C535 "Preface" [revised]. In Reach for Tomorrow. New York:
      Harcourt, Brace & World, pp. vii-viii. A82

C536 "A Post-Apollo Preface to Prelude to Space." In Prelude to
      Space. New York: Harcourt, Brace & World, pp. ix-xii.
      A41

      New York: Ballantine, 1976, paper. [Revised.]

C537 "The Fascination of Space." American Review [United States
      Information Service, New Delhi] 14 (April):84-90.

      American Review 15 (January 1979):93-99.

C538 "Hal Jr. Has Arrived." Measure [Hewlett-Packard in-house
      magazine], April, pp. 6-8. [Correspondence over new gift
      H-P computer.]

C539 "Foreword to the 1962 [sic] Edition." In <u>Prelude to Space</u>.
      New York: Lancer, pp. 9–12, paper. A41

      Originally "Foreword," 1961. C348

C540 "The Great Teacher in the Sky." <u>Boston Sunday Globe Magazine</u>,
      5 April, pp. 23, 25–28, 30.

      Excerpt from "Beyond Babel," 1969. C528

C541 "Beyond Apollo." Epilogue to <u>First on the Moon: A Voyage
      with Neil Armstrong, Michael Collins, Edwin E. Aldrin, Jr.</u>
      Written with Gene Farmer and Dora Jane Hamblin. Boston:
      Little, Brown, pp. 371–419.

      London: Michael Joseph, 1970.
      Excerpt, "Man's Future in Space," 1970. C543
      Excerpt, "Man's Destiny in Space," 1970. C545

C542 "An Evening With." <u>ERB-Dom</u> [fanzine] 36 (July):8–9. [Report
      on lecture and question period by Stanley Wiater.]

C543 "Man's Future in Space." <u>True</u> 51 (July):31–35, 86–92.

      Excerpt from "Beyond Apollo," 1970. C541

C544 "Introduction." In The <u>Panic Broadcast: Portrait of an
      Event</u> by Howard Koch. Boston: Little, Brown, pp. 3–8.
      [Interview with Clarke.]

C545 "Man's Destiny in Space." <u>Sunday Telegraph</u>, 9 August, p. 6.

      Excerpt from "Beyond Apollo," 1970. C541

C546 "Arthur C. Clarke Went on a Whirlwind Tour Promoting <u>2001</u>."
      In <u>The Making of Kubrick's 2001</u>.by Jerome Agel. New York:
      New American Library, pp. 310–12, paper. [Excerpts from
      interviews, undocumented.] D95

C547 <u>Space, the Unconquerable</u>. Colombo, Sri Lanka: Lake House
      Investments, paper. ["The Uses of the Moon," C347; "To
      the Stars," C448; "Ages of Plenty," C394; "Space, the Un-
      conquerable," C392; title page lists last item first.]

                                1971

C548 "At the Interface: Technology and Mysticism." <u>Playboy</u> 19
      (January):94–97, 130, 256–58, 260–64, 270–74. [Dialogue
      with Alan Watts.]

C549   "Moon Strike." Science Students Magazine, 1969-70
            [Vidyalankara University of Ceylon, Kalaniya, March 1971],
            pp. 1-2.

C550   "Whatever Happened to Flying Saucers?" Saturday Evening Post
            243 (Summer):10.

            Daily Mail, 6 July 1971, p. 6.
            UFO Thirtieth Anniversary Issue (1977), pp. 10-11.

C551   "Space Shuttle: Key to Future." Congressional Record 117
            (23 June):21757. [Letter to New York Times (15 May 1971).]

C552   "2001: An Earth Odyssey." Rotarian 118-19 (July):15-17.
            [Condensed.]

            Originally "Next: on Earth, the Good Life?" 1968. C487
            Retitled "Speech Delivered in Columbus," 1969. [Oral
                transcription.] C529
            Retitled "The World of 2001," 1977. C643

C553   Into Space: A Young Person's Guide to Space. [Revised by
            Robert Silverberg.] New York: Harper & Row.

            Originally The Young Traveller in Space, 1954. C200
            Retitled Going into Space, 1954. C201
            Retitled The Scottie Book of Space Travel, 1957. C258

C554   "Schoolmaster Satellite." Daily Telegraph Magazine, 7 Decem-
            ber, pp. 9-10, 12.

            Retitled "Promise of Space," 1972. C572
            Retitled "India Reaches for the Stars," 1973. [Condensed.]
                C587
            Retitled "Star of India," 1974. C609
            Retitled "Satellites and Saris" [second part], 1977. C647

                              1972

C555   "Mars and the Mind of Man." Engineering and Science 35
            (January):17-19. [Highlights of panel discussion at
            California Institute of Technology, 12 November 1971.]

            In Mars and the Mind of Man, 1973. [Complete discussion.]
                C594

C556   "Foreword." In The Lost Worlds of 2001. New York: New
            American Library, p. 11, paper. A200

C557   "Son of Dr. Strangelove." In The Lost Worlds of 2001, pp. 17-
            18. A200

                              111

C558 "Christmas, Shepperton." In The Lost Worlds of 2001, pp. 29–
      40. A200

      Untitled excerpt, liner notes to Arthur C. Clarke Reads
          from His "2001: A Space Odyssey," 1976. B41

C559 "Monoliths and Manuscripts." In The Lost Worlds of 2001, pp.
      41–49. A200

C560 "The Dawn of Man." In The Lost Worlds of 2001, pp. 50–52.
      A200

C561 "The Birth of HAL." In The Lost Worlds of 2001, pp. 76–79.
      A200

C562 "Mission to Jupiter." In The Lost Worlds of 2001, pp. 124–27.
      A200

C563 "The Worlds of the Star Gate." In The Lost Worlds of 2001,
      pp. 188–91. A200

C564 "Epilogue." In The Lost Worlds of 2001, pp. 239–40. A200.

C565 Report on Planet Three and Other Speculations. New York:
      Harper & Row. ["Preface," C566; "Report on Planet Three,"
      C313; "The Men on the Moon," C291; "Meteors," C307; "The
      Star of the Magi," C308; "Vacation in Vacuum," C304; "So
      You're Going to Mars," C306; "Next--The Planets!" C517;
      "The Planets Are Not Enough," C223; "When the Aliens Come,"
      C567; "Possible--That's All!" C508; "God and Einstein,"
      C531; "Across the Sea of Stars," C311; "The Mind of the
      Machine," C511; "Technology and the Future," C568; "Beyond
      Babel," C528; "More than Five Senses," C486; "Things That
      Can Never Be Done," C569; "The World We Cannot See," C570;
      "Things in the Sky," C315; "Which Way is Up?" C312;
      "Haldane and Space," C507; "Son of Dr. Strangelove; or How
      I Learned to Stop Worrying and Love Stanley Kubrick," C571;
      "The Myth of 2001," C519.]

      London: Victor Gollancz, 1972.
      New York: New American Library, 1973, paper.
      London: Corgi, 1973, paper.

C566 "Preface." In Report on Planet Three, pp. xi–xii. C565

C567 "When the Aliens Come." Report on Planet Three, pp. 93–107.
      [Minor revisions.] C565

      Originally "When Earthman and Alien Meet," 1968. C479

C568 "Technology and the Future." In Report on Planet Three,
      pp. 138–51. C565

Originally "A Glimpse of the Future--Near and Otherwise,"
1967. C474
Retitled "Some Startling Predictions for the 21st Century,"
1967. [Condensed.] C475

C569 "Things That Can Never Be Done." In Report on Planet Three,
pp. 180-90. C565. [Original publication in Cavalier or
Why Not not confirmed.]

C570 "The World We Cannot See." In Report on Planet Three, pp.
191-202. C565. [Original publication in Cavalier or Why
Not not confirmed; includes postscript possibly added after
first publication.]

C571 "Son of Dr. Strangelove; or, How I Learned to Stop Worrying
and Love Stanley Kubrick." In Report on Planet Three, pp.
238-46. C565

Originally "Destination: 2001--Kubrick at the Controls,"
1968. C497
Damon Knight, ed. Turning Points: Essays on the Art of
Science Fiction. New York: Harper & Row, 1977.

C572 "Promise of Space." Congressional Record 118 (27 January):
1604-5. [Condensed.]

Originally "Schoolmaster Satellite," 1971. C554
Retitled "India Reaches for the Stars," 1973. [Condensed.]
C587
Retitled "Star of India," 1974. C609
Retitled "Satellites and Saris" [second part], 1977. C647
No connection with C505.

C573 "Satellites and the United States of Earth." Futurist 6
(April):61. [Adapted from an address at the signing of
the world satellite communications system agreements, 20
August 1971.]

Retitled "Satellites and Saris" [first part], 1977. C647

C574 "Introduction." In The Peculiar Exploits of Brigadier
Ffellowes by Sterling E. Lanier. New York: Walker, p.
[vii].

C575 "Ceylon: An Adventurer's Retreat." True, no. 419 (April),
pp. 38-39, 42-43.

C576 "Preface." In The Wind from the Sun. New York: Harcourt
Brace Jovanovich, pp. vii-viii. A201

C577 "Foreword." In <u>Challenge of the Stars</u> by Patrick Moore [text]
      and David A. Hardy [paintings]. London: Mitchell Beazley,
      p. 5.

C578 "Preface." In <u>Earthlight</u>. New York: Harcourt Brace
      Jovanovich, pp. ix-x. A76

C579 "Foreword." In <u>Of Time and Stars: the Worlds of Arthur C.
      Clarke</u>. London: Victor Gollancz, p. 5. A206

C580 Untitled answers to questionnaire. In <u>Focus on the Science
      Fiction Film</u>. Edited by William Johnson. Englewood Cliffs,
      N.J.: Prentice-Hall, pp. 154-55.

C581 "Out of this World." <u>London Observer Magazine</u>, 29 October,
      pp. 22-27.

          Retitled "Call it Sri Lanka or Ceylon," 1973. [Condensed.]
            C593
          Retitled "Sri Lanka Land of No Sorrows," 1973. C600
          Retitled "A Land Without Enemies," 1974. C604
          Retitled "Sri Lanka: A Land Without Enemies," 1974. C608
          Retitled "The Sea of Sinbad" [second part], 1977. [Re-
            vised.] C648

C582 "The Future City is Not Manhattan, but Disney World." <u>Chicago
      Tribune Magazine</u>, 26 November, pp. 108-11.

          Retitled "The Next Twenty Years," 1977. C646

C583 "Voices from the Sky." <u>Literary Cavalcade</u> 25 (December):26-
      27.

          Excerpt from "The Social Consequences of the Communications
            Satellites," 1962. C349
          No connection with C398, C446, or C483.

C584 "Epilogue." In <u>The Electron</u> by George Thomson. Washington,
      D.C.: United States Government Printing Office, pp. 80-86,
      paper.

          Originally "Spark of the Second Industrial Revolution,"
            1962. C406
          Retitled "The Electronic Revolution," 1965. C460

C585 "The World of Water." In <u>Mysterious Wisteria</u>. Edited by
      Theodore L. Harris et al. Oklahoma City: Economy Co.,
      pp. 193-99.

          Excerpt [adapted from chapter 1], <u>The Challenge of the Sea</u>,
            1960. C330

C586   "Ayu Bowan, Ceylon." Welcome Aboard [BOAC in flight magazine],
       no volume no. or month, pp. 22-28.

      Retitled "The Sea of Sinbad" [first part], 1977. [Revised.]
      C648

1973

C587   "India Reaches for the Stars." Reader's Digest 102 (January):
       33-37. [Condensed.]

      Originally "Schoolmaster Satellite," 1971. C554
      Retitled "Promise of Space," 1972. C572
      Retitled "Star of India," 1974. C609
      Retitled "Satellites and Saris" [second part], 1977. C647

C588   "A Look at Futures Past." Washington Post, 16 March, pp. B1,
       B8. [Interview by Jean M. White.]

C589   "An Unheard Melody Keeps Mona Smiling." Los Angeles Times,
       17 March, Section I, p. 2. [Anonymous third-person report
       on Smithsonian Institute lecture.]

C590   "A Mathematical Genius in Sarong and Bare-Toed Sandals." San
       Francisco Chronicle, 25 March, p. 17. [Interview by
       William Otterburn-Hall.]

C591   Beyond Jupiter: The Worlds of Tomorrow. Boston: Little,
       Brown. [With Chesley Bonestell.]

      Excerpt, "Beyond Jupiter." Science Digest 74 (September
        1973):72-76.
      Excerpt, "Beyond Jupiter." Sunday Times Magazine, 24
        April 1974, pp. 30-35, 37-39.

C592   "Preserving Sri Lanka." Ceylon Daily News, 5 June, p. 4.

C593   "Call it Sri Lanka or Ceylon." Travel and Leisure 3 (June-
       July):40-43.

      Originally "Out of this World," 1972. C581
      Retitled "Sri Lanka Land of No Sorrows," 1973. C600
      Retitled "A Land Without Enemies," 1974. C604
      Retitled "Sri Lanka: A Land Without Enemies," 1974. C608
      Retitled "The Sea of Sinbad" [second part], 1977. [Re-
        vised.] C648

C594   Mars and the Mind of Man. New York: Harper & Row. [Edited
       transcript of conference, 12 November 1971, with "After-
       thoughts" solicited prior to November 1972.] With Ray

Bradbury, Bruce Murray, Carl Sagan, Walter Sullivan. [In-
cludes "Mars and the Mind of Man" (highlights), C555, and
"Whether or Not There is Life on Mars Now, There Will Be
by the End of This Century," C595.]

C595 "Whether or Not There is Life on Mars Now, There Will Be by
the End of This Century." In Mars and the Mind of Man,
pp. 26-28. [Discussion pp. 29-39, "Afterthoughts" pp. 79-
87.] C594

Retitled "Mars and the Mind of Man," 1977. [Discussion
omitted.] C650

C596 "Arthur C. Clarke." Publishers Weekly 204 (10 September):24-
25. [Interview by Alice K. Turner.]

Retitled "Clarke Interviewed," 1974. C605

C597 "1933: A Science Fiction Odyssey." In The Best of Arthur C.
Clarke. Edited by Angus Wells. London: Sidgwick &
Jackson, pp. 9-14. A209

C598 "Arthur C. Clarke: A Space Homer." Radio Times, 18 October
1973, p. 24. [Interview by Donald Lehmkuhl.]

C599 "A Man in His Element." Sunday Mail Colour Magazine, 18 November, p. 6. [Interview by Jan Modder.]

C600 "Sri Lanka Land of No Sorrows." Sri Lanka Tourist Bulletin,
2d week of December [year not given], pp. 8-10.

Originally "Out of this World," 1972. C581
Retitled "Call it Sri Lanka or Ceylon," 1973. C593
Retitled "A Land Without Enemies," 1974. C604
Retitled "Sri Lanka: A Land Without Enemies," 1974. C608
Retitled "The Sea of Sinbad" [second part], 1977. [Re-
vised.] C648

C601 "Closing in on Life in Space." In Nature/Science Annual 1974.
New York: Time/Life Books, pp. 98-111.

Retitled "Life in Space," 1977. [Minor revisions.] C651

1974

C602 "Arthur C. Clarke: Ceylonese by Choice." Asian Student 11
(May):8. [Interview by Eric Ranawake.]

C603 "About the Author." In Rendezvous with Rama. New York:

Ballantine, pp. 275-76, paper. A207 [Third person, but revises C336.]

Retitled "Arthur C. Clarke," 1976. [Minor revisions.] C625
See also "About Arthur C. Clarke," 1953. C187

C604 "A Land Without Enemies." Tourmaline: The Magazine of Sri Lanka 1, no. 2 (n.d.):2-17.

Originally "Out of this World," 1972. C581
Retitled "Call it Sri Lanka or Ceylon," 1973. C593
Retitled "Sri Lanka Land of No Sorrows," 1973. C600
Retitled "Sri Lanka: A Land Without Enemies," 1974. C604
Retitled "The Sea of Sinbad" [second part], 1977. [Revised.] C613

C605 "Clarke Interviewed." Algol [fanzine] 12 (November 1974):14, 16. [Interview by Alice K. Turner.]

Originally "Arthur C. Clarke," 1973. C573

C606 "From a Speech: Rio, 1969." Algol [fanzine] 12 (November): 17. ["rio" on title page.]

Originally, "The Future Isn't What it Used to Be," 1969. C532

C607 "The Future of Man in the Sea." In Oceans 2000: Third World Congress of Underwater Activities. [London]:British Sub-Aqua Club, n.d., pp. 1-4. [Proceedings of conference held 8-14 October 1973; additional comments by Clarke on pp. 7, 10, 11, 15-18, 20-21, 70.]

C608 "Sri Lanka: A Land Without Enemies." Ceylon News, 24 November, p. 6. [First half of original article, "to be continued."]

Originally "Out of This World," 1972. C581
Retitled "Call it Sri Lanka or Ceylon," 1973. C593
Retitled "Sri Lanka Land of No Sorrows," 1973. C600
Retitled "A Land Without Enemies," 1974. C604
Retitled "The Sea of Sinbad" [second part], 1977. [Revised.] C648

C609 "Star of India." Voice Across the Sea. [Revised ed.; added chapter 26.] C273

Originally "Schoolmaster Satellite," 1971. C554
Retitled "Promise of Space," 1972. C572
Retitled "India Reaches for the Stars," 1973. [Condensed.] C587

Retitled "Satellites and Saris," [second part], 1977. C647

C610 "The Snows of Olympus." Playboy 21 (December):161.

Retitled "Fired by the Red Planet," 1975. C616
In The View from Serendip, 1977. C638

C611 "The World of Arthur C. Clarke." New Scientist 64 (12 December):822-23. [Interview by Michael Kenward.]

C612 "Foreword." In The World in Focus by William MacQuitty.
Edinburgh: John Bartholomew, p. 7.

Retitled Our World in Colour. Surrey, England: Colour
Library International, 1977.

1975

C613 "Introducing Isaac Asimov." Magazine of Fantasy and Science
Fiction 48 (January):113-16.

In The View from Serendip, 1977. C638
See B39 for earlier recording.

C614 Technology and the Frontiers of Knowledge. Garden City, N.Y.:
Doubleday. [Frank Nelson Doubleday Lectures, 1972-1973.]
With Saul Bellow, Daniel Bell, Edmundo O'Gorman, and Sir
Peter Medawar. [Includes "Technology and the Limits of
Knowledge," C615.]

C615 "Technology and the Limits of Knowledge." In Technology and
the Frontiers of Knowledge, pp. 111-13. C614

In The View from Serendip, 1977. C638

C616 "Fired by the Red Planet." Daily Telegraph Magazine, 11
April, p. 7.

Originally "The Snows of Olympus," 1974. C610

C617 "UFO'S Explained by Philip J. Klass, The UFO Controversy in
America by David Michael Jacob." New York Times Book Review, 27 July, pp. 4-5.

Retitled "Last (?) Words on UFO's," 1977. C652

C618 "Arthur C. Clarke Looks at ATS-6 Dream Come True." Fairchild
World [in-house magazine] 12 (November-December):1-2.
[Anonymous interview/profile/report on visit to Fairchild
Co.]

C619 "Next 100 Years." Senior Scholastic 17 (16 December):10.

    Originally "Chart of the Future," 1973. C402

C620 "Acknowledgements and Notes." In Imperial Earth: A Fantasy
    of Love and Discord. London: Victor Gollancz, pp. 285-87.

    Imperial Earth. New York: Harcourt Brace Jovanovich,
      1976, pp. 273-75. [Expanded.] A216

C621 Untitled testimony. Future Space Programs 1975: Hearings
    Before the Subcommittee on Space Science and Applications
    [House of Representatives]. Washington, D.C.: Government
    Printing Office, pp. 190-200 [discussion, pp. 200-207].

    Retitled "To the House Subcommittee on Space Science and
      Applications," 1975. C622
    Retitled "Man, Space, and Destiny," 1976. [Omits discus-
      sion.] C626
    Retitled "To the Committee on Space Science," 1977. C654

C622 "To the House Subcommittee on Space Science and Applications."
    Science Fantasy Correspondent 1 (1975):22-30.

    Originally untitled testimony, 1975. C621
    Retitled "Man, Space, and Destiny," 1976. [Omits discus-
      sion.] C626
    Retitled "To the Committee on Space Science," 1977. C654

                    1976

C623 "Communications in the Second Century of the Telephone."
    Technology Review 78 (May):83-122. [Address to the tele-
    phone centenary conference, 10 March 1976.]

    Retitled "The Second Century of the Telephone," 1977.
      [Minor revisions.] C655
    Retitled "Communications in the Future," 1977. [Condensed,
      footnotes added.] C668
    Congressional Record 122 (14 June 1976):17931-35.
    Galileo, no. 1 (September 1976), pp. 16-21, 66-67.
    The Telephone's First Century and Beyond, 1977. C633
    Across the Board 14 (August 1977):58-65.

C624 "A Word from Arthur C. Clarke." Publishers Weekly 209 (14
    June):47. [Interview by J.F. B(aker).]

C625 "Arthur C. Clarke." In Childhood's End. 33d printing. New
    York: Ballantine, pp. [219-20], paper. [Minor revisions.]
    A64

Originally "About the Author," 1974. C603
In <u>Tales from the "White Hart</u>." 12th printing. New York:
   Ballantine, 1977, paper, pp. [149-50].
See also "Arthur C. Clarke," 1953. C187

C626 "Man, Space, and Destiny." <u>Analog Science Fiction/Science
      <u>Fact</u> 96 (July):5-9, 171-78.

      Originally, untitled testimony, 1975. C621
      Retitled "To the House Subcommittee on Space Science and
         Applications," 1975. C622
      Retitled "To the Committee on Space Science," 1977. C654

C627 "Why Men Should Explore the Planets." <u>Sunday Observer</u> (Sri
      Lanka), 3 October, p. 1.

C628 "Introduction." In <u>The Complete Venus Equilateral</u> by George
      O. Smith. New York: Ballantine, pp. ix-xi, paper.

      Originally "Foreword," 1967. C477

C629 "Additional Note." In <u>Imperial Earth</u>. New York: Ballantine,
      p. 305, paper. A216

C630 "The Legacy of Viking--A Taste of Things to Come." <u>Space-
      <u>flight</u> 18 (December):429-31.

C631 "What Star Was This?" <u>Saturday Evening Post</u> 248 (December):
      48-49, 96. [Abridged, longer than C211.]

      Originally "What Was the Star of Bethlehem?" 1954. C207
      Retitled "Does the Star of Bethlehem Still Shine?" 1955.
         [Condensed.] C211
      Retitled "The Star of the Magi," 1959. [Footnote, post-
         script added.] C308

C632 "Satellite Communication." In <u>Postal Training Institute of
      <u>Sri Lanka 1977 Annual</u>. Colombo: Postal Training Institute,
      pp. 23, 25.

                              1977

C633 <u>The Telephone's First Century and Beyond</u>. New York: Thomas
      Y. Crowell. [Symposium on the one hundredth anniversary
      of the telephone, 9-10 March 1976.] With Michael L.
      Dertouzos, Morris Halle, Ithiel de Sola Pool, and Jerome B.
      Wiesner. [Includes "Communications in the Second Century
      of the Telephone," C623.]

C634 "Sri Lanka and Me." <u>Millimeter</u> 5 (March):41.

C635 "Could You Solve Pentominoes?" <u>Sunday Telegraph Magazine</u>,
8 May, pp. 30-32, 34.

C636 "An 'Earth' in Outer Space in 50 Years." <u>Ceylon Observer</u>,
10 May, p. 2. [Interview by H.P. Mama.]

C637 [Untitled introduction to section 2.14, "Computers and Cybernetics."] <u>The Visual Encyclopedia of Science Fiction</u>.
Edited by Brian Ash. New York: Harmony House, p. 181.

C638 <u>The View from Serendip</u>. New York: Random House. [Auto-
biographical passages surrounding the following: "Con-
cerning Serendipity," C639; "Dawn of the Space Age," C640;
"Servant Problem--Oriental Style," C363; "The Scent of
Treasure," C641; "The Stars in their Courses," C642; "How
to Dig Space," C442; "A Breath of Fresh Vacuum," C469;
"The World of 2001," C643; "And Now--Live from the
Moon. . . ," C644; "Time and the Times," C645; "The Next
Twenty Years," C646; "Satellites and Saris," C647; "The
Sea of Sinbad," C648; "Willy and Chesley," C649; "Mars and
the Mind of Man," C650; "The Snows of Olympus," C610;
"Introducing Isaac Asimov," C613 "Life in Space," C651;
"Last (?) Words on UFO's," C652; "When the Twerms Came,"
A204; "The Clarke Act," C653; "Technology and the Limits of
Knowledge," C615; "To the Committee on Space Science,"
C654; "The Second Century of the Telephone," C655; "Ayu
Bowan!" C656; "About the Author," D188.]

London: Victor Gollancz, 1978. [Omits "About the
Author."]
New York: Ballantine, 1978, paper. [Omits "About the
Author."]
London: Pan, 1979, paper. [Omits "About the Author."]

C639 "Concerning Serendipity." In <u>The View from Serendip</u>, pp. 3-8.
C638

C640 "Dawn of the Space Age." In <u>The View from Serendip</u>, pp. 9-12.
C638

C641 "The Scent of Treasure." In <u>The View from Serendip</u>, pp. 27-
32. [Revised.] C638

Originally "Their Skin Diving Paid Off," 1962. C360
Adapted from <u>The Treasure of the Great Reef</u>, 1964. C429

C642 "The Stars in their Courses." In <u>The View from Serendip</u>, pp.
33-39. C638

Originally "Commonsense and the Planets," 1962. C354

121

C643 "The World of 2001." In The View from Serendip, pp. 59-71.
      C638

      Originally "Next--on Earth, the Good Life?" 1968. C487
      Retitled "Speech Delivered in Columbus," 1969. [Oral
         transcript.] C529
      Retitled "2001: An Earth Odyssey," 1971. [Condensed.]
         C552

C644 "And Now--Live from the Moon. . . ." In The View from Seren-
      dip, pp. 73-79. C638

C645 "Time and The Times." In The View from Serendip, pp. 81-92.
      C638

      First part originally "Will Advent of Man Awaken a Sleeping
         Moon?" 1969. C523
      Retitled "Beyond the Moon's Horizon," 1969. C525
      Second part originally "Beyond the Moon: No End," 1969.
         [Condensed.] C524

C646 "The Next Twenty Years." In The View from Serendip, pp. 93-
      104. C638

      Originally "The Future City is Not Manhattan, but Disney
         World," 1972. C582

C647 "Satellites and Saris." In The View from Serendip, pp. 105-
      16. C638

      First part originally "Satellites and the United States of
         Earth," 1971. C573
      Second part originally "Schoolmaster Satellite," 1971.
         C554
      Retitled "Promise of Space," 1972. C572
      Retitled "India Reaches for the Stars," 1973. [Condensed.]
         C587
      Retitled "Star of India," 1974. C609

C648 "The Sea of Sinbad." In The View from Serendip, pp. 117-30.
      C638

      First part originally "Ayu Bowan Ceylon," 1972. C586
      Second part originally "Out of this World," 1972. C581
      Retitled "Call it Sri Lanka or Ceylon," 1973. C593
      Retitled "Sri Lanka Land of No Sorrows," 1973. C600
      Retitled "A Land Without Enemies," 1974. C604
      Retitled "Sri Lanka: A Land Without Enemies," 1974. C608

C649 "Willy and Chesley." In The View from Serendip, pp. 131-37.
      C638

C650 "Mars and the Mind of Man." In The View from Serendip, pp. 139-46. C638

> Originally "Whether of Not There is Life on Mars Now, There Will Be by the End of This Century," 1973. C595

C651 "Life in Space." In The View from Serendip, pp. 159-74. C638

> Originally "Closing in on Life in Space," 1974. C616

C652 "Last (?) Words on UFO's." In The View from Serendip, pp. 175-78. C638

> Originally "UFO's Explained by Philip J. Klass, The UFO Controversy in America by David Michael Jacob," 1975. C617

C653 "The Clarke Act." In The View from Serendip, pp. 183-85. C638

C654 "To the Committee on Space Science." In The View from Serendip, pp. 211-39. C638

> Originally untitled testimony, 1975. C621
> Retitled "To the House Subcommittee on Space Science and Applications," 1975. C622
> Retitled "Man, Space, and Destiny," 1976. [Omits discussion.] C626

C655 "The Second Century of the Telephone." In The View from Serendip, pp. 241-65. [Minor revisions.] C638

> Originally "Communications in the Second Century of the Telephone," 1976. C623
> Retitled "Communications in the Future," 1978. [Condensed, footnotes added.] C668

C656 "Ayu Bowan!" In The View from Serendip, pp. 267-73. C638

> Excerpt, "Coping with Correspondents," 1980. C690

C657 "Preface." In The Best of Arthur C. Clarke, 1955-1972, p. 9. A209

C658 "Next--The Wandering Executive." COMSAT General Marifacts 3 (October):2-3.

1978

C659 "The Challenge of Change." Sunday Observer (Sri Lanka), 22 January, p. 14. [Report on Clarke speech.]

C660 "Tourism--The Challenge of Change." Ceylon Daily Mirror, 23
        January, p. 4.

        Sri Lanka Travel News n.s. 2 (April):4.

C661 "A Look Forward to Encountering New Neighbors." Science
        Digest 83 (February):8-11. [Interview by Mark Davidson and
        Nirmali Ponnamperunal.]

C662 "The Destruction of Sri Lanka." Times Weekender (Sri Lanka),
        25 February, p. 1.

C663 "On Moylan on The City and the Stars." Science-Fiction
        Studies 5 (March):88-90. [Letter in response to D204;
        further discussion, D222, 239.]

C664 "Beyond Infinity with Arthur C. Clarke." Bangkok Post, 12
        March, no page on clipping. [Interview by Jeffrey Shane.]

C665 "Men Only Interview: Arthur C. Clarke." Men Only 43 (April):
        20-22, 24, 30. [Interview by David S. Garnett.]

        Retitled "An Interview with Arthur C. Clarke," 1978. C667
          [Interview by David Garnett.]

C666 "Arthur C. Clarke: At a Turning Point in Paradise." Future:
        The Magazine of Science Adventure 1 (May):20-26. [Inter-
        view by David Houston and the editors of Future.]

C667 "An Interview with Arthur C. Clarke." Locus [fanzine] 11
        (July):9, 11. [Interview by David Garnett; introductory
        material, magazine title as interviewer omitted.]

        Originally "Men Only Interview: Arthur C. Clarke," 1978.
          [Interview by David S. Garnett.] C665

C668 "Communications in the Future." Handbook of Futures Research.
        Edited by Jib Fowles. Westport, Conn.: Greenwood Press.
        [Condensed, footnotes added.]

        Originally "Communications in the Second Century of the
          Telephone," 1976. C623
        Retitled "The Second Century of the Telephone," 1977.
          [Minor revisions.] C655

C669 "The Man with Space for Development." Guardian, 30 August,
        p. 8. [Interview by Martin Walker.]

        Retitled "The Distant Worlds of Arthur C. Clarke," 1978.
          C670
        Retitled "Arthur C. Clarke in Sri Lanka," 1978. C671

C670   "The Distant Worlds of Arthur C. Clarke." <u>Washington Post</u>,
       4 September, pp. C1, C3. [Interview by Martin Walker.]

       Originally "The Man with Space for Development," 1978.
         C669
       Retitled "Arthur C. Clarke in Sri Lanka," 1978. C671

C671   "Arthur C. Clarke in Sri Lanka." <u>Los Angeles Times</u>, 14
       September, section IV, p. 8. [Interview by Martin Walker.]

       Originally "The Man with Space for Development," 1978.
         C669
       Retitled "The Distant Worlds of Arthur C. Clarke," 1978.
         C670

C672   [Untitled liner notes.] In <u>"Transit of Earth" and "The Nine
       Billion Names of God"--"The Star" Read by the Author,
       Arthur C. Clarke</u>. New York: Caedmon. [Disc/cassette.]
       B50

C673   "Introduction." In <u>My Four Feet on the Ground: Memories of
       Exmoor and Ballifants</u> by Nora Clarke. London: Rocket Pub-
       lishing Co., pp. 6-7, paper.

C674   "Introduction." In <u>Writing to Sell</u> by Scott Meredith. 2d rev.
       ed. New York: Harper & Row, pp. xv-xx.

C675   "The Future." In <u>COMSAT at 15</u>. [Clarkson, Md.]: Communica-
       tions Satellite Corp., pp. 54-55. [Of two pamphlets with
       this title, this is 32 pages long, glossy, color-illustrated,
       with no subtitle; the other is subtitled "Chronology of
       Significant Events 1962-1977."]

                              1979

C676   "A Visit with Arthur C. Clarke." <u>Writer's Digest</u> 59 (January):
       24-25. [Interview by Billye Cutcheon.]

C677   "How One Man Found His Way to the Stars." <u>Telegraph Sunday
       Magazine</u>, 21 January, pp. 32-33, 35-36, 39. [Interview by
       Philip Purser.]

C678   "Foreword." In <u>The Fountains of Paradise</u>. London: Victor
       Gollancz, p. 11. A224

       Retitled "Preface," 1979. C680

C679   "Sources and Acknowledgements." In <u>The Fountains of Paradise</u>.
       London: Victor Gollancz, pp. 251-55. A224

C680   "Preface." In <u>The Fountains of Paradise</u>. New York: Harcourt

Brace Jovanovich, p. xiii. A224

Originally "Foreword," 1979. C678

C681 "Spaceships." Omni 1 (February):76-85. [Condensed.]

Originally "The Challenge of the Spaceship," 1946. C64
Ben Bova, and Don Myers, eds. The Best of Omni Science
    Fiction 2. New York: Omni, 1980.

C682 "Interview: Arthur C. Clarke." 100-103, 139-41. [Interview
    by Malcolm Kirk.] Omni 1 (March),

C683 "The View from Sri Lanka." Locus [fanzine] 12 (April):9.

C684 "From Arthur C. Clarke." Science Fiction Review [fanzine] 8
    (May):8. [Letter excerpted in "Letter from Charles
    Sheffield."]

Retitled "An Open Letter to the Science Fiction Writers of
    America," 1979. C685

C685 "An Open Letter to the Science Fiction Writers of America."
    Bulletin of the Science Fiction Writers of America 14
    (Summer):45-46.

Originally "From Arthur C. Clarke," 1979. C684
Charles Sheffield. The Web Between the Worlds. New York:
    Ace, 1979.

C686 "The Best is Yet to Come." Time 114 (16 July):27.

C687 "A Cable Car to Outer Space." Daily Telegraph, 24 September,
    p. 12. [Anonymous report on paper delivered at Munich
    conference.]

C688 "Sri Lanka--Pearl of the Orient." Animal Kingdom 82 (October-
    November):4-5.

1980

C689 "Law Giver." Omni 2 (April):80-87. [Pictorial.]

C690 "Electronic Tutors." Omni 2 (June):76-78, 96.

C691 "Coping with Correspondents." Author 91 (Summer):89-90.

Excerpt from "Ayu Bowan!" 1977. C656

C692 "Foreword," "Introduction." In Arthur C. Clarke's Mysterious
    World by John Fairley and Simon Welfare. London: William
    Collins Sons, pp. 7, 11. [Brief comments also close each
    of twelve chapters; based on Yorkshire Television series,
    B58.]

New York: A & W Publishing, 1980.

C693 "Say Hello and Good Morning to Mr. Chips." Electronic Times,
      11 September, no page on clipping. [Report by Joan Gray on
      Cambridge lecture.]

C694 "The Man in the Sarong Who is Building a Ladder to the Moon."
      Family Scene, 25 September, pp. 2-3, 79. [Interview by
      Jane Ennis.]

C695 "The White Hart Series." In The Great Science Fiction Series.
      Edited by Frederik Pohl, Martin Harry Greenberg, and Joseph
      D. Olander. New York: Harper & Row, pp. 154-55.

      Originally "Preface," 1957. C236.

C696 "Arthur C. Clarke: Down to Earth." Observer Sunday Magazine
      (Sri Lanka), 6 December, pp. 8, 10. [Interview by Eustace
      Rulach.]

C697 "Einstein and Science Fiction." In Einstein: The First
      Hundred Years. Edited by Maurice Goldsmith, Alan MacKay,
      and James Woudhuysen. Oxford: Pergamon Press, pp. 159-61.
      [Expanded.]

      Originally "God and Einstein," 1969. C531

C698 "Interview with Arthur C. Clarke." In Future Imperfect: Sci-
      ence Fact and Science Fiction. Edited by Rex Malik.
      London: Frances Pinter, pp. 115-22. [Interview by Rex
      Malik, based on a filmed "entertainment" including Clarke
      responses for July 1969 Sperry-Univac conference.]

                              Undated

C699 "The Fourth Dimension." Probe [fanzine], no. 60A [six, "con-
      tinued from no. 29A], pp. 1-3. [Probably 1950; see Appen-
      dix 4.]

C700 "Underwater Holiday." [11" by 14" British magazine, illustra-
      tions by Edward Osmond], pp. 14-15, 45. [Ca. 1954-1960.]

      Originally "Undersea Holiday," 1954. C197
      Excerpt from The Challenge of the Sea, 1960. C330

C701 "When Earthmen Become the 'UFO' of Other Planets." [8 1/2"
      by 11" UFO magazine], pp. 8-17. [Concerns 2001, bylined
      Arthur C. Clarke, but with references to him in third
      person--ca. 1970?]

C702   "Future Perfect." <u>She</u> [no volume no. or date on clipping],
       pp. 80-81. [Ca. 1970-1975? mention of "Hal Jr." Inter-
       view by A.J. Venter.]

Secondary Material

Part D: Biography, Bibliography, Criticism

1936

D1 "Personalia" column. Huish Magazine 25 (Summer):27.
      Clarke placed 26th of 1,469 civil service candidates.
    Job assured, prospects bright for "Archie."

1949

D2 "Know Your Council." Journal of the British Interplanetary
      Society 8 (January):21-22.
        Clarke's first published vita stresses his education,
    radar work, scientific societies, publications since 1944.

1952

D3 FADIMAN, CLIFTON. "The Exploration of Space." Book-of-the-
      Month-Club News, June, pp. 4-5.
        Promotional "review" for an "Alternate Selection."

D4 HUTCHENS, JOHN K. "On the Books--On an Author." New York
      Herald-Tribune Book Review, 10 August, p. 8.
        Profile/interview stresses The Exploration of Space.

1954

D5 "Arthur C. Clarke: From Here to Infinity." Leica Photography
      7 (Summer):9.
        Clarke's photographic exploits described, using Leica
    equipment.

D6 BREIT, HARVEY. "Lunar Man" [column segment, "In and Out of
      Books"]. New York Times Book Review, 14 March, p. 8.
        Brief discussion of The Exploration of Space, The Ex-
    ploration of the Moon (forthcoming), skindiving.

D7   CARNELL, JOHN.   "Arthur C. Clarke." New Worlds 8 (April):
      no page number [inside front cover].
         Brief profile.

*D8   TUCK, DONALD H., comp. A Handbook of Science Fiction and
      Fantasy. Hobart, Tasmania: privately mimeographed, paper.
      [Source: RR.]

         "Clarke, Arthur C.," annotated checklist.
         2d ed., 1959, paper, 2 vols. 1:61-62.
         Retitled The Encyclopedia of Science Fiction and Fantasy:
         A Bibliographical Survey of the Fields of Science Fiction,
         Fantasy and Weird Fiction through 1968. Vol. 1. Chicago:
         Advent, 1974, pp. 100-3.

            "Clarke, Arthur C.(harles)," résumé and checklist.

                                1955

D9   KUNITZ, STANLEY, ed. Twentieth Century Authors: A Biblio-
      graphical Dictionary of Modern Literature, First Supple-
      ment. New York: H.W. Wilson, pp. 205-6.
         "Clarke, Arthur C.," résumé including short paragraph by
      author.

                                1956

D10   BLISH, JAMES. "Arthur C. Clarke: An Appreciation." Journal
      of the World Science Fiction Society 14 [convention progress
      report no. 1]:5-8.
         "Episodic, fact-centered, rambling, seemingly discursive,"
      Clarke's stories legitimate their surprise endings and
      coincidences. His prose can be "evocative and poetic,"
      but he has a journalist's sincerity and desire to convince.
      This first critical survey of Clarke's work acknowledges
      Blish supplied ending for "Guardian Angel" (American ver-
      sion).

D11   DONAHO, BILL.   Untitled profile. Journal of the World Sci-
      ence Fiction Society 14 [convention progress report no. 1]:
      4.
         Résumé promoting Clarke as guest of honor at forthcoming
      14th World Science Fiction Convention in New York.

D12   KNIGHT, DAMON. In Search of Wonder. Chicago: Advent, pp.
      125-27.
         Collected from magazines, Expedition to Earth suggests
      incompetence of editors rejecting early Clarke stories.
      Prelude to Space "the definitive story of the first space-

ship launching." Thin in content, The City and the Stars
features vivid images; its real protagonist is time.

2d ed., 1967 (subtitled Essays on Modern Science Fiction), pp. 187-92. [Expanded.] D49

1957

D13 "Arthur C. Clarke." Wonder Stories 45 (no month):n.p.
     [inside front cover].
         Brief profile.

D14 FADIMAN, CLIFTON. "Party of One" (column). Holiday 21 (May):
     6.
         Rare among science fiction writers, Clarke uses futuristic
     gadgets for impressive purposes.

1958

D15 "Mr. Arthur C. Clarke, B.Sc., F.R.A.S." Britian Enters the
     Space Age (A Discussion on Guided Missile and Space Travel).
     [Program for 14 April conference in Royal Festival Hall.]
     p. 18.
         Short biography and précis of lecture.

D16 "Dear Reader." Coronet 44 (May):5.
         Brief profile.

D17 "Duke of Edinburgh on Rival Views of Space Travel." Times
     (London), 15 April, p. 5.
         Clarke stole the show at youth conference held by Air
     League of the British Empire, "Britain Enters the Space
     Age."

1959

D18 AMORY, CLEVELAND, ed. International Celebrity Register.
     American ed. New York: Celebrity Register, p. 155.
         "Clarke, Arthur C.," résumé includes author's comments,
     sees him purveying "grim views" of future.

D19 FADIMAN, CLIFTON. Introduction to Across the Sea of Stars.
     New York: Harcourt, Brace & World, pp. ix-xii.
         Stressing space, parallels with H.G. Wells, sees Clarke
     among "new mental species" living in future. See A142.

1960

D20 The Author's and Writer's Who's Who. 4th ed. London: Burke's
     Peerage, p. 73. [Error in year Clarke was assistant editor
     of Science Abstracts appears in 5th (1963) and 6th (1971)
     eds.]

D21 BROWNING, D.C., ed. Everyman's Dictionary of Literary Biog-
     raphy. Rev. ed. London: J.M. Dent; New York: E.P.
     Dutton, p. 139.
          "Clarke, Arthur Charles," résumé.

D22 "Publisher's Note." In Against the Fall of Night. New York:
     Pyramid, p. 4.
          Brief explanation of reissuing earlier version of a
     book already in print (The City and the Stars). See A63.

D23 von BRAUN, WERNHER. Introduction to The Challenge of the Sea.
     New York: Holt, Rinehart, Winston, pp. 7-8. See C330.

1961

D24 "Clarke of Ceylon." Newsweek 58 (30 October):74-75.
          Profile quotes Clarke: "I rebel against categorizing."

1962

D25 C[ARNELL], J[OHN]. "Arthur C. Clarke." New Worlds 42
     (November):n.p. (both inside covers).
          Brief profile.

D26 "Comment from the Editors." Elks 41 (October):5.
          Brief profile.

D27 "Kalinga Prize to Space Writer." UNESCO Courier 15 (June):16.
          Announcement of award presentation.

D28 No entry.

D29 "The Man Who Foresaw Telstar." Daily Telegraph and Morning
     Post, 30 July, p. 13.

1963

D30 ASH, LEE. "WLB Biography: Arthur C. Clarke." Wilson Library
     Bulletin 37 (March):598.
               Influences cited: H.G. Wells, Herman Melville, James
     Branch Cabell, Olaf Stapledon.

D31 BERNSTEIN, JEREMY. "The Future is Already Here." New Yorker
38 (5 January):94, 96-97.
"All the essentials" of a science-fiction writer, sci-
entific training, imagination, energy, make Clarke's fic-
tion exciting, instructive, possible guide to the future.
The City and the Stars represents him at his best. "Pure
fantasy," Childhood's End has a "strange plausibility."
Short stories blend real and unreal. Compares well with
Jules Verne, H.G. Wells, Karel Čapek, Olaf Stapledon, A.E.
Van Vogt.

Retitled "The Future is Practically Here: A Tribute to
Arthur C. Clarke." A Comprehensible World: On Modern
Science and Its Origins. New York: Random House, 1967.

D32 "About the Author." In Dolphin Island. New York: Holt,
Rinehart, Winston, p. [187].
Brief profile. See A169.

D33 FRENCH, CEDRIC. "Prophet of the Space Age." Men Only 82
(April):19-22.
Aims and achievements set against interviews with family
and friends. "Exiled" in Ceylon, disinterested in people,
he turned to the sea because he was born too soon for space.

D34 MOSKOWITZ, SAM. "Arthur C. Clarke." Amazing Stories Fact and
Science Fiction 37 (February):67-77.
Career traced to background in British Interplanetary
Society, science education, fanzines, previous fantasy
writers (Lord Dunsany, John W. Campbell, Jr., Olaf
Stapledon). Wide popularity attributed to optimism, sin-
cerity, clear and authentic science, thought-provoking
ideas poetically expressed.

In Seekers of Tomorrow: Modern Masters of Science Fiction. Cleveland and New York: World, 1966. [Revised
and expanded.]

D35 "A Prophet Honored." Triton 8 (November-December):25.
Profile emphasizes work concerned with the sea.

1964

D36 MADSDEN, ALAN. "That Starlit Corridor." English Journal 53
(September):405-12.
Clarke among "core of talented science fiction writers"
recommended by authors and critics, used in 9th grade
literature class.

D37 Who's Who 1964. 116th ed. London: Adam & Charles Black,

p. 574.
  "Clarke, Arthur Charles," résumé.

D38 WILLIAMS, W.T. "Science in Science Fiction: Alien Biology."
     Listener and BBC Television Review 72 (24 December):1003-4.
        Debunks concept of disembodied mind in Childhood's End
     and The City and the Stars.

                              1965

D39 "About the Author." In The Coast of Coral. New York: Harper
     Perennial Library, p. 209.
        Brief profile. See C230.

                              1966

D40 BERNSTEIN, JEREMY. "Profiles: How About a Little Game?" New
     Yorker 42 (November):70-72, 74, 76, 79-80, 85-86, 88, 91,
     93-94, 97-98, 100, 103-4, 106, 108, 110.
        Interview of Stanley Kubrick stresses Clarke's involve-
     ment throughout the making of 2001 (pp. 82ff.).

        A Comprehensible World: On Modern Science and Its
        Science and Its Origins. New York: Random House, 1967.
        [Title omits "Profiles."]
        The Making of Kubrick's 2001, 1970. D95

*D41 "Clarke, Arthur C[harles]." Current Biography, October.
        Profile (including list of publications) calls Child-
     hood's End a "space novel" by "the most commercially suc-
     cessful and highly respected contemporary science fiction
     writer."

        [Source: Current Biography Yearbook 1966. Edited by
        Charles Moritz. New York: H.W. Wilson, pp. 49-52.]

D42 "Kubrick, Farther Out." Newsweek 68 (12 September):106.
        Anonymous preview of 2001 cites Clarke-Kubrick collabora-
     tion on novel and screenplay, anticipation that film will
     visualize aliens.

D43 SMITH, GODFREY. "Astounding Story! about a Science Fiction
     Writer." New York Times Magazine, 6 March, pp. 28-29, 75-
     77.
        The possibly highest paid writer of science and science
     fiction liked his early years as an auditor, had a marriage
     "explode" on him, and reacts equably to Brian Aldiss's
     charge of vanity. Close friend A.V. Cleaver sees Clarke's
     head in the clouds, not in human relations. Influences

                              136

acknowledged: Jacques Cousteau, Louis Leakey, H.G. Wells, Jonathan Swift, J.B.S. Haldane. Perhaps a "crypto-Buddhist" (Clarke's term), he longs for proof of extraterrestrial intelligence, a dolphin for a friend, and the world's biggest Meccano set. 2001 novel expected in 1966, film in 1967, both co-authored.

D44   Who's Who in America 1966-1967. Chicago: Marquis Who's Who, 34:393.
      "Clarke, Arthur Charles," résumé.

1967

D45   "Arthur C. Clarke: He's So Far Out, He's In." Forbes 99 (15 April):75.
      Value for businessmen in Clarke's talks and bull sessions. Brief interview comments included.

D46   DEMPEWOLFF, R.F. "2001: Backstage Magic for a Trip to Saturn." Popular Mechanics 127 (April):106-9, 218-19.
      Special effects surveyed with Clarke as tour guide.

      Retitled "How They Made 2001" [by Richard Dempewolff]. Science Digest 63 (May 1968):34-39. [Condensed.]

D47   ETHRIDGE, JAMES M., and BARBARA KOPALA, eds. Contemporary Authors: A Bio-Bibliographical Guide to Current Authors and their Works. 1st rev. Detroit: Gale Research, 4:179-80.
      "Clarke, Arthur C[harles]," résumé includes 2001 "in press."

      Updated, 1980. D268

D48   HILLEGAS, MARK R. The Future as Nightmare: H.G. Wells and the Anti-Utopians. New York: Oxford University Press, pp. 152-53.
      "Wellsian utopian vision . . . stated directly . . . in Arthur C. Clarke's near classic, Childhood's End," attacked by many science-fiction writers in the 1950s.

D49   KNIGHT, DAMON. In Search of Wonder: Essays on Modern Science Fiction. Chicago: Advent, pp. 187-92.
      D12 expanded. Though flawed, Childhood's End still an "amazing achievement" in reworking magazine material; its scope impressed mainstream critics. The Deep Range mostly background. Gadget stories, Tales from the White Hart flimsy but fun.

1968

D50 [Untitled note.] The Coast of Coral. New York: Avon Camelot,
     p. ii.
          Extremely brief vita. See C230.

D51 ADLER, RENATA. "2001 is Up, Up and Away." New York Times,
     4 April, p. 58.
          Film review. Boring film displays Clarke's concept of
     a world-mind.

               Renata Adler. A Year in the Dark: Journal of a Film
               Critic 1968-1969. New York: Random House, 1969.
               Film Facts 11 (May 1968):95-99. [Excerpt.]
               The Making of Kubrick's 2001, 1970. D95
               A.W. Strickland. A Collection of Great Science Fiction
               Films. Bloomington, Ind.: TIS Publications, pp. 205-8.
               [Excerpt.]

D52 ANDERSON, RAY LYNN. "Persuasive Functions of Science Fiction:
     A Study in the Rhetoric of Science." Ph.D. dissertation
     (speech), University of Minnesota.
          Major themes of Clarke, Isaac Asimov, Fred Hoyle emerge
     from normative vision of role of science as advice for
     future action. Specific Clarke stories attack government
     secrecy; advocate social investment in science; argue only
     scientists, not politicians, qualified to evaluate sci-
     entific problems; show science-military hostility; accept
     dependency on ideal and infallible computer; rank characters
     by facility with scientific language. Overall, social per-
     suasiveness undercuts power of scientific language to under-
     score fiction's credibility. All three writers fail to
     mediate between scientific and nonscientific establishments.
     Contrary to Kingsley Amis and Reginald Bretnor, analysis
     suggests science fiction an unlikely moral and social guide.

               Dissertation Abstracts 29 (1969):3698A.

D53 BERNSTEIN, JEREMY. "Chain Reaction." New Yorker 44 (21
     September):180-84.
          Clarke novel among his best, "full of poetry, scientific
     imagination, and . . . wit." Clarifies puzzling parts of
     film, for which soundstage tour had not been enough prepara-
     tion.

D54 B., R. "Pathfinder." Incentive/68 (BOAC in-house publica-
     tion), no. 14 (November), pp. 14-15.
          Clarke's lifestyle includes use of BOAC transport.

D55 BRADBURY, RAY. "Space Odyssey 2001." Psychology Today 2

(June):10.
Film review. Kubrick blamed for ruining Clarke potential.

The Making of Kubrick's 2001, 1970. [Excerpt.] D95

D56 BREEN, WALTER. "The Blown Mind on Film." Warhoon [fanzine],
     no. 24 (August), pp. 16-24, 62.
       Symbolic reading of 2001 demands esoteric context for
     Clarke's vision of what the universe is really like:
     dangerous voyage, incomprehensible alien, effect of contact
     on humanity.

       Supplement. Warhoon [fanzine], no. 26 (February), pp.
       48-49, 56. Claims Clarke called Prelude to Space his last
       "materialistic" book, discounts novel's explanation of
       2001 light show.

D57 DANIELS, DON. "2001: A New Myth." Film Heritage 3 (Summer):
     1-11.
       Clarke's novel explains Hal's motivation.

       Supplement. "Letter to the Editor." Film Heritage 4
       (Winter 1968-1969):31-32.

D58 DELANEY, MARSHALL [pseud. for Robert Fulford]. "2001: A
     Space Obfuscation." Saturday Night 83 (September):33.
       Announced nonrational, religious objectives of film-
     makers an attempt to disarm criticism. Film infatuated
     with own ideas, like Clarke short story and novel.
     Clarke's prosaic limitations contrast with Kubrick's mumbo-
     jumbo.

       Robert Fulford. Marshall Delany at the Movies: The
       Contemporary World as Seen on Film. Toronto: Peter
       Martin, 1974.

D59 EBERT, ROGER. "2001: A Masterpiece by Accident?" Chicago
     Sun-Times, 6 October, "Showcase," p. 2.
       Compares film and novel.

D60 EISENSTEIN, ALEX. "2001: A Parable Detailed, and a Devilish
     Advocacy (Part 1)." Trumpet [fanzine], no. 9 [February-
     March], pp. 37-41.
       Comparison of film and novel shows Clarke misjudging
     symbolic ending, Kubrick making technical bobbles in cen-
     tral sequence; novel otherwise a "remarkable job of plastic
     surgery." Plot outweighs science for Clarke; drama out-
     weighs both for Kubrick. [No part 2.]

       Supplement. "2001 Errata." Trumpet [fanzine], no. 10
       [ca. May], p. 2. Corrects minor factual errors.

D61   "From Icarus to Arthur Clarke." Forbes 102 (1 July):112-14.
          Science-fiction films good business: 2001, Planet of
      the Apes, forthcoming Barbarella. "Top popularizer of
      space" is Dr. [sic] Clarke.

D62   GEDULD, HARRY. "Return to Melies: Reflections on the Science
          Fiction Film." The Humanist 28 (November–December):23-24,
          28.
          Clarke story complicated by film's monolith, relating
      aliens and man both externally and internally. Novel
      argues man can earn his destiny; film challenges progress,
      takes self too seriously.

          William Johnson, ed. Focus on the Science Fiction Film.
          Englewood Cliffs, N.J.: Prentice-Hall, 1972.

D63   HODGENS, RICHARD. "Notes on 2001: A Space Odyssey." Trumpet
          [fanzine], no. 9 [February–March], pp. 30-37.
          Comprehensive analysis claims explicit novel improves
      HAL sequence, but not the film's beginning or end.

D64   HUNTER, TIM, with Stephen Kaplan, and Peter Jaszi. "2001: A
          Space Odyssey." Harvard Crimson, 12 April, pp. 3-5.
          Film review. Lengthy critique accepts some Clarke
      terminology, not Ahab parallel.

          Film Heritage 3 (Summer 1968):12-20.
          The Making of Kubrick's 2001, 1970. D95

D65   International Who's Who. 32nd ed. London: Europa Publica-
          tions, pp. 257-58.
          "Clarke, Arthur Charles," résumé.

D66   JAMES, CLIVE. "2001: Kubrick vs. Clarke." Cinema (London),
          no. 2 (March), pp. 18-21.
          Novel reverts to Clarke's thematic emphases; film has
      few Clarkean elements. Kubrick's consistency visual,
      Clarke's scientific. Kubrick's film poetry less fanciful,
      more economical, more reliable than Clarke's purple prose.
      Clarke's assumptions suspect, as in Childhood's End.
      Bowman gains insight for Kubrick, power for Clarke. Novel
      shows two kinds of verbal language; only spoken jargon re-
      mains in film. Lack of enthusiasm for space divides
      Kubrick from science-fiction writers.

          Film Society Review 5 (January 1970):27-35.

D67   KAUFFMAN, STANLEY. "Lost in the Stars." New Republic 158
          (4 May):24, 41.
          Film review. Kubrick "sloughed off" Clarke influence.

The Making of Kubrick's 2001, 1970. D95
Stanley Kauffman. Figures of Light: Film Criticism
and Comment. New York: Harper & Row, 1971, pp. 70-75.

D68 "Latter-Day Jules Verne." Time 92 (19 July):56-57.
Emphasizes predictions of space travel to the stars.

*D69 MACDOWELL, DAVID. "2001: A Critique." Photon, no. 16
[August], pp. 25-37. [Source: WC, confirmed by publisher.]
Detailed critique includes praise of Clarke screenplay
and novel, in "flatter" medium.

Photon, no. 24 (March 1974), pp. 25-37.

D70 NATHAN, PAUL. "Now Read the Book." Publishers Weekly 194
(26 August):263.
Novel clears up film's confusion.

D71 NORDEN, ERIC. "Playboy Interview: Stanley Kubrick." Playboy
15 (September):85-86, 88, 90, 92, 94, 96, 158, 180, 182-84,
190, 192, 195.
Two brief explicit references, but exposure to Clarke's
ideas evident throughout.

The Making of Kubrick's 2001, 1970. D95
Hugh Hefner, ed. The Twentieth Anniversary Playboy
Reader. [Chicago]:Playboy Press, 1974.

D72 PARKINSON, BUD. "The Authentic Vision: A Study of the
Writing of Arthur C. Clarke." Vector: The Journal of the
British Science Fiction Association [fanzine], no. 49
(June), pp. 2-6.
Style transparent, like space paintings of Chesley
Bonestell, comparable to Hemingway. Poetic, but "an older
poetry," not words for their own sake. Envisions new
Renaissance of "Science, Exploration, and Evolutionary
Humanism." Extrapolates spaceflight toward infinity, with
man not at universe's center. Whereas Walter M. Miller,
Jr., foresees pain in spaceflight, Clarke sells it optimis-
tically, but exhibits "terrible intensity of vision," as
George Orwell said of Jonathan Swift.

D73 PREHODA, ROBERT W. "2001: A Space Odyssey." Futurist 2
(June):52-53.
Film review. Emphasizing sound technological forecasting, accepts Clarke interpretation of "Star Gate"
sequence [pictured with Clarke at world premiere].

The Making of Kubrick's 2001, 1970. D95

D74 ROSENFELD, ALBERT. "Perhaps the Mysterious Monolith is Really

Moby Dick." Life 64 (5 April):34-35.
  Profile of Clarke and Kubrick and their intentions for
  2001 discusses their speculations, cinema technology,
  Melville parallel, "Clarke's Third Law" comparing high
  technology to magic.

D75   STINE, G. HARRY. "2001: A Space Odyssey." Analog Science-
        Fiction--Science Fact 82 (November):167-68.
        Film review. Ninety percent gadgets, ten percent fan-
        tasy, film combines Kubrick's opposition to science with
        Clarke's mysticism.

D76   STRICK, PHILIP. "2001: A Space Odyssey." Sight and Sound
        37 (Summer):153-54.
        Film review. Emphasizes philosophical nature of science
        fiction, use of "The Sentinel," optimism and pessimism.

        The Making of Kubrick's 2001, 1970. D95

D77   WHITE, TED. "2001: A Metaphysical Fantasy." Shangri
        L'Affaires [fanzine], no. 73 (1 June), pp. 29-36.
        Visual effects nonfunctional but impressive, underlining
        point of mystical Clarke novels.

D78   WILLIAMS, MICHAELA. "Where Did It Go Right?" Chicago Daily
        News, 13 July, "Panorama," pp. 1, 3.
        2001 a surprise hit, Clarke novel now available for com-
        parison.

        The Making of Kubrick's 2001, 1970. D95

                              1969

D79   "Arthur C. Clarke Will Speak at October Meeting." Courier
        (General Dynamics of Fort Worth), October, p. 3.
        Brief profile and summary of upcoming speech.

D80   BATES, DAN. "Some Thoughts on Kubrick's 2001." Castle of
        Frankenstein 4 (Spring):8-11.
        Warns against using novel for elucidation: "Clarke's
        'interpretation' . . . [is] earthbound and cloddish."

D81   BEJA, MORRIS. "2001: Odyssey to Byzantium." Extrapolation
        10 (May):67-68.
        Parallels with Yeats's poem, "Sailing to Byzantium."

        Thomas D. Clareson, ed. SF: The Other Side of Realism:
        Essays on Modern Fantasy and Science Fiction. Bowling
        Green, Ohio: Bowling Green University Popular Press,
        1971.
          See responses, D88, D111.

D82   BERNSTEIN, JEREMY. "Profiles: Out of the Ego Chamber." New
      Yorker 45 (9 August):40-42, 44, 46, 51-52, 54-56, 58-63.
            After his father died in Clarke's early teens, reading
      Olaf Stapledon's Last and First Men "transformed my life."
      Early interest in prehistoric animals connected to his
      menagerie in Ceylon, and the more human status of animals,
      robots, and aliens in his fiction. Less interest in people
      than ideas, hated early auditing job, liked editing Science
      Abstracts. World War II radar work a turning point. Dis-
      cusses partnership with photographer Mike Wilson, short-
      lived marriage, emigration to Ceylon, where he is held by
      the sea and a considerable retinue dependent on him. Neo-
      colonial lifestyle described, as well as his office or "ego
      chamber." Location of Ceylon with regard to synchronous
      satellites considered. Characteristic note of Clarke's
      writing "the sense of sadness and loneliness that man must
      feel over living for so brief a time in such a vast uni-
      verse of which he can have so limited a glance."

            Retitled "Extrapolators: Arthur C. Clarke." Experienc-
            ing Science. New York: Basic Books, 1978.

D83   BOWERS, DOROTHY W. "Science Fiction for College Libraries."
      Choice 6 (June):478-83.
            Eight books cited for Clarke as writer of fiction, sci-
      ence, and "criticism" (Time Probe), evoking "sense of
      wonder" and terming Stapledon most imaginative of science-
      fiction writers.

D84   GRAHAM, COLIN. "2001: A Space Odyssey--An Appreciation."
      Supernatural Horror Filming, no. 1 [May], pp. 24-27.
            2001 to second half of century what Things to Come was
      to first. Film misunderstood out of anthropocentric pride.
      If others cause our progress, aliens more believable than
      gods. Book argues man's self-destruction of no account.
      Man's lot is dissatisfaction. Clarke transcends science-
      fiction medium, of which he is one of the "founders."
      Poetic novel a "milestone in literature as a whole."

D85   MACKLIN, F. A[NTHONY]. "The Comic Sense of 2001." Film Com-
      ment 5 (Winter):10-14.
            Novel and pronouncements of Clarke should be seen as
      coming from film's "first critic."

D86   MCKEE, MEL. "2001: Out of the Silent Planet." Sight and
      Sound 38 (Autumn):204-7.
            Parallels with C.S. Lewis novel: "silence" of Earth
      broken by spaceflight, aliens depicted as [sic] monoliths,
      2001 visual motif of worlds in alignment featured on

Lewis's monoliths, essence of life treated as visual,
strange guest house, apotheosis of hero. Lewis and Clarke
friendship makes parallels seem more than coincidence.

D87 O'MEARA, ROBERT. "2001: A Space Odyssey." Screen 10
     (January-February):104-12.
          Film review. Digest of other articles notes screenplay
     parallels "Moon Watcher" with "Star Child."

D88 PLANK, ROBERT. "1001 Interpretations of 2001." Extrapolation
     11 (December):23-24.
          Facetious riposte dismisses numerology of Beja [D81].
     Ambiguity of artwork leads to numerous undemonstrable
     interpretations.

          Thomas D. Clareson, ed. SF: The Other Side of Realism:
          Essays on Modern Fantasy and Science Fiction. Bowling
          Green, Ohio: Bowling Green University Popular Press,
          1971.
          See response, D111.

D89 _____. "Sons and Fathers, A.D. 2001." Hartford Studies in
     Literature 1 [ca. March]:26-33.
          Paradoxical change from "The Sentinel" in which man
     awaits superior aliens; in 2001 he seeks them. HAL neces-
     sarily male, in "double bind," afflicted with hubris. Man
     is father to HAL, son to aliens. "Jealousy" attributed to
     aliens by short story is Oedipally charged.

          Joseph D. Olander, and Martin Harry Greenberg, eds.
          Arthur C. Clarke. New York: Taplinger, 1979. [Comma
          in title replaced by "in."] D206

D90 "Prophet of the Space Age Comes Home to Ceylon." Ceylon
     Travel Newsletter, July, p. 3.
          Review of accomplishments, preferred residence.

D91 REDDY, JOHN. "Arthur C. Clarke: Prophet of the Space Age."
     Montrealler 44 (March):16-18.
          Summarizes Clarke's whirlwind schedule, prophecies, in-
     terest in aliens, early life, reputation, lifestyle, 2001:
     A Space Odyssey, television documentaries, and effects of
     communication satellites.

          Reader's Digest 94 (April 1969):134-36, 138, 140. [Con-
          densed.]
          Reader's Digest (U.K.) 95 (November 1969):74-78. [Con-
          densed.]

D92 RICHARDSON, KENNETH R., ed. Twentieth Century Writing:
     Reader's Guide to Contemporary Literature. London: Newnes,

p. 129.
"Clarke, Arthur C.," résumé.

D93 SAMUELSON, DAVID NORMAN. "Arthur C. Clarke: <u>Childhood's End</u>."
In "Studies in the Contemporary American and British Science Fiction Novel." Ph.D. dissertation (comparative
literature), University of Southern California, pp. 84-119.
   Familiar genre motifs guide readers "from predictable
technological advances to prophetic eschatological fantasy,"
stunning reviewers. Novel extols reason, downplays technology, implying rational utopias must stagnate. Alien
contact theme evokes apocalyptic and demonic image patterns,
setting up a "morality play" contradicting the rational
message on the surface. Exponents of reason and science,
the Overlords live up to their devilish appearance, de-
ceiving man in the reluctant service of the godlike Overmind.
Unified theme, imagery, tone, and Clarkean "cosmic viewpoint" but rationalization, plotting, and motivation flawed.

   <u>Dissertation Abstracts</u> 30 (1969):1181A.
   Retitled "<u>Childhood's End</u>: A Median Stage of Adolescence?" 1973. D146
   Dissertation retitled <u>Visions of Tomorrow: Six Journeys</u>
   <u>from Outer to Inner Space</u>. New York: Arno Press, 1975.

D94 SUTTON, THOMAS C., and MARILYN SUTTON. "Science Fiction as
Mythology." <u>Western Folklore</u> 28 (October):230-37.
   "The Star" illustrates Clarke's "mythopoeic vision,"
composed of religion, psychology, and science, invented to
delight technological man.

                              1970

D95 AGEL, JEROME, ed. <u>The Making of Kubrick's 2001</u>. New York:
New American Library, paper.
   Scrapbook of still photos from film footage, reviews,
interviews, excerpts from Clarke works, fan letters, etc.;
no index or contents pages, minimal documentation. [Con-
tents include A68, C546, D40, 51 (excerpt), 55 (excerpt),
64, 67, 71, 73, 76, 78.]

D96 ATHELING, WILLIAM, Jr. [pseud. for James Blish]. <u>More Issues</u>
<u>at Hand</u>. Chicago: Advent, pp. 47-48.
   Clarke's success due in part ot his "unashamed use . . .
of . . . semi-erotic, semi-irresponsible daydreams, . . .
told as soberly as though they were as worth taking seri-
ously as hard truths."

   Excerpt, <u>Contemporary Literary Criticism</u>, 1973. D147

                              145

D97 BAXTER, JOHN. Science Fiction in the Cinema. New York: A.S.
     Barnes, pp. 181-85, paper.
          Conveying Clarke's mysticism, and the beauty of science
     and technology, 2001 joins science fiction's optimism with
     pessimism of science-fiction film.

D98 BERADUCCI, MICHELE C. "A Content Analysis of the Science Fic-
     tion Writing of Arthur C. Clarke, Lester del Rey, and Isaac
     Asimov." M.S. thesis (library science), Long Island Uni-
     versity, esp. pp. 10-43, 143-46.
          Chapter on Clarke depends on Moskowitz biography (D34),
     summarizes eight novels. Notes 1984 twist in Childhood's
     End with Big Brother good for us. Conclusion finds high
     scientific credibility, optimism, romance subplots, moral
     and social lessons, stress on Buddhist "philosophy," sci-
     entific debunking of revealed religion, belief that man is
     neither alone nor the highest life form in the universe.

D99 The Blue Book: Leaders of the English-Speaking World, 1970.
     Chicago and London: St. James, p. 144.
          "Clarke, Arthur Charles," résumé.

D100 CLARESON, THOMAS D. Foreword to "The Sentinel." In The
     Mirror of Infinity: A Critics' Anthology of Science Fic-
     tion. Edited by Robert Silverberg. New York: Harper &
     Row, pp. 131-33.
          "Essential Clarke" story more reflective than dramatic,
     domesticating scene with familiar details, enunciating one
     of two basic Clarke themes, alien contact (the other one,
     loss, best exhibited in "'If I Forget Thee, Oh
     Earth . . .'").

D101 "Coin Haul." Times (London), 23 June, p. 10.
          Spoils of Wilson-Clarke treasure hunt on sale.

D102 DRAKE, PHYLLIS. "Homer in 2001: Comparisons between The
     Odyssey and 2001: A Space Odyssey." English Journal 59
     (December):1270-71.
          Numerous parallels help introduce ancient literature in
     classroom (e.g., Bowman as Odysseus; HAL as Scylla, Athena,
     and Poseidon; aliens as Zeus; next-to-last section the
     Land of the Dead).

D103 GELMIS, JOSEPH. The Film Director as Superstar. Garden City,
     N.Y.: Doubleday, pp. 293-316.
          Includes interview in which Kubrick rationalizes plot
     ending science fictionally, calls Clarke novel an indepen-
     dent creation, based on rushes, admirably accommodated to
     different medium.

D104 GREENLAW, MARY JANE. "A Study of the Impact of Technology on

Human Values as Reflected in Modern Science Fiction."
Ph.D dissertation (Education), Michigan State University.
Clarke works among recommended reading to help children
consider-technology's effects on quality of life (especially
individualism and privacy).

Dissertation Abstracts International 31 (1971):5665A.

D105   REGINALD, R[OBERT] [pseud. for Michael Burgess]. *Stella
       Nova: The Contemporary Science Fiction Writers.* Los
       Angeles: Unicorn Books, pp. 51-52, paper.
          "Arthur C. Clarke," brief résumé (checklist includes
       nonexistent collection, *The Mind Masters*).

              Retitled *Contemporary Science Fiction Authors.* New York:
              Arno Press, 1975.
              Retitled *Science Fiction and Fantasy Literature: A
              Checklist, 1700-1974, with Contemporary Science Fiction
              Authors II.* 2 vols. Detroit: Gale Research, 1979,
              1:105-6; 2:855. "Arthur C. Clarke" résumé and check-
              list corrected and updated.

D106   ROSE, LOIS, and STEPHEN ROSE. *The Shattered Ring: Science
       Fiction and the Quest for Meaning.* Richmond, Va.: John
       Knox Press, pp. 73-76.
          Childhood's End and *2001: A Space Odyssey* exhibit
       Platonic antagonism toward matter, favoring pure mind over
       individual and social history.

              Excerpt, *Contemporary Literary Criticism*, 1976. D170

D107   SRAGOW, MICHAEL. "2001: A Space Odyssey." *Film Society Re-
       view* 5 (January):23-26.
          Film review. Attempts to bridge "two cultures," compar-
       ing film and novel on "Dawn of Man" time-span, HAL's
       motivation to kill. Kubrick captured Clarke's world-view
       of technology and spirit, as seen in *Childhood's End*.

D108   WARD, A.C. *Longman Companion to Twentieth Century Literature.*
       London: Longman, pp. 130-31.
          "Clarke, Arthur C. (Arthur Charles Clarke)," résumé.

D109   *Who's Who in the World.* 1st ed. Chicago: Marquis Who's
       Who, p. 186.
          "Clarke, Arthur Charles," résumé.

                              1971

D110   DANIELS, DON. "A Skeleton Key to *2001.*" *Sight and Sound* 40
       (Winter):28-33.
          2001's art and mystery deserve better treatment than

                              147

Agel [D95]. More borrowed than music: ideas from
Koestler, Stapledon, for example. A "study of various
capacities for consciousness": machine, alien, human (both
intuitive and rational). Clarke's utopian element opposed
by Kubrick. Structure and motif suggest symphonic form.
Monolith an artifact, also symbol of inevitable growth of
consciousness, science-fiction shortcut, causal force,
goal, and source. Novel sometimes throws light on film,
"if only in contrast." Compares "subhuman" HAL with super-
human machines in Clarke nonfiction. Verbal critiques of
this film may ultimately be futile.

D111 EISENSTEIN, ALEX. "The Academic Overkill of 2001." In SF:
The Other Side of Realism: Essays on Modern Fantasy and
Science Fiction. Edited by Thomas D. Clareson. Bowling
Green, Ohio: Bowling Green University Popular Press, pp.
267-71.
    Response to D81 and D89. Beja's methodology questioned.
Plank, though facetious, also strains for correspondences,
Freudian rather than numerological.

D112 Encyclopedia Americana. New York: Americana Corporation,
7:20.
    "Clarke, Arthur C.," brief profile.

D113 Encyclopedia Britannica. Chicago: Encyclopedia Britannica,
"Micropedia," 2:969-70.
    "Clarke, Arthur C.," brief profile.

D114 "It is Ceylon that Now Seems Home." Horizons (United States
Information Service, Manila) 20 ([Spring]):48-49.
    Introduction to Clarke for Philippine audience.

D115 KAGLE, STEVEN EARL. "The Societal Quest." Extrapolation 12
(May):79-85.
    Childhood's End among novels developing group objectives
beyond an individual's lifespan, keeping alive the nine-
teenth century's "cosmic optimism."

D116 MOORE, PATRICK. Introduction to Islands in the Sky. Philadelphia: Winston, pp. [1-4].
    Memoir of British Interplanetary Society early days,
when Clarke helped make both space research and science
fiction respectable. His factual novels (like this one)
no longer seem futuristic, but his imagination roams in
others. Varied career includes science writing, helping
to revolutionize undersea exploring, film-making. 'Not
another Verne or Wells, but in their class. See A54.

D117 SCHWARTZ, SHEILA. "The World of Science Fiction." New York
State English Record 21 (February):27-40.

Childhood's End and 2001 "hypothesize a superior intelligence which has grave concern about what man will do
with his new ability to conquer space. In the film, the
black stone flies away shrieking when man comes upon it.
At the end of Space Odyssey [sic], the space explorer who
has survived is returned to perfect and superior childhood."

D118   STRICK, PHILIP. "Time, Transplants, and Arthur Clarke."
       Sight and Sound 40 (April):190.
           Clarke promoting television documentary, The Promise of
       Space, at Trieste Film Festival.

D119   THOMPSON, WILLIAM IRWIN. At the Edge of History: Speculations
       on the Transformation of Culture. New York: Harper & Row,
       pp. 152-63.
           What H.G. Wells was to another generation, Clarke is to
       this one. Science and engineering students profoundly
       moved by his aesthetic mysticism. The City and the Stars
       idealizes the present in Diaspar, contrasting it with the
       Hopi-like culture of Lys. Popularity spread by 2001: A
       Space Odyssey, which explores transforming conflict of man
       with machine, nature, and interstellar beings. Clarke,
       Edgar Cayce, C.S. Lewis, and Mexican myth contribute to a
       "universal myth of human nature" welcoming an apocalyptic
       transformation.

D120   WALKER, ALEXANDER. Stanley Kubrick Directs. New York:
       Harcourt, Brace, Jovanovich.
           "The humanist in Kubrick hopes that man will survive
       his own rationality; the intellectual doubts it." Both
       attitudes led to considerations of space, extraterrestrials,
       2001. Chief concern: "intelligence and its transforma-
       tions." Communications, computers interest pre-dated
       Clarke encounter, but HAL minor in early script. Kubrick
       "already shared Clarke's belief in the power of myths and
       legends to set up echoes in human awareness." Odyssey,
       nonverbal concepts grew gradually as teaching machines,
       orbiting bombs, female computer (Athena) were deleted from
       early drafts. HAL's vengeance like Gen. Mireau's in Paths
       of Glory.

D121   WARD, MARTHA E., and DOROTHY A. MARQUARDT, comps. Authors of
       Books for Young People. 2nd ed. Metuchen, N.J.: Scare-
       crow Press, p. 101.
           "Clarke, Arthur Charles," brief listing (four books).

D122   WOLLHEIM, DONALD A. The Universe Makers. New York: Harper &
       Row, pp. 97-99.
           The "best publicized science-fiction writer in the
       world," a popularizer of spaceflight whose faith in tech-
       nology is less interesting than his imagination.

Excerpt, <u>Contemporary Literary Criticism</u>, 1973. D147

1972

D123 BABRICK, JEAN. "The Possible Gods: Religion in Science Fiction." <u>Arizona English Bulletin</u> 15 (Fall):37–42. [Special
issue, "Science Fiction and the English Class."]
<u>The City and the Stars</u> illustrates how "man without
death and without reproduction becomes somehow less than he
was."

D124 BARRETT, WILLIAM. <u>Time of Need: Forms of Imagination in the
Twentieth Century</u>. New York: Harper & Row, pp. 353–61.
At opposite ends of time and technology, <u>2001</u> and <u>The
Sky Above, The Mud Below</u> dramatize art's inadequacy today
for dealing with transcendence. Contrasting with film's
immediacy, Clarke novel emphasizes metaphysics of transcen-
dent machines. Teilhard de Chardin connection.

Excerpt, <u>Contemporary Literary Criticism</u>, 1976. D170

D125 "Bibliography: Books by Arthur C. Clarke." In <u>Of Time and
Stars: The Worlds of Arthur C. Clarke</u>. London: Victor
Gollancz, pp. 205–7.
Fiction and nonfiction, emphasizing British editions.
See A206.

D126 BOYD, BEULAH. "Science Fiction and Films About the Future."
<u>Arizona English Bulletin</u> 15 (Fall):62. [Special issue,
"Science Fiction and the English Class.]
<u>Against the Fall of Night</u> and <u>Childhood's End</u> arouse
class discussion, improve vocabulary.

D127 CARY, MEREDITH. "Faustus Now." <u>Hartford Studies in Litera-
ture</u> 4, no. 2 ([mid-year]):167–73.
"Saturn Rising" refurbishes Faust theme with thoroughly
modern tempter and enduringly grateful "victim."

D128 CLARESON, THOMAS D. "Notes" on "'If I Forget Thee, O [sic]
Earth.'" In <u>A Spectrum of Worlds</u>. Garden City, N.Y.:
Doubleday, pp. 178–79.
Sources include "By the Waters of Babylon" by Stephen
Vincent Benet and Psalm 137. Scene graphically visualized:
lunar colony life, wasteland terrain, "lost" Earth, "anguish
of exile," pilgrimage.

D129 DEAKIN, MICHAEL. "Gentle Prophet Behind the Men on the Moon."
<u>TV Times</u> (London), 6 April, pp. 16–17.
Profile by producer of television documentary (B28).

D130 <u>Dictionary of International Biography</u>. London: Melrose Press,

part 1, 8:254.
"Clarke, Arthur Charles," résumé.

D131 KAGAN, NORMAN. <u>The Cinema of Stanley Kubrick</u>. New York:
Holt, Rinehart, Winston, esp. pp. 145-66.
Discounts novel, facetiously suggests film may be seen
as sexual allegory, that is, "Arthur C. Clarke's ultimate
liberated science fiction story, in which two precocious
boys go off in their space ship looking for adventure, and
wind up having a baby."

D132 KATZ, JOHN STUART (with the assistance of Curt Oliver and
Forbes Aird). <u>A Curriculum in Film</u>. Curriculum Series,
no. 13. Toronto: Ontario Institute for Studies in Education, 1972, paper.
<u>2001</u> novel summarized in terms suggesting more familiar-
ity with film, as part of "Reading Options" for Film-
Literature Study Project.

D133 KELLER, ELAINE J., and DEBORAH H. ROSEN (supervised by Dorothy
Matthews). "Yesterday and Tomorrow: A Study of the
Utopian and Dystopian Vision." <u>Arizona English Bulletin</u> 15
(Fall):5-23. [Special issue, "Science Fiction and the
English Class."]
<u>Childhood's End</u> listed as dystopia, briefly summarized,
"recommended for science fiction addicts."

D134 OGAN, JANE. "Science Fiction Selection for Jr. High."
<u>Arizona English Bulletin</u> 15 (Fall):32-36. [Special issue,
"Science Fiction and the English Class."]
Three brief story summaries from <u>Expedition to Earth</u>.

D135 PRIESTLEY, J.B. Introduction to <u>Of Time and Stars: The
Worlds of Arthur C. Clarke</u>. London: Victor Gollancz, pp.
7-10.
In love with space, fascinated by gadgets, Clarke pro-
duces convincing, audacious, vivid, memorable images. A
variety of work reveals a "civilized" writer, not content
with satirical extrapolations or melodramatic formulas
shifted to outerspace. See A206.

D136 SMITH, CURTIS C. "Clarke, Arthur C." In <u>Contemporary Novel-
ists</u>. Edited by James Vinson. London: St. James; New
York: St. Martin's, pp. 267-70.
Clarke's protagonist the "romantic maverick," his theme
"the eternal renewal of childhood in a never-ending expansion into the unknown." Claims frequent use of a "second-
person persona." Brief comment by Clarke identifies as
sources W. Somerset Maugham, Rudyard Kipling, H.G. Wells,
Alfred Lord Tennyson, Algernon Swinburne, A.E. Housman,
Georgian poets, Olaf Stapledon.

D137 SMITH, JEANNE K. "A Sampler of Science Fiction for Junior
      High." Arizona English Bulletin 15 (Fall):91-96. [Special
      issue, "Science Fiction and the English Class."]
          Islands in the Sky summarized as a "tour of satellite
      life."

                              1973

D138 ALDISS, BRIAN W. Billion Year Spree: The True History of
      Science Fiction. Garden City, N.Y.: Doubleday, pp. 259-
      61.
          Though his predominant tone is elegiac, Clarke remains
      exceptionally "faithful to a boyhood vision of science as
      saviour of mankind, and of mankind as a race of potential
      gods destined for the stars."

D139 ALLEN, L[OUIS] DAVID. Science Fiction: An Introduction.
      Lincoln, Neb.: Cliff's Notes, pp. 47-55, 128-30, paper.
          Childhood's End praised for sweeping vision, details of
      reality, despite detached narrator, minimal action. Cycli-
      cal nature of time, efficient use of power among ideas sub-
      ordinated to a "religious vision" of man's potential, in
      contrast to the Overlords. 2001: A Space Odyssey shows
      how science fiction can also concern the past and can sug-
      gest explanations for the unexplained.

          Retitled Science Fiction Reader's Guide. Lincoln, Neb.:
          Centennial Press, 1974, paper.

D140 ATCHITY, KENNETH JOHN. "SF: Literary Frontiers." Occidental
      College Occasional Paper, June, four unnumbered pages.
          Citing Childhood's End, Reach for Tomorrow, and 2001:
      A Space Odyssey, connects Clarke to myth and fable, alien
      visitors, and the identity of God, in a wide-ranging genre
      survey.

D141 BISHOP, GERALD. "The Science Fiction Books of Arthur C.
      Clarke." In The Best of Arthur C. Clarke. Edited by Angus
      Wells. London: Sidgwick & Jackson, pp. 333-36.
          Includes multiple editions, Three for Tomorrow as
      "edited by Clarke" (British publisher's error). See A209.

          [Updated to 1977 in two-volume edition, 1976-1977.]

D142 DeVRIES, DANIEL. The Films of Stanley Kubrick. Grand Rapids,
      Mich.: William B. Eerdmans, esp. pp. 45-56.
          "Dully written and overintellectualized" novel compli-
      cates interpretation. Seeking truth in the film is con-
      fusing, finding it in the novel is boring.

D143 GEDULD, CAROLYN. Filmguide to "2001: A Space Odyssey."
Bloomington, Ind.: Indiana University Press, paper.
Film noir leanings, predestination, technology versus
humanism consistent throughout Kubrick's career. Resources
available in 2001 "to expand his vision to epic scale."
Concerned with "mythology of intelligence," philosophical
versus unconscious ideas. Most plot material traced to
early Clarke stories.

D144 GOSHGARIAN, GARY, and CHARLES O'NEILL. "The Future Isn't
What It Used to Be." In Order and Diversity: The Craft of
Prose. Edited by Robert Parker and Peter L. Sandberg.
New York: Wiley, pp. 132-39.
Optimistic ending (as in Childhood's End) leaps beyond
mind and body.

D145 LEARY, DANIEL J. "The Ends of Childhood: Eschatology in
Shaw and Clarke." Shaw Review 16 (May):67-78.
Notes minor personal connection, allusions to Shaw in
2001: A Space Odyssey and Childhood's End, parallels in
The City and the Stars. Alien consciousness freed from
bodies a Shavian concept. Both mythographers, battling
fear of change, offering hope and consolation if we have
the strength to live by our dreams. Accepting Shaw's
Lamarckian biology, sees evolution at work in Childhood's
End.

D146 NICHOLLS, PETER. "Introduction: An ABC of British Science
Fiction--Apocalypse, Bleakness, Catastrophe." In Beyond
this Horizon: An Anthology of Science Fiction and Science
Fact. Edited by Christopher Carrell. Sunderland, England:
Ceolfrith Press, pp. 18-25, paper.
Clarke an exception to British pessimism and apocalypse.
Renowned in other fields, but true fame is in science fiction. Perhaps obsessed "by the necessity and inevitability
of some sort of spiritual growth and evolution of the human
race, guided perhaps by other forms of life, but ultimately
growing from a seed that we hold within us now."

D147 RILEY, CAROLYN, ed. Contemporary Literary Criticism: Excerpts from Criticism of Today's Novelists, Poets, Playwrights, and other Creative Writers. Detroit: Gale Research, 1:58-59.
Excerpts from "Atheling" (D96), Wollheim (D122).

D148 SAMUELSON, DAVID N. "Childhood's End: A Median Stage of
Adolescence." Science-Fiction Studies 1 (Spring):4-17.
[Revised.]
Originally "Arthur C. Clarke: Childhood's End." In
"Studies in the Contemporary American and British Science
Fiction Novel," 1969, [chapter 3]. D93

R[ichard] Dale Mullen, and Darko Suvin, eds. Science
Fiction Studies: Selected Essays 1973-1974. Boston:
Gregg Press, 1976.
Arthur C. Clarke, 1977. D206
See response, D156.

D149 WEINKAUF, MARY S. "The Escape from the Garden." Texas Quarterly 16 (Autumn):66-72.
Like many utopian writers, Clarke has reservations about
his social creations. The main drawback in Childhood's End,
Against the Fall of Night, and The Lion of Comarre is bore-
dom.

D150 WESTERBACK, COLIN L. "Looking Backward at the film 2001."
In Favorite Movies: Critics' Choice. Edited by Philip
Nobile. New York: Macmillan, pp. 225-35.
Logical Clarke interpretation satisfies linear critics.

1974

D151 CLARESON, THOMAS D. "The Early Novels" (in symposium, "Arthur
C. Clarke: Man and Writer"). Algol [fanzine] 12 (November):7-10.
Overshadowed by critical attention to Childhood's End,
other early novels show Clarke's central concerns from
spreading gospel of space exploration to making "a symbolic
statement about the future of mankind."

Retitled "The Cosmic Loneliness of Arthur C. Clarke,"
1976. [Expanded.] D176

D152 DAILEY, JENNIE ORA MARRIOTT. "Modern Science Fiction." Ph.D.
dissertation (English), University of Utah, pp. 12, 17, 33,
Appendix.
Report on offering university level course. Sees
"History Lesson" as parody of scientific community's pro-
pensity to overgeneralize, Childhood's End defending
brotherhood of all intelligence. Chose "The Star" for
class, "an unquestionable example of myth-making science
fiction," rationalizing a religious phenomenon. Questions
for class note symbolism, ideas, surprise ending, clear
scientific explanation, otherwise weak style. Appendix
also cites as myths 2001: A Space Odyssey, "The Nine
Billion Names of God."

Dissertation Abstracts International 35 (1974):1095A.

D153 del REY, JUDY-LYNN BENJAMIN. "Clarke, Arthur C." In World
Book Encyclopedia. Chicago: World Book--Childcraft
International, 4:498.
Brief summary, last date 1968.

D154 GILLINGS, WALTER. "Modern Masters of Science Fiction, 1:
Arthur C. Clarke." Science Fiction Monthly 1 (July):8-9.
Bio-bibliographical profile.

Retitled "The Man from Minehead" (in symposium, "Arthur
C. Clarke: Man and Writer"). Algol [fanzine] 12
(November):12-14.

D155 HEFNER, HUGH, ed. The Twentieth Anniversary Playboy Reader.
[Chicago]: Playboy Press, p. 316.
Brief anonymous, untitled profile.

D156 HUNTINGTON, JOHN. "The Unity of Childhood's End." Science-
Fiction Studies 1 (Spring):154-64.
Like 2001: A Space Odyssey and The City and the Stars,
Childhood's End is unified by mythic structure that pre-
sents "rational, technological progress" en route to "tran-
scendent evolution." Rebutting Samuelson (D146), asserts
success of patterns, despite clumsiness and banal style.

Retitled "From Man to Overmind: Arthur C. Clarke's
Myth of Progress." In Arthur C. Clarke, 1977. D206

D157 KETTERER, DAVID. New Worlds for Old: The Apocalyptic Imagination, Science Fiction, and American Literature. Garden
City, N.Y.: Doubleday, pp. 19-20, 45, 47, 62, 163-65, 265-
66, paper.
Several Clarke stories and novels show apocalyptic theme
material, amid Stapledonian evolutionary scheme and ac-
ceptance of machines as improvement on man. Influence of
Poe, Melville also detected.

D158 NICHOLLS, PETER. "Science Fiction and the Mainstream, Part 2:
The Great Tradition of Proto Science Fiction." Foundation:
The Review of Science Fiction, no. 5 (January), pp. 9-43,
esp. 15, 21, 29, 32.
Clarke novels invert Plato, play with metaphysics, em-
ploy pastoral motifs, revamp theme of Samuel Johnson's
Rasselas.

D159 OWER, JOHN B. "Manacle-Forged Minds: Two Images of the Computer in Science Fiction." Diogenes, no. 85 (Spring), pp.
47-61.
2001: A Space Odyssey and Harlan Ellison's "I Have No
Mouth and I Must Scream" vary theme of the Fall of Man.
Pride versus guilt in HAL's "subliminal self-awareness."
Lobotomy begins with "cognitive feedback," computational,
not emotional. Incapacity for moral choice tied to Clarke
reinterpretation of the fall; inability to love contrasts

with Bowman's empathy for HAL. "Both authors judge the
gifts of modern science from the viewpoint of a theology
which it has supposedly rendered obsolete." Possible shift
from "liberal faith in an advance through science and technology" to "a more 'traditional' sense of man's fallen
nature, and his inherent limitations as a creator."

*D160 Science Fiction: Jules Verne to Ray Bradbury [no. 261-156].
       White Plains, N.Y.: Center for Humanities. 3 discs/
       cassettes and 3 slide sets. [Source: MT.]
          Childhood's End and 2001: A Space Odyssey among works
       discussed.

D161   THOMPSON, WILLIAM IRWIN. Passages About Earth: An Exploration
       of the New Planetary Culture. New York: Harper & Row,
       pp. 144-48, 174.
          Clarke shares with Teilhard de Chardin vision of twen-
       tieth-century culture giving birth to cosmic man. Like
       Hopi myth and Doris Lessing in Briefing for a Descent into
       Hell, shows "evolutionary mutants being taken away by gods."
       Clarke, Teilhard, Paolo Soleri, Sri Aurobindo contribute
       to age's self-fulfilling prophecy.

*D162 Uncertain Worlds: The Literature of Science Fiction. Stam-
       ford, Conn.: Educational Dimensions. 4 discs/cassettes
       and 4 filmstrips. [Source: MT.]

                              1975

D163   ALLEN, L[OUIS] DAVID. The Ballantine Teacher's Guide to Sci-
       ence Fiction: A Practical Creative Approach to Science
       Fiction in the Classroom. New York: Ballantine, pp. 189-
       208, 309-26, paper.
          Childhood's End provides double-edged vision of man's
       potential, dwarfed by rationality of Overlords, transcended
       through parapsychology. Interweaves comedy, tragedy,
       irony, social commentary, Christian symbolism. With heavy
       technological emphasis, Rendezvous with Rama combines
       story elements of starship, exploration, alien world, with
       archaeological overtones. Despite some hostility, human
       reactions to visiting craft mainly awe, curiosity.

          *Part of The Cosmic Classroom, multi-media package.
          New York: Ballantine, [publisher unable to confirm
          precise date, possibly 1975].

D164   ASH, BRIAN. Faces of the Future: The Lessons of Science
       Fiction. New York: Taplinger, pp. 114-16, 119, 174-75,
       184-98.
          Computers' powers illustrated in "The Nine Billion Names

of God" and <u>2001: A Space Odyssey</u>. HAL's murders due to
"an electrical fault . . . in one of its circuits." Sober
speculation of <u>Prelude to Space</u> supplements very short
stories of colonization, relates to test of man's potential
in "The Sentinel." "The Star" compares well with other
religious science fiction. <u>Childhood's End</u> suggests re-
lieving man of tyranny of his own nature.

*D165   <u>Classics of Science Fiction</u>. Stamford, Conn.: Educational
Dimensions. 4 discs/cassettes and 4 filmstrips. [Source:
MT.]
     <u>Childhood's End</u> one of four novels explored.

D166   GREEN, PAUL. <u>The Cyclic Obsession in Science Fiction</u>. North
Hollywood, Calif." Center for Cassette Studies. [CBC467],
four lectures on audiocassette.
     Lecture three cites "The Nine Billion Names of God" as
the most ingenious apocalypse so far devised."

D167   KAFKA, JANET. "Why SF?" <u>English Journal</u> 64 (May):46-53.
     Identifies <u>Childhood's End</u> as "optimistic," <u>Rendezvous
with Rama</u> as "traditional space opera" with subordinate
woman doctor. Clarke "acknowledged master of the explora-
tion-colonization theme," who "extrapolates from pure science" in some stories.

D168   MILLIES, SUZANNE. <u>Science Fiction Primer for Teachers</u>.
Dayton, Ohio: Pflaum, pp. 34-35 and passim.
     Credits influence of John W. Campbell, Jr., on Clarke,
summarizes several works, claiming <u>2001</u> film made from
book. He would free man from matter, but "underestimates
the importance of nature . . . [and] denies the importance
of individual freedom or consciousness." Three novels,
sixteen short stories listed under several thematic
headings.

D169   PHILLIPS, GENE D. <u>Stanley Kubrick: A Film Odyssey</u>. New
York: Popular Library, esp. pp. 129-51, paper.
     Analyzes "The Sentinel," summarizes film at length,
aided by Clarke and Kubrick writings and interviews.
Earlier drafts featured female computer Athena, Dawn of
Man as flashback, other forms of artifact, voiceover.
Odyssean parallels in mind from start, also man-machine
congruence. "Kubrick originally envisioned <u>2001</u> . . .
along more conventional lines." Internal conflict explicit
in earlier emotional treatments of HAL. Background im-
plicit, but viewer participation demanded.

D170   RILEY, CAROLYN, ed. <u>Contemporary Literary Criticism: Excerpts from Criticism of Today's Novelists, Poets, Playwrights, and other Creative Writers</u>. Detroit: Gale

Research, 4:104-5.
Excerpts from Rose (D106), Barrett (D124), reviews of
Rendezvous with Rama in Best Sellers and Virginia Quarterly
Review (see Section E).

D171 ROTTENSTEINER, FRANZ. The Science Fiction Book: An Illustrated History. New York: Seabury Press, pp. 106-8.
Brief profile stresses mystical side of Clarke's fiction,
far less important than his nonfiction.

1976

D172 AQUINO, THOMAS. Science Fiction as Literature. Washington,
D.C.: National Education Association, pp. 45-48.
Childhood's End's "topical, episodic structure . . .
unified by the development of understanding of . . . the
nature of the Overlords." Little people play important
roles, dominated by the Overlord, Karellen. Among many
Judeo-Christian images, explanation of Devil unconvincing.
Classroom comparisons suggested: "The Devil and Daniel
Webster," Rosemary's Baby, Visit to a Small Planet.

D173 ASH, BRIAN, comp. Who's Who in Science Fiction. New York:
Taplinger, pp. 69-70.
"Arthur C. Clarke," profile emphasizes significance of
science at expense of character. Contrived but effective
"last-line twists" to his short stories. Childhood's End
"strikingly imaginative."

D174 BAILEY, J[AMES] O[SLER]. "Some Comments on Science Fiction."
Journal of General Education 28 (Spring):75-82.
"Metaphysical Will" of Hardy (The Dynasts) recurs in
Shaw, Stapledon, Clarke. Childhood's End least scientific,
most mystical in line of descent. Mechanics of mutation
unclear, blurring motivation for climax, suspending belief.

D175 BAINBRIDGE, WILLIAM SIMS. The Spaceflight Revolution: A
Sociological Study. New York: John Wiley & Sons, pp. 37-
44, 145-57, 217-18.
Clarke among fourteen representative pioneers of space
travel who shared independent fathers, early commitment to
space, interest in astronomy, influence of science fiction,
but otherwise varied. Clarke's role in British Interplanetary Society that of propagandist. Opinions recounted
on other science fiction and space writers, as well as
"invention" of communication satellites in synchronous
orbit.

D176 CLARESON, THOMAS D. "The Cosmic Loneliness of Arthur C.
Clarke." In Voices for the Future: Essays on Major Sci-

ence Fiction Writers. Edited by Thomas D. Clareson.
Bowling Green, Ohio: Bowling Green University Popular
Press, pp. 216-37, 276-80.
   Clarke emphasizes man's need to explore the universe to
find his own soul. Nonfiction provides foundation for
speculative vision, especially of space colonization fueling
cultural renaissance. Early fiction didactic (selling
space travel), or magical (indebted to Olaf Stapledon and
John W. Campbell, Jr.). Celebrates intelligence, plus
reverence and anxiety for life. Bodiless mind of Against
the Fall of Night recalled in 2001: A Space Odyssey, H.G.
Wells's "The Star" in Rendezvous with Rama. Most artistic
achievement "A Meeting with Medusa."

   Excerpt, "The Early Novels," 1974. D151
   In Arthur C. Clarke, 1977. D206

D177   de BOLT, JOE, and JOHN PFEIFFER. "The Modern Period, 1938-
       1975." In Anatomy of Wonder: Science Fiction. Edited by
       Neil Barron. New York and London: R.R. Bowker, pp. 162-66.
          Summaries and mini-critiques of Childhood's End (mediocre
       narrative), The City and the Stars (inadequate prose), The
       Deep Range, Expedition to Earth, A Fall of Moondust, The
       Other Side of the Sky, Prelude to Space (accurate science),
       Reach for Tomorrow, Rendezvous with Rama (juvenile), Tales
       from the White Hart, 2001: A Space Odyssey (substandard),
       and The Wind from the Sun. Comparisons suggested with T.J.
       Bass, Ben Bova, Kenneth Bulmer, Martin Caidin, Avram
       Davidson, Barry Malzberg, Larry Niven, Eric Frank Russell,
       Kurt Vonnegut, Jr.

D178   ERLICH, RICHARD D. "Strange Odyssey: From Dart and Ardrey to
       Kubrick and Clarke." ("SF in the Classroom" series.)
       Extrapolation 17 (May):118-24.
          2001 helps illustrate change in anthropological ideas
       about the ancestry of man.

D179   FERLITA, ERNEST, and JOHN R. MAY. Film Odyssey: The Art of
       Film as the Search for Meaning. New York and Toronto:
       Paulist Press, pp. 140-45.
          2001 primarily a visual experience, each episode a
       crucial "interface": mind/matter, man/technology, man/God
       (or the Infinite). Film elevates monolith above novel's
       narrative level. Visual experience of conclusion belied
       by novel. Starchild "called to be" in the sense of reli-
       gious vocation.

*D180 Getting Hooked on Science Fiction. White Plains, N.Y.:
       Guidance Associates. 1 disc/cassette and 1 filmstrip.
       [Source: MT.]
          Dolphin's Island among works discussed.

D181 HOLLOW, JOHN. "2001 in Perspective: The Fiction of Arthur C.
      Clarke." Southwest Review 61 (Spring):113-29.
          Clarke's poignant desire to know the unknowable echoed
      in Kubrick's film, "Son of Dr. Strangelove" to Clarke.
      Novel emphasizes creation, film self-realization. Clarke
      typically concerned with man-machine relationships, alien
      contact, minor place of man in universe, mistrusting such
      ultimates as divine plan and pure mind. Clarke accepts
      machines as logical successors to man; Kubrick shows danger
      of men becoming machines. Clarke's astronauts not machines,
      his Bowman does not change; Kubrick's Bowman both transcends
      and remains himself, because Kubrick obsessed with personal
      immortality. Film's final scene ambiguous enough to sug-
      gest both immortality and new beginning. In The City and
      the Stars, "clearly the center of [Clarke's] work," death
      is natural. Clarke "should have ended the novel at the
      moment of contact with the extraterrestrials." But
      "Kubrick's demand for some ultimate answer . . . forced
      Clarke to borrow from Childhood's End to complete 2001."
      Rendezvous with Rama and Imperial Earth return to Clarkean
      glimpses of something beyond us, but no ultimate answers.

D182 KRAFT, DAVID ANTHONY. "2001: A Space Retrospective." In
      2001: A Space Odyssey. New York: Marvel Comics, pp. 73-
      82. B40
          Retrospective review incorporates material from novel,
      Lost Worlds of 2001, Clarke and Kubrick comments, imputes
      debt to Disney's Fantasia.

D183 KYLE, DAVID. A Pictorial History of Science Fiction. London:
      Hamlyn, passim.
          Inspired by Hugo Gernsback, a "discovery" of John W.
      Campbell, Jr., Clarke appeared in Playboy in "late forties."
      Helped found Nova Publications (British SF magazine pub-
      lisher). Star attraction at 1956 World Science Fiction
      Convention, Tokyo's First International Science Fiction
      Symposium (Expo '70). 2001: A Space Odyssey given
      European premiere in Vienna at United Nations Conference on
      the Peaceful Uses of Space (August 1968).

D184 MAYHEW, PAULA C. "Science in Science Fiction Mini-Course."
      Science Teacher 43 (April):36-37.
          Sands of Mars, "History Lesson," "The Wind from the
      Sun" helpful.

D185 MOLSON, FRANCIS J. "Juvenile Science Fiction." In Anatomy of
      Wonder: Science Fiction. Edited by Neil Barron. New York
      and London: R.R. Bowker, p. 314.
          Dolphin Island and Islands in the Sky seen as thoroughly
      extrapolated, but routine stories.

D186 RABKIN, ERIC S. The Fantastic in Literature. Princeton, N.J.: Princeton University Press, pp. 127–33.

Childhood's End, like Theodore Sturgeon's More than Human, projects man's next evolutionary step. Sturgeon's unity greater, using the fantastic as a Wellsian paradigm. Clarke's book more popular, rejecting modern evolution in favor of the "Christian fantasy of the descent of Grace."

D187 RHODE, ERIC. A History of the Cinema from its Origins to 1970. New York: Hill & Wang, p. 612.

Kubrick's ballets, Clarke's mystical ideas seem high-flown nonsense," engage enduring problems: machines both beautiful and repugnant, impossibility of foolproof plans, Kubrick's anxiety over his own death. Resultant "journey into the self's awareness of its own annihilation" carries message that "only by accepting the inevitably [sic] of death . . . will mankind be able to come to terms with its inherited impulse to destroy."

D188 SCHMIDT, STANLEY. "Science Fiction and the High School Teacher." ("SF in the Classroom" series.) Extrapolation 17 (May):141–50.

In scientific context, "A Meeting with Medusa" useful for explaining Jupiter to astronomy class.

*D189 Science Fiction and Fantasy. Pleasantville, N.Y.: Educational Audio-Video. 2 discs/cassettes and 2 filmstrips. [Source: MT.]

Clarke featured as part of post-1945 development.

D190 The Writers Directory, 1976–1978. London: St. James; New York: St. Martin's Press, p. 148.

"Clarke, Arthur C[harles]," résumé.

1977

D191 "About the Author." In The View from Serendip. New York: Random House, p. [275].

Brief résumé. See C638.

D192 "Arthur C. Clarke: A Biographical Note." In Arthur C. Clarke. New York: Taplinger, pp. 245–47. D206.

Basic facts of the author's public life.

D193 ASIMOV, ISAAC. "Asimov's Corollary." Magazine of Fantasy and Science Fiction 52 (February):102–12.

Partially rebuts Clarke's claim [in Profiles of the Future] that "distinguished, elderly [i.e., over thirty] scientists" are usually wrong saying something is impossible. If the public rallies around a [crackpot] belief, scientists are probably right.

Isaac Asimov. Quasar, Quasar, Burning Bright. Garden
City, N.Y.: Doubleday, 1978.
Excerpt, "Clarke's Law and Asimov's Corollary." Science
Digest 83 (October):16-17.

D194 BRIGG, PETER. "Three Styles of Arthur C. Clarke: the Pro-
      jector, the Wit, and the Mystic." In Arthur C. Clarke.
      New York: Taplinger, pp. 15-51. D206.
         The Projector extrapolates: structure and tone allow
      him to reveal a great deal of scientific matter. The Wit
      relates a quirk or fantasy to a point of science. The
      Mystic movingly expresses his desire to explore the un-
      known. A limited stylist, Clarke uses to advantage strengths
      inherent in each mode.

         Excerpt, Contemporary Literary Criticism, 1980. D264

D195 CORNISH, EDWARD et al. The Study of the Future: An Introduc-
      tion to the Art and Science of Understanding and Shaping
      Tomorrow's World. Washington, D.C.: World Future Society,
      pp. 152-57.
         Bio-biliographical sketch emphasizes forecasting.

D196 CRAVEN, TOM. "2076: A Sri Lankan Odyssey." Millimeter 5
      (March):40-42, 46, 48, 50, 78-79.
         Describes filming commercials (B42) with Clarke, touring
      Sri Lanka, visiting the author's "neo Somerset Maugham"
      residence.

D197 GALLAGHER, EDWARD J. "From Folded Hands to Clenched Fists:
      Kesey and Science Fiction." Lex et Scientia 13 (January-
      March):46-50.
         One Flew Over the Cuckoo's Nest parallels science fic-
      tion films and stories in depicting a mechanical womb or
      coffin against which it is natural to rebel. Clarke
      parallels include The City and the Stars and 2001: A Space
      Odyssey (only Kubrick credited).

D198 HARFST, BETSY. "Of Myths and Polyominoes: Mythological Con-
      tent in Clarke's Fiction." In Arthur C. Clarke. New York:
      Taplinger, pp. 87-120. D206.
         In Childhood's End, 2001: A Space Odyssey, Rendezvous
      with Rama, and Imperial Earth, Clarke uses myths from East
      and West, in an attempt to reconcile opposites as well as
      to examine and explain "ideas common to all times and
      cultures."

D199 HOWES, ALAN B. "Expectation and Surprise in Childhood's End."
      In Arthur C. Clarke. New York: Taplinger, pp. 149-71.
      D206.

Literary conventions normally signal what type of story
to expect, but Clarke entertains in part with surprise
twists, confounding expectations of genre, character and
theme in this novel.

D200 KYLE, DAVID. The Illustrated Book of Science Fiction Ideas
      and Dreams. London: Hamlyn, passim.
          Jules Verne, Olaf Stapledon major influences on the
      best-known science-fiction writer alive. Emphasizes
      Clarke's belief in human progress, hard-core extrapolation,
      overlapping nonfiction, but religious questioning also
      evident.

D201 LEHMAN-WILZIG, SAM N. "Science Fiction as Futurist Prediction:
      Alternative Visions of Heinlein and Clarke." Literary Re-
      view 20 (Winter):133-51.
          Clarke and Robert A. Heinlein heirs, respectively, of
      Jules Verne and H.G. Wells. Of British science-fiction
      writers, Clarke least given to literary and material Ameri-
      canisms, uninfluenced by frontier mythology. Team effort
      stressed in Prelude to Space, Islands in the Sky. Clarke
      faces threat of annihilation equably, compared to rage,
      denial, withdrawal of Heinlein. Aliens can be superior
      for Clarke, seeing mankind as one race, accepting that
      "the stars are not for man" (Childhood's End) as presently
      constituted. Clarke foresees birth of true superman not
      far off, man merging with, then giving way to machines.
      Also expressed in nonfiction (Profiles of the Future), his
      sobering view sounder than Heinlein's, despite Clarke's
      extrapolation giving way to metaphysics.

D202 LUNDWALL, SAM J. Science Fiction: An Illustrated History.
      New York: Grosset & Dunlap, pp. 118, 121, 185, paper.
          Like Stanislaw Lem's Solaris, Rendezvous with Rama
      "manages . . . to depict something so totally different
      from us that it is virtually unexplainable." Science fic-
      tion's best story of immortality, Childhood's End compares
      with Huxley and Capek.

D203 MENVILLE, DOUGLAS, and R[OBERT] REGINALD [pseud. for Michael
      Burgess]. Things to Come: An Illustrated History of the
      Science Fiction Film. New York: Times Books, p. 146.
          2001 gave respectability to science-fiction films.
      Clarke's effect waned as production progressed. Confused
      ending may be due to post-production cuts.

D204 MOYLAN, TOM. "Ideological Contradiction in Clarke's The City
      and the Stars." Science-Fiction Studies 4 (July):150-57.
          Falsely promising liberation, science fiction often
      only compensates and co-opts. Clarke typically prophesies

American-dominated space program. Mystical and technological extremes of his fiction both compatible with postwar
"end of ideology" movement. In The City and the Stars, the
"dialectical tension" between flawed city of Diaspar and
perfect utopia of Lys "a product of cold-war ideology."
Of Clarke's disembodied minds, Vanamonde, like Alvin and
Hilvar, is an adventurous youth; "Mad Mind" symbolizes
both capitalism's failure and socialism's menace. This
novel best illustrates Clarke's technocratic vision.
Clarke also downgrades politics and economics in nonfiction
(Profiles of the Future).

See Clarke response, C663; discussion D222, 239.

D205 NAHA, ED. Science Fiction Aliens. New York: Starlog Magazine, p. 60 ["Contents" claims p. 61], paper.
Entry for 2001 notes aliens not seen in film, claims
they were in "The Sentinel."

D206 OLANDER, JOSEPH D., and MARTIN HARRY GREENBERG, eds. Arthur
C. Clarke. "Writers of the 21st Century" series. New
York: Taplinger.
[Contents: Introduction, Brigg (D194), Clareson (D177),
Thron (D215), Harfst (D198), Plank (D89), Howes (D199),
Tranzy (D216), Samuelson (D148), Huntington (D156), Notes,
"Selected Bibliography" (D212), "Arthur C. Clarke: A
Biographical Note" (C192).]

D207 PARKER, HELEN NETHERCUTT. "Biological Themes in Modern Science Fiction." Ph.D. dissertation (English), Duke University, esp. pp. 17, 22, 25, 49, 52-56, 174.
Kalinga Speech shows Clarke's view of universe like
John W. Campbell, Jr.'s, but with reduced role for man.
Childhood's End best known positive representation of
human evolution replaced by or merging with the alien (seen
also in Clifford Simak, Olaf Stapledon). Overmind "totally
alien, totally indifferent to life it may destroy," transformation "immediate and total," human identity lost.
Despite technical flaws, "an unforgettably powerful novel."
Demonstrates extrapolative method, like Ursula K. Le Guin's
The Left Hand of Darkness, but Clarke more traditional and
conservative.

Dissertation Abstracts International 38 (1978):7347A.

D208 Random House Encyclopedia. New York: Random House, p. 2049.
"Clarke, Arthur Charles," brief listing.

*D209 ROSENHAUSE, SHARON. "Writer Arthur C. Clarke Leads Tax-Free
Life on Sri Lanka." Los Angeles Times, 9 June, part I A,
p. 1. [Source: clipping seen; Los Angeles Times Index

citation not verified on microfilms (1 June-3 August).]

Retitled "Sri Lanka Finally Gives Writer Tax-Free Status." Houston Chronicle, 3 August, Section 1, p. 23. [Numerous other titles in various reprints.]

D210 ROVIN, JEFF. From Jules Verne to Star Trek. New York and London: Drake, pp. 122-23, paper.
    Deliberately obscure, 2001 demands viewer participation. Clarke novel explains subtleties.

D211 SCHOLES, ROBERT, and ERIC S. RABKIN. Science Fiction: History, Science, Vision. New York: Oxford University Press, pp. 65-66, 85-86, 216-20.
    Childhood's End related to Olaf Stapledon's Odd John and the ominous warning closing Robert A. Heinlein's "Future History" chart. A critique of utopian dreams, it subordinates evolution to "Grace." Like Stanislaw Lem's The Invincible, Rendezvous with Rama deals with first contact; stressing courage, endurance, resourcefulness, both evoke "awe at the possibilities of the cosmos--in which humanity is just a single possibility." Transcending science and science fiction, Clarke has influence outside the field, notably British novelist Doris Lessing.

D212 "Selected Bibliography." [No compiler credited.] In Arthur C. Clarke. New York: Taplinger, pp. 237-44. D206.
    Fiction and critiques of it, drawn mainly from Tuck (D8) and Contento's "forthcoming" Index to Science Fiction Anthologies and Collections (Boston: G.K. Hall, 1978).

D213 SLUSSER, GEORGE EDGAR. The Space Odysseys of Arthur C. Clarke. San Bernardino, Calif.: Borgo Press, paper.
    Odyssey pattern central to Clarke oeuvre: voyages and returns, fathers and sons seeking each other, overt Homeric allusions. Past Britain's age of conquest, Clarke "doomed to chronicle progress and deny it at the same time." Progress leads him repeatedly to stagnant utopias, evolutionary blind alleys and metamorphoses he must reject, committed as he is to man in his present biological and cultural form. A spectator, he writes elegies for man's paralysis in a huge cosmos. Bound to this theme, emblematic of his age, Clarke can vary only the size, complexity, self-consciousness and satire of his works.

    Excerpt, Contemporary Literary Criticism, 1980. D264

D214 SNYDER, GENE. "Caution: Science Friction [sic] Causes Heat." Media and Methods 14 (November):28-29.
    Among several comparisons/contrasts, suggests Childhood's End with The Midwich Cuckoos by John Wyndham. Asks how we

would react to Clarke's "next, natural step in human evolution"?

D215   THRON, E. MICHAEL. "The Outsider from Inside: Clarke's
       Aliens." In Arthur C. Clarke. New York: Taplinger, pp.
       72-86. D206.
            In 2001: A Space Odyssey, Childhood's End and Rendezvous
       with Rama, Clarke writes within traditional forms but uses
       the alien to shatter our "mundane technological and psycho-
       logical world and the fictional devices that created the
       mundane in the process." The alien is Clarke's answer to
       the threat of stagnation, as we progressively domesticate
       nature and even ourselves.

D216   TRANZY, EUGENE. "Contrasting Views of Man and the Evolutionary
       Process: Back to Methuselah and Childhood's End." In
       Arthur C. Clarke. New York: Taplinger, pp. 172-95. D206.
            Both Clarke and Bernard Shaw domesticate Darwin, sug-
       gesting a belief in human potential and a nonmechanistic
       counter-theory. Shaw limits his discussion (Back to
       Methuselah) to the earth; Clarke needs the universe to
       show human evolutionary potential.

D217   WARRICK, PATRICIA. "The Cybernetic Imagination in Science
       Fiction." Ph.D. dissertation (English), University of
       Wisconsin--Milwaukee, pp. 158, 216-20, 226.
            Brief comments on 2001 and "The Nine Billion Names of
       God." Focus on The City and the Stars in which Clarke
       transforms information and technology into images and im-
       plications of computerized society. Storing genetic infor-
       mation, chance and game theory, time travel utilized.
       Lackin sexual reproduction, however, "utopian" city lacks
       creativity.

            Dissertation Abstracts International 40 (1979):253A.
            The Cybernetic Imagination in Science Fiction. Cam-
            bridge, Mass.: M.I.T. Press, 1980.

D218   WEIDEMANN, A.J. "Three Journeys: One Tradition." Standpunte
       (Union of South Africa) 30, no. 4 [Autumn?]:55-62.
            2001: A Space Odyssey, like James Joyce's Ulysses,
       modernizes Homer's Odyssey. Classical motifs include sea
       imagery, oracular prophecy (monolith), Polyphemus (HAL).
       "If Ulysses is an expression of the credo, 'l'art pour
       l'art,' then 2001 . . . is art for the sake of sanity."
       But Clarke's novel lacks "verisimilitude and the complexity
       of everyday life." Ulysses offers "playful and mundane
       scepticism"; 2001 represents "excesses of humanistic opti-
       mism and unchecked faith in human progress."

D219   WOLFE, GARY K. "The Known and the Unknown: Structure and

Image in Science Fiction." In Many Futures, Many Worlds.
Edited by Thomas D. Clareson. Kent, Ohio: Kent State
University Press, pp. 94-116, esp. pp. 104-14.

The City and the Stars shows the "archetypal science-
fictional city," Diaspar. This city as icon interacts with
spaceships, robots, alien creatures, computers, all bridging
the known and the unknown. Barriers broken successfully
transform oppositions into higher ones, until the protagonist Alvin himself finally comes to represent the unknown.
Opposing scientific progress to the unknowable other,
Clarke "consistently pushes the process of extrapolation
to the limits of rationality and beyond." Diaspar counter-
poses human potential to wasteland beyond; extrapolated
from the familiar and rational, its power comes from our
"subrational" fear of the unknown within, as well as without.

In The Known and the Unknown: The Iconography of Science Fiction. Kent, Ohio: Kent State University Press,
1979. [Slightly revised.]

1978

D220 "Arthur C. Clarke." In Against the Fall of Night. New York:
Jove, p. [2], paper.
Brief profile. See A63.

D221 ASHLEY, MICHAEL. "Pulps." In Encyclopedia of Science Fiction.
Edited by Robert Holdstock. London: Octopus, pp. 50-67,
paper.
Clarke's first fiction sold to Walter Gillings, who ad-
vised him to seek United States markets.

D222 ASTLE, RICHARD. "Dear Professor Mullen." Science-Fiction
Studies 5 (November):303-4.
Letter. Clarke letter (C663) ill-advised, actually
supports Moylan reading (D204) of The City and the Stars,
despite factual misstatements.

Editor's response, D239.

D223 BOTSFORD, WARD. Untitled liner notes. "Transit of Earth"
and "The Nine Billion Names of God"--"The Star" Read by
the Author, Arthur C. Clarke. New York: Caedmon. B50.
Brief profile.

Reprinted without identification on other Clarke recordings (B51, B55).

D224 BOYD, DAVID. "Mode and Meaning in 2001." Journal of Popular

Film 6 (Summer):202-15.
Cultists would reduce 2001 to materials and medium,
but its meaning resides in myth and satire. Film superior
because unexplained, but novel provides terms of analysis:
Moon Watcher, Stargate Corridor, Starchild. "The" monolith
may be several. Images too rich and ambiguous: title,
monolith(s), broken goblet. Major allusions to Nietzsche,
Homer, D.W. Griffith's film "Man's Genesis." Myth hard to
miss, satire often overlooked, including cruel inversion of
man and machine. Three "gods" apparent: alien force, HAL,
Starchild. Clarke misreads HAL's motivation; paralleling
the Dawn of Man, it connects to evolution. HAL becomes
vanquished rival; David Bowman (Jewish-Greek combination of
names) survives outer, faces inner space.

D225 BROSNAN, JOHN. Future Tense: The Cinema of Science Fiction.
New York: St. Martin's, pp. 174-81.
"In Stanley Kubrick, Clarke found the perfect collabora-
tor. Both men are technology-fixated, have high energy
drives, are perfectionists, and are insatiably curious, and
both share similar ideas on God." Hostile critics (many in
science fiction) upset by picture of humanity as pathetic,
technology as toys, man at a dead end. "Kubrick's aim was
to force his audiences to . . . re-examine their own per-
ceptions of the Universe . . . which would have been ob-
scured by . . . emotionally involving, real characters."
In correspondence, John Baxter stressed getting the background right; Michael Moorcock found film barren of ideas,
topheavy with technology, due to Clarke.

D226 COMMIRE, ANNE, ed. Something About the Author: Facts and
Pictures about Contemporary Authors and Illustrators of
Books for Young People. Detroit: Gale Research, 13:22-24.
"Clarke, Arthur C(harles)," profile with author's allu-
sions to W. Somerset Maugham and Ernest Hemingway.

D227 EDWARDS, MALCOLM. "Yesterday, Today and Tomorrow." In Encyclopedia of Science Fiction. Edited by Robert Holdstock.
London: Octopus, pp. 174-89, paper.
Notes Clarke, Asimov, Heinlein "superstars" of science
fiction in 1970s. Of them, Clarke still evokes the "sense
of wonder," in Rendezvous with Rama, "A Meeting with
Medusa," less so in Imperial Earth.

D228 FARMER, PHILIP JOSÉ, and BEVERLY FRIEND. "The Remarkable Ad-
venture." In Science Fiction: Contemporary Mythology.
Edited by Patricia Warrick, Martin Harry Greenberg, and
Joseph Olander. New York: Harper & Row, pp. 39-48.
"Before Eden" compared with "Brightside Crossing" by
Alan E. Nourse and "The Game of Rat and Dragon," by
Cordwainer Smith to illustrate the fantastic journey of

Joseph Campbell's "monomyth." In the Clarke story, the
lesson not to despoil another world (or this one?) is for
the reader, too late for the fictional explorers.

D229 FEENBERG, ANDREW. "The Politics of Survival: Science Fiction
in the Nuclear Age." Alternative Futures 1 (Summer):3-23.
If Campbellian science fiction straitjacketed humanity
with its view of scientific (and literary) limits, the new
science fiction of the 1960s tried to define human limits
in terms of "a dialectic of progress which promises certain
self-destruction." Like Clifford Simak, Clarke prefigured
this movement in his novels, seeking a place for mankind
"in a universe of rational or even super-rational minds."
The City and the Stars requires reuniting mechanical and
psychic potential. Childhood's End, its transfiguration
of the species fueled by self-doubt, points toward genre's
mutation in next decade.

D230 FOX, JORDAN R. "Childhood's End Hits Legal Snag." Cinefan-
tastique 8 (December):31.
Clarke reported suing Universal to stop production of
film for television.

D231 FRANK, ALAN. Sci-Fi Now. London: Octopus, pp. 8, 22-29,
paper.
"A special effects movie in search of a plot," also a
sign of "the coming of age of the genre in the cinema."
Clarke story "barely visible under the surrounding padding"
and willful obscurity.

D232 HARRISON, HARRY. Foreword to Future Tense: The Cinema of
Science Fiction, by John Brosnan. New York: St. Martin's,
pp. 6-8.
Involving real science-fiction writers (like Wells and
Clarke) eliminates the need for quotation marks in "science
fiction" films. See D225.

D233 _____. "Machine as Hero." In Encyclopedia of Science Fiction.
Edited by Robert Holdstock. London: Octopus, pp. 86-103,
paper.
Cites Clarke variations on time travel ("Time's Arrow"),
matter transmission ("Travel by Wire"), danger of computers
("The Nine Billion Names of God"), alien contact (Rendezvous with Rama, "The Sentinel").

D234 HILL, DOUGLAS. "Major Themes." In Encyclopedia of Science
Fiction. Edited by Robert Holdstock. London: Octopus,
pp. 28-49, paper.
Scientists as heroes, aware of risks, common in Clarke
works. Advanced aliens in "The Sentinel," "Loophole,"
Childhood's End.

D235 LABAR, MARTIN. "Arthur C. Clarke: Humanism in Science Fic-
        tion." Christianity Today 22 (2 June):27.
              Author of several "religious" stories, Clarke created
        in Rendezvous with Rama "a metaphor for an atheist's view
        of existence . . . big, imperturbable, and inexplicable,
        coming from who-knows-what purpose." Clarke's supermind
        part of insidious Manichean heresy that evolution is purging
        us of our bodies.

D236 MENGER, LUCY. "The Appeal of Childhood's End." In Critical
        Encounters: Writers and Themes in Science Fiction. Edited
        by Dick Riley. New York: Frederick Ungar, pp. 87-108.
              More than the sum of its episodic parts, this novel is
        welded together by suspense and overall theme of reason and
        the irrational. Discusses super race, utopia, star travel,
        slight but basically decent characters, and a clear style
        that sometimes rises to poetry. Beginning with an ending,
        ending with a beginning, the novel at its core is a myth.

D237 MOORE, PATRICK. "Fiction to Fact." In Encyclopedia of Sci-
        ence Fiction. Edited by Robert Holdstock. London:
        Octopus, pp. 142-51, paper.
              Clarke's "invention" of communication satellites pre-
        dated in fiction by over a century. Sober scientific pro-
        jections in A Fall of Moondust, Earthlight, The Sands of
        Mars, "Icarus Ascending" [sic], 2001: A Space Odyssey,
        Imperial Earth, and Rendezvous with Rama.

D238 MORGAN, CHRIS. "Alien Encounter." In Encyclopedia of Science
        Fiction. Edited by Robert Holdstock. London: Octopus,
        pp. 104-21, paper.
              Childhood's End, The City and the Stars, "The Sentinel"
        cited as Clarke variations on this theme.

D239 MULLEN R[ICHARD] DALE. "In Response to Mr. Astle." Science-
        Fiction Studies 5 (November):304-6.
              Editorial apology for not catching specified errors in
        carelessly tendentious article by Moylan (D204) attacked
        by Clarke (C663), defended by Astle (D222).

D240 TOMPKINS, BOYLSTON. Introduction to Alien Creatures by
        Richard Siegel and Jean-Claude Suares. Los Angeles: Reed
        Books, pp. 7-32, paper.
              Parallels monolith-makers in 2001: A Space Odyssey to
        mythical Apollo. Apeman sequence "a masterful celebration
        of the ancient victory of human reason over brute strength
        which continues to form the theme of the invasion type of
        s-f film." Central Clarke concern from Childhood's End to
        Rendezvous with Rama is to undermine anthropocentrism.
        Comfortable with technology in 2001, we may be dehumanized,
        but the answer is more technology, albeit higher, alien,

"raised into mysticism, as much pure mind as machine."

D241 WYMER, THOMAS L. et al. Intersections: The Elements of Fic-
      tion in Science Fiction. Bowling Green, Ohio: Bowling
      Green University Popular Press, pp. 51, 53, 60-62, 89, 113-
      14, paper.
           "The Sentinel" suggests vastness, comparing "a carefully
      extrapolated moon base" with artifact "billions" [sic] of
      years old. It speculates on human destiny, like Childhood's
      End. "History Lesson," anchored in archaeology, illustrates
      omniscient third person viewpoint, gradually revealing in-
      formation, like an impersonal historian. Playing with
      myth, "The Star" could be called an "anti-myth."

                                1979

D242 ANTCZAK, JANICE. "The Mythos of a New Romance: A Critical
      Analysis of Science Fiction for Children." Ph.D. disserta-
      tion (library science), Columbia University, pp. 39, 69,
      78.
           In Dolphin Island, computer helps dolphins speak as
      animals do in myth and fairy tale, sharks and killer whales
      stand for dragons, sea works for and against the hero.
      Islands in the Sky in bibliography.

D243 ASIMOV, ISAAC. Untitled liner notes. "Childhood's End"
      Excerpts Read by the Author, Arthur C. Clarke. New York:
      Caedmon. B51.
           Clarke's imagination disciplined, doesn't depend on sex,
      violence, or purple prose. Childhood's End a huge success,
      its superrace notion reused in 2001: A Space Odyssey and
      Rendezvous with Rama. Now "Sri Lanka's natural wonder,"
      Clarke continually ranks with Asimov and Robert A. Heinlein
      atop science-fiction reader surveys.

D244 BEJA, MORRIS. Film and Literature: An Introduction. New
      York and London: Longman, passim.
           For 2001 as one of 25 case studies, cites literary germ,
      coincident writing of screenplay and novel, special effects
      breakthroughs. "Topics to think about" include comments by
      reviewers (and by Kubrick and Clarke), myth, film versus
      novel, music, lack of dialogue, motivation of HAL, Bowman's
      feat and risk, attitudes toward science, comparisons with
      A Clockwork Orange (another case study).

D245 BOSSAY, LYSSA DIANE. "Religious Themes and Motifs in Science
      Fiction." Ph.D. dissertation (English), University of
      Texas (Austin), esp. pp. 97-111.
           Vision of Childhood's End "sharpened and made intelli-
      gible through an unfamiliar use of a great many familiar

                                171

patterns." Evolutionary stance sees true passage into
adulthood as simultaneously an apotheosis. Hero is the
human race, whose birth is our ending. Study examines
"dramatic irony, reversals of traditional motifs, structural
parallels which reiterate the primary motif on a human
scale, and . . . believable and generally sympathetic characters." At great cost, "a form of divine grace" is ac-
cepted, this "Fall" delivering promise of Eden's serpent:
"Ye shall be as gods." Stormgren, Overlords, like Moses,
will not see Promised Land. Contrasting journeys of children, Jan Rodericks, begun at seance. Unlike Jonah, Jan
seeks his mission, sees "tree of fire," plays mediating
role at end.

Dissertation Abstracts International 40 (1980):5857A.

D246 FULLER, BUCKMINSTER. Untitled liner notes. "Fountains of
      Paradise" [sic] Read by the Author, Arthur C. Clarke. New
      York: Caedmon. B55.
           Clarke's strategy in fiction compared to archery, finding
      underpinnings in history from which to extrapolate and pro-
      ject parallel behaviors. Sound scientific basis for The
      Fountains of Paradise.

D247 HARDESTY, WILLIAM H., IV. "Rendezvous with Rama." In Survey
      of Science Fiction Literature. Edited by Frank N. Magill.
      Englewood Cliffs, N.J.: Salem Press, 4:1759-63.
           Vigorously extrapolated with sense of wonder at first
      contact, novel weakened by romantic and melodramatic sub-
      plots. "Adventure, mystery and scientific gadgetry" made
      it an "instant classic."

D248 HIRSCH, FOSTER. Introduction to Arthur C. Clarke, The Lost
      Worlds of 2001. Boston: Gregg Press, pp. v-xv.
           Clarke's book illuminates by contrast Kubrick's wisdom
      in not explaining. Film challenges traditional relation-
      ship of audience to film and to science fiction. Elliptical
      structure, motivation by concept compared to D.W. Griffith's
      Intolerance, illustrated by obelisk [sic], HAL's breakdown,
      hotel room. Suggests HAL sabotaged by aliens. Praises
      handling of Jungian archetypes, hypnotic rhythm, aesthetic
      distance. "Ultimately . . . 2001 is not primarily a satire,
      or a discourse on human limitation, but a poetic evocation
      of human possibility." See A200.

D249 KITTREDGE, WILLIAM, and STEVEN M. KRAUZER. "'The Sentinel'
      (2001: A Space Odyssey)." In Stories into Film. New
      York: Harper & Row, pp. 221-22.
           Traditional story, innovative film. Kubrick's visceral
      response to Clarke's story: "His central character is . . .
      a stark black monolith." Wrestling with same questions as

Blow-Up, but attacked by many Antonioni supporters. "Clarke's sentinel finally speaks, but its voice is complex and elevated. It is our responsibility to make the effort to understand." Nineteen-sixties "Flower children" may have seen themselves in the Starchild.

D250 LAWLER, DONALD L. "Imperial Earth." In Survey of Science Fiction Literature. Edited by Frank N. Magill. Englewood Cliffs, N.J.: Salem Press, 3:1019-25.

Drawing heavily on predecessors, shows unusual emphasis on interpersonal relations and fully developed symbolism. Vivid moments and technological verisimilitude in a vague tapestry, sentimental and contrived. Strong on forecasting, but predictions date, like traditional image of Saturn as only ringed planet.

D251 MARTIN, DAVID THOMAS. "Religious Dimensions of Representative Science Fiction." Ph.D. dissertation (English education), Ohio State University, esp. pp. 49-55, 93-95, 117.

Childhood's End offers "a different twist of the resurrection theme," reminiscent of Hinduism or Buddhism. Rendezvous with Rama suggests the possibility of resurrecting a whole civilization. In The City and the Stars, "resurrection is part of the cycle of life for the multitudes, alternating with a period of mock death" overseen by a computer. This novel also shows moral character development, transcending material security supplied by technology leaving "important spiritual needs unheeded."

Dissertation Abstracts International 40 (1980):5430A.

D252 P[ETER] N[ICHOLLS]. "Clarke, Arthur C(harles)." In The Science Fiction Encyclopedia. Edited by Peter Nicholls. Garden City, N.Y.: Doubleday, pp. 121-23.

Wooden prose of early genre stories enlivened by scientific imagination. "The Sentinel" first exposed paradoxical combination of hardcore technological science fiction and mystical transcendence. The City and the Stars probably his most perfect work. Popular science writing, often related to his fiction, compares with Isaac Asimov's. More recent fiction less voluminous, more controversial.

D253 P[ETER] N[ICHOLLS], and J[OHN] B[ROSNAN]. "2001: A Space Odyssey. In The Science Fiction Encyclopedia. Edited by Peter Nicholls. Garden City, N.Y.: Doubleday, p. 618.

"Kubrick's unique production lays a gloss of metaphysics over a number of traditional sf themes, including the idea, derived from Charles Fort, that 'we are property.'" Novel written after film's completion.

D254 PERAKOS, PETER S. "Arthur C. Clarke's The Fountains of

Paradise." <u>Cinefantastique</u> 8 (July):35.
   Book originally conceived as film, negotiations pending.
Update on <u>Childhood's End</u> [see D230] sugggests Clarke now
supporting production.

D255 POLLOCK, KARL. "An Interview with Charles Sheffield." <u>Sci</u>-
      <u>ence Fiction Review</u> [fanzine], no. 33 (November), pp. 10-
      15 (pt. 1); no. 34 (February 1980), pp. 24-29 (pt. 2).
         Sheffield notes similarities with Clarke, emphasizing
      overlap of central idea in novels published almost simul-
      taneousley [cf. C683-684]. Sees Clarke as the rare science
      fiction writer accepted by scientists, because he "invented"
      communications satellites.

D256 PRIEST, CHRISTOPHER. "British Science Fiction." <u>Science Fic</u>-
      <u>tion: A Critical Guide</u>. Edited by Patrick Parrinder.
      London and New York: Longman, pp. 187-202; 196 on Clarke.
         Naive, homely, authentically English, Clarke overrated.
      Effectively simplified style can be poetic; plots pedestrian,
      character motivations unbelievable.

D257 "A Prophet of Hope." <u>Asiaweek</u>, 10 August, p. 23.
         Profile.

D258 PURSER, PHILIP. "Where UFOs are Unwanted." <u>Sunday Telegraph</u>,
      26 August, p. 3.
         Discussion of World Science Fiction Convention in
      Brighton spotlights Clarke's optimism on prospects in space
      and energy crisis.

D259 RABKIN, ERIC S. <u>Arthur C. Clarke</u>. West Linn, Ore.: Starmont
      House, paper.
         "No 'mere' entertainer," Clarke is "polished . . .
      humane . . . [with an] open and fundamentally optimistic
      view of humankind and its potential in a universe which
      dwarfs us in physical size but which we may hope some day
      to match in spirit." Debts to Olaf Stapledon, H.G. Wells,
      J.D. Bernal. Faith in science best exemplified in <u>A Fall</u>
      <u>of Moondust</u>, but "most pervasive theme" is communication.
      "No strong father-son relationships," possibly due to early
      bereavement. Biology deliberately falsified in three
      novels. Consoling myth in <u>Childhood's End</u>: abandoning
      science makes "much more vivid its homocentric map of the
      spiritual universe." Jungian synchronicity, fairytale
      motifs recalled. Repetitive image of pylon or monolith in
      his works achieves "phallic potency" in <u>2001: A Space</u>
      <u>Odyssey</u>. <u>Rendezvous with Rama</u>, the "most mature explora-
      tion of his constant theme of the meaning for mankind of
      science, echoes "two wives" motif of <u>The Deep Range</u>, and
      arrives at "overhanging stairway" of progress or evolution.
      "Clarke was only able to achieve this unique repudiation of

his homocentrism after he had worked his way past the
haunting imagery of 2001." Shorter forms include tall tale,
ghost story, love story, joke, lecture; fiction always more
important than science.

   Revised second edition (Mercer Island, Washington, 1980)
   adds The Fountain of Paradise to existing lines and
   generalizations.

D260 SAMUELSON, DAVID N. "Childhood's End." In Survey of Science
   Fiction Literature. Edited by Frank N. Magill. Englewood
   Cliffs, N.J.: Salem Press, 1:337-41.
      Projects end of strife, initiative, human race. Tech-
   nology advanced but utopia inadequate. Characters, melo-
   drama transcended by theme. Choosing sides in the ending,
   many readers prefer the godlike Overmind to an extrapolation
   of mankind into the devilish Overlords. Mood, imagery well
   chosen, helping morality play to dominate. Appeals to a
   sense of fragility of the human race.

D261 SHEFFIELD, CHARLES. Letter to the editor. SFWA Bulletin
   [fanzine] 4 (Summer):47.
      Notes coincidental parallels in scientific speculation
   between his The Web Between the Worlds and Clarke's The
   Fountains of Paradise [cf. C683-684].

   Excerpt, Science Fiction Review [fanzine], no. 31 (May),
   p. 8. [Expanded.]

D262 SLUSSER, GEORGE EDGAR. "2001: A Space Odyssey." In Survey
   of Science Fiction Literature. Edited by Frank Magill.
   Englewood Cliffs, N.J.: Salem Press, 5:2343-49.
      Clarke's novel written after the fact to reassert his
   own vision, tainted by Kubrick's insistence that man is
   doomed to repeat past behaviors. Voyage forward perpetually
   frozen in a film which "does not even pretend to tell a
   story." Sexual imagery emphasized: focus on sexual division and killing to live makes it clear no Eden existed for
   man to fall from, or from which to look satirically at
   today. Clarke theme of fathers and sons shortcircuited,
   divided against itself. Star Child's eyes "weary," hotel
   room from Bowman's own time, HAL feminine-voiced, hermaphro-
   ditic. Inevitable sequel: more violence.

D263 WILLIAMSON, JACK. "The City and the Stars." In Survey of
   Science Fiction Literature. Edited by Frank N. Magill.
   Englewood Cliffs, N.J.: Salem Press, 1:374-77.
      Clarke's optimism contrasts with Wells's pessimism. In
   utopian context, Alvin's search may seem religious. "Drama
   of life and mind against time" marks the book Clarke spent
   the most time on. Suffers from pulp cliches, may be "his
   most characteristic and most enduring."

D264   WOLFE, GARY K. "The Short Fiction of Arthur C. Clarke." In
       Survey of Science Fiction Literature. Edited by Frank N.
       Magill. Englewood Cliffs, N.J.: Salem Press, 4:1926-29.
           Clarke's stories often mirror or anticipate his novels;
       both divide into short and long range futures. Early
       stories "steeped in . . . cosmic irony." Middle period
       "dominated by his humorous tall tales of loony scientists
       and bizarre inventions." Later stories show "growing con-
       cern with the political implications of technology and
       space travel."

                              1980

D265   Academic American Encyclopedia. Princeton, N.J.: Arete, 5:
       40.
           "Clarke, Arthur C.," brief listing.

D266   BRYFONSKI, DEDRIA, ed. Contemporary Literary Criticism: Ex-
       cerpts from Criticism of Today's Novelists, Poets, Play-
       wrights, and other Creative Writers. Detroit: Gale Re-
       search, 14:148-56.
           Excerpts from Brigg (D194), Slusser (D213), reviews of
       The Fountains of Paradise in New Statesman and New York
       Times Book Review (see Section E).

D267   COYLE, WALLACE. Stanley Kubrick: A Guide to References and
       Resources. Boston: G.K. Hall, esp. pp. 6-7, 23-25, 49-52.
           Invaluable source for 2001: A Space Odyssey; lacks some
       newspaper and all fanzine reviews, de-emphasizes Clarke's
       contribution.

D268   EVERY, ANN, ed. Contemporary Authors: A Bio-Bibliographical
       Guide to Current Writers in Fiction, General Non-Fiction,
       Poetry, Journalism, Drama, Motion Pictures, Television and
       Other Fields. New Revision Series. Detroit: Gale Re-
       search, 2:118-19.
           "Clarke, Arthur C(harles)," profile updated (from D47),
       hints at second film with Stanley Kubrick.

D269   GRIFFITHS, JOHN. Three Tomorrows: American, British and
       Soviet Science Fiction. Totowa, N.J.: Barnes & Noble, pp.
       12, 16, 26, 48, 75-76, 93, 106, 109, 133, 143, 174, 176,
       180.
           One of few science fiction writers with a really inter-
       national reputation, Clarke, like Wells, has an "uncon-
       scious recognition that the elimination of intrahuman con-
       flict creates a need for external alien aggression as the
       sole alternative to stagnation." His short stories are

highest quality, even his "less safe" stories being trans-
lated into Russian.

D270 MEYERS, WALTER E. <u>Aliens and Linguists: Language Study and
Science Fiction</u>. Athens: University of Georgia Press, pp.
20, 27, 41, 65-66, 97, 117.
Linguistic naiveté concerning language suggested in
overrated <u>Childhood's End</u> (universal English use, difficulty
of learning language), and in <u>The City and the Stars</u>
(changeless languages of Diaspar and Lys). "People of the
Sea," however, the "first well-done long story of talking
dolphins," foreshadows actual devices built by researchers.

D271 NEDELKOVICH, ALEXANDER. "The Stellar Parallels: Robert
Silverberg, Larry Niven, and Arthur C. Clarke." <u>Extrapola-
tion</u> 21 (Winter):348-60.
"The Star" by Clarke, "Neutron Star" by Larry Niven, "To
the Dark Star" by Robert Silverberg exhibit similar central
images, major differences in literary handling (largely to
Clarke's credit).

D272 OTTEN, TERRY. "The Fallen and Evolving Worlds of <u>2001</u>."
<u>Mosaic: A Journal for the Interdisciplinary Study of Liter-
ature</u> 13 (Spring/Summer):41-50.
Concerned more with novel than film, finds its roots in
Romantic (especially Blakean) rendering of man's Fall.
Monolith a Tree of Knowledge, Bowman's forced entrance a
rape of the mother-ship, his triumph an achievement of
Chardinian self-consciousness.

D273 PARRINDER, PATRICK. <u>Science Fiction: Its Criticism and
Teaching</u>. London and New York: Methuen, pp. 108-10.
<u>Rendezvous with Rama</u> illustrates "the language of
novelty." Science fiction's reason for being, seldom con-
fronted directly, novelty is domesticated here partly by
the rarely noted future displacement of the narrator.

D274 ROBERTSON, STEVEN. "<u>2001: A Space Odyssey</u>." In <u>Magill's
Survey of Cinema</u>. English Language Films, 1st series.
Edited by Frank N. Magill. Englewood Cliffs, N.J.: Salem
Press, 4:1798-1800.
Commercial success for both film and Clarke's "interpre-
tation" despite early negative reviews. Film relied heavily
on nonverbal elements, music, and "documentary quality of
the special effects."

D275 SEARLES, BAIRD et al. <u>A Reader's Guide to Science Fiction</u>.
New York: Facts on File, pp. 33-35.
British maverick with American appeal writes hard science
fiction with philosophical humanism. <u>Childhood's End</u> a
campus cult book in 1960s, later novels largely "extended

tours of various speculative locales." Good starting point
for novices. (Frequent cross-references from other writers
of "mystical" or "hard science" fiction.)

D276   SEYMOUR-SMITH, MARTIN, ed. <u>Novels and Novelists: A Guide to
the World of Fiction</u>. New York: St. Martin's Press, p.
116.
    "Clarke, Arthur C.," mini-profile.

D277   SLESS, DAVID. "Arthur C. Clarke." <u>The Stellar Gauge: Essays
on Science Fiction Writers</u>. Edited by Michael J. Tolley
and Kirpal Singh. Carlton, Victoria, Australia: Norstrilia
Press, pp. 91-107.
    The archetypal example of the science-fiction writer as
technological prophet, Clarke uses humor and mysticism
primarily as background for an "act of celebration" of the
physical world. In at least six novels, some short stories
and nonfiction, nature is the hero, its "landscapes" always
fresh. Through them the typical Clarkean hero, nature's
"insignificant byproduct," takes his odyssey of observation
and "solitary contemplation." Success in this fictional
universe requires intelligence, but little or no social in-
volvement. Clarke's technophilic optimism is economically
naive, morally insensitive, bereft of any consideration of
social evolution.

D278   SOBCHACK, THOMAS, and VIVIAN C. SOBCHACK. <u>An Introduction to
Film</u>. Boston: Little, Brown, 1980, passim.
    Novel of <u>2001</u> capitalized on film's popularity and
viewers' confusion about its narrative issues.

Part E: Book Reviews

    In the table which follows, reviews of each book (and a couple of essays) are listed in chronological order under each book title. The sequence for each line is periodical title (usually abbreviated), volume (if available) and page(s), date, name(s) of reviewer(s). Fanzines are indicated by [f]. Newspapers unidentified as to city were published in London. If no page numbers are given, only a press clipping was seen. If no reviewer's name is given, none is apparent in the original document. Names for which initials stand have been supplied when possible. The compilation of reviews is preceded by a listing of abbreviations for periodicals, alphabetized by the letters in the abbreviation.

ABBREVIATIONS

AA	American Artist	BL	Booklist
AER	Aeronautical Engineering Review	BM	Bookman
		BS	Best Sellers
Aeron	Aeronautics	BT	Books Today
Aerop	Aeroplane	BWd	Book World
AMZ	Amazing Science Fiction, Amazing Stories, Amazing Stories Fact and Science Fiction	BWk	Book Week
		CCB	Children's Book Center, Chicago, Bulletin
		CDN	Chicago Daily News, "Panorama"
ASF	Astounding Science Fiction, Analog Science Fiction--Science Fact	CLW	Catholic Library World
		CMWL	Commonweal
		COS	Cleveland Open Shelf
		CSM	Christian Science Monitor
Atl	Atlantic Monthly	CST	Chicago Sunday Tribune, "Magazine of Books"
AUT	Authentic Science Fiction, Authentic Science Fiction Monthly		
		Disc	Discovery
		DMl	Daily Mail
BAS	Bulletin of the Atomic Scientists	DMr	Daily Mirror
		DSFR	Delap's Science Fiction and Fantasy Review
BB	Books and Bookmen		
BE	British Engineer	DT	Daily Telegraph

179

Econ	Economist	LATC	Los Angeles Times, "Calendar"
EN	Evening News		
Enc	Encounter	LJ	Library Journal
FAU	Fantastic Universe Science Fiction	LM	Luna Monthly [f]
		ME	Mechanical Engineering
FOU	Foundation: The Review of Science Fiction	MM	Media and Methods
		NEB	Nebula Science Fiction
		NH	Natural History
FSF	The Magazine of Fantasy and Science Fiction	NO	National Observer
		NR	National Review
GAL	Galaxy Magazine, Galaxy Science Fiction	NRP	New Republic
		NRV	New Review
GDN	Guardian (Manchester and London)	NS	New Statesman
		NSN	New Statesman and Nation
GLO	Galileo	NST	New Scientist
GT	Grade Teacher	NWB	New Worlds
HB	Horn Book	NYHT	New York Herald-Tribune
HCt	Hartford (Connecticut) Courant	NYHTB	New York Herald-Tribune, "Books"
HR	Hudson Review	NYHTBR	New York Herald-Tribune Book Review
IASFM	Isaac Asimov's Science Fiction Magazine		
		NYkr	New Yorker
IndRsch	Industrial Research	NYP	New York Post
INF	Infinity Science Fiction	NYT	New York Times
		NYTBR	New York Times Book Review
INT	Intellect		
IntRel	International Relations	Obs	Observer
ISF	Imagination Science Fiction, Imagination Stories of Science Fantasy	OSFS	Original Science Fiction Stories
		PH	Penthouse
		PL	Playboy
JARS	Journal of the American Rocket Society	PS	Prairie Schooner
		PW	Publishers Weekly
JAS	Journal of Astronautical Sciences	SCF	Science Fantasy
		SciAm	Scientific American
JBAA	Journal of the British Astronomical Association	SciBks	Science Books
		SciProg	Science Progress
		SciRsch	Science Research
JBIS	Journal of the British Interplanetary Society	SeaF	Sea Frontiers
		SFA	Science Fiction Adventures
JR	Journal of Reading	SFAd	Science Fiction Advertiser [f]
JRAS	Journal of the Royal Aeronautical Society		
		SFBL	Science Fiction Booklog [f]
JSF	Journal of Science Fiction [f]	SFC	San Francisco Chronicle
KPG	Kliatt's Paperback Book Guide	SFCTW	San Francisco Chronicle, "This World"
KR	Kirkus Reviews	SFF	Science Fiction Fortnightly
LATBR	Los Angeles Times, "Book Review"	SFFBR	Science Fiction and

	Fantasy Book Review [f]		S[cience] F[iction] A[ssociation] Journal [f]
SFaN	Science-Fantasy News [f]	TAC	The Alien Critic [f]
SFO	Science Fiction Commentary [f]	TLS	Times Literary Supplement
SF+	Science Fiction Plus	TON	Top of the News
SFR	Science Fiction Review [f]	TS	Sunday Telegraph
SFRSL	Science Fiction: A Review of Speculative Literature [f]	TSM	Sunday Telegraph Magazine
SFST	Science-Fiction Studies	TWS	Thrilling Wonder Stories
Sky	Sky and Telescope	UNC	UNESCO Courier
SL	School Librarian	VAR	Views and Reviews
SLJ	School Library Journal	VEN	Venture Science Fiction
SM1	Sunday Mail	VOT	Visions of Tomorrow
SMR	Springfield (Massachusetts) Republican	VQR	Virginia Quarterly Review
SN	Saturday Night	VYA	Voice of Youth Advocates
SNL	Science News-letter	WFSB	World Future Society Bulletin
Spec	Spectator	WIF	If, Worlds of Science Fiction
SPF	Spaceflight		
SPS	Space Stories	WLB	Wisconsin Library Bulletin
SR	Saturday Review	WP	Washington Post
SSM	Space Science Fiction	WSFAJ	W[ashington] S[cience] F[iction] A[ssociation] Journal [f]
ST	Sunday Times		
STL	Startling Stories	WSJ	Wall Street Journal
STM	Sunday Times Magazine	YRR	Young Readers Review
SWSFAJ	Son of W[ashington]		

E1		Across the Sea of Stars		
	KR	27:470	1 July 1959	
	CSM	p. 7	20 Aug. 1959	Peter J. Henniker-Heaton
	SFC	p. 35	21 Aug. 1959	Robert McCary
	NYHTBR	p. 11	30 Aug. 1959	H.H. Holmes
	Time	74:70	31 Aug. 1959	
	BL	56:30	1 Sept. 1959	
	LJ	84:2519	1 Sept. 1959	E.M. Oboler
	ASF	64:144-45	Dec. 1959	P. Schuyler Miller
	WIF	9:84	Jan. 1960	Frederik Pohl
	NR	8:208	26 Mar. 1960	C.R. Morse
	GAL	18:142	Apr. 1960	Floyd C. Gale

E2		Against the Fall of Night		
	JSF	pp. 22-23	Fall 1952	Arthur Jean Cox
	BL	49:376	July 1953	
	FSF	5:96	Aug. 1953	Anthony Boucher and J. Francis McComas

	NYHTBR	p. 12	30 Aug. 1953	H.H. Holmes
	FAU	1:192	Aug.-Sept. 1953	Sam Merwin, Jr.
	NYTBR	p. 13	6 Sept. 1953	J. Francis McComas
	SR	36:50	12 Sept. 1953	Fletcher Pratt
	ASF	52:149-50	Nov. 1953	P. Schuyler Miller
	GAL	7:80	Nov. 1953	Groff Conklin

E3   An Arthur C. Clarke Second Omnibus

Punch	256:35	1 Jan. 1969	B.A. Young

E4   Arthur C. Clarke's Mysterious World

PW	218:40	22 Aug. 1980	
Spec	245:25-26	4 Oct. 1980	Jeffrey Bernard

E5   The Best of Arthur C. Clarke

Obs	p. 36	11 Nov. 1973	Henry Tilney
SFBL	no. 8:16	Mar./Apr. 1976	R. Laurraine Tutihasi
Times	p. 9	7 Aug. 1976	Tom Hutchinson
IASF	1:152	Spring 1977	Charles N. Brown
TLS	p. 662	16 June 1978	Thomas M. Disch

E6   Beyond Jupiter: The Worlds of Tomorrow

PW	203:50	16 Apr. 1973	
CSM	p. 11	19 May 1973	Robert C. Cowen
AA	37:65	Oct. 1973	Ralph Fabri
SPF	15:476	Dec. 1973	G.E. Perry
SciBks	9:291	Mar. 1974	

E7   Boy Beneath the Sea

CSM	p. 14	6 Nov. 1958	Robert C. Cowen
BL	55:266	15 Jan. 1959	
LJ	84:255	15 Jan. 1959	Jane Manthorne
HB	35:36	Feb. 1959	Virginia Haviland

E8   The Challenge of the Sea

KR	28:630	1 Aug. 1960	
HB	36:415	Oct. 1960	Isaac Asimov
CSM	p. 9B	3 Nov. 1960	Robert C. Cowen
CST	sec. 2, p. 44	6 Nov. 1960	Vernon Ives

NYHTBR ("Children's Book Week" section)

	p. 26	13 Nov. 1960	Margaret S. Libby
NYTBR	p. 18	13 Nov. 1960	Henry W. Hubbard
LJ	85:4230	15 Nov. 1960	Elaine Simpson
BL	57:247	15 Dec. 1960	
AMZ	35:136	Jan. 1961	S.E. Cotts
WIF	10:85-86	Jan. 1961	Frederik Pohl
ASF	67:153	Mar. 1961	P. Schuyler Miller
GAL	19:97	June 1961	Floyd C. Gale

PW	109:78	18 July 1966	B.A. Bannon

E9 The Challenge of the Spaceship

KR	27:297	1 Apr. 1959	
LJ	84:1906	1 June 1959	R.M. Drury
NYTBR	p. 18	21 June 1959	Jonathan N. Leonard
NYHTBR	p. 7	5 July 1959	Gerald Wendt
CSM	p. 9	21 July 1959	Robert C. Cowen
PL	6:26	Aug. 1959	
BL	56:111	15 Oct. 1959	
SFCTW	p. 33	25 Oct. 1959	Caspar W. Weinberger
ASF	64:142-44	Dec. 1959	P. Schuyler Miller
WIF	9:83-84	Jan. 1960	Frederik Pohl
Sunday Times of Ceylon			
	p. 6	3 June 1960	"The Bookman"
NWB	38:127	Nov. 1961	John Carnell
AMZ	36:138-39	Jan. 1962	S.E. Cotts
BS	21:408	1 Jan. 1962	
KPG	14:64	Fall 1980	Valentin R. Livada

E10 Childhood's End

KR	21:459	15 July 1953	
NYTBR	p. 9	23 Aug. 1953	H.H. Holmes
NYTBR ("Children's Books" section)			
	p. 19	23 Aug. 1953	Basil Davenport
NYT	p. 23	27 Aug. 1953	William Dubois
CSM	p. 7	10 Sept. 1953	Peter J. Henniker-Heaton
NYTBR	p. 2	13 Sept. 1953	J. Donald Adams
FSF	5:72	Oct. 1953	Anthony Boucher and J. Francis McComas
BL	50:58	1 Oct. 1953	
SFCTW	p. 23	18 Oct. 1953	Don Fabun
Atl	192:112	Nov. 1953	
SFAd	p. 15	Winter 1954	Anthony More
GAL	7:128-29	Jan. 1954	Groff Conklin
WIF	2:113	Jan. 1954	
ASF	52:151-52	Feb. 1954	P. Schuyler Miller
SR	37:61	20 Feb. 1954	Fletcher Pratt
ISF	5:147	Mar. 1954	Mark Reinsberg
NWB	8:127	June 1954	Leslie Flood
AUT	no. 47:112	July 1954	
NEB	no. 9:116-17	Aug. 1954	Kenneth F. Slater
BS	23:26-27	15 Apr. 1963	Rudy A. Hornish
DSFR	2:16	June 1976	Alan Brennert
Locus [f]	no. 190:4	30 June 1976	Charles N. Brown
Cresset	41:23-24	Oct. 1978	Ronald J. Sommer

E11 The City and the Stars

NYHTBR	p. 10	5 Feb. 1956	H.H. Holmes
NYTBR	p. 21	5 Feb. 1956	J. Francis McComas

	FSF	10:78	Apr. 1956	Anthony Boucher
	BL	53:364	1 May 1956	
	SFCTW	p. 22	6 May 1956	Don Fabun
	LJ	81:1554	1 June 1956	Grace P. Slocum
	AMZ	39:117	July 1956	Villiers Gerson
	ASF	57:155	July 1956	P. Schuyler Miller
	GAL	12:108-9	Aug. 1956	Floyd C. Gale
	ISF	7:123	Aug. 1956	Henry Bott
	INF	1:106-7	Aug. 1956	Damon Knight
	NWB	17:126	Sept. 1956	Leslie Flood
	AUT	no. 74:153 -54	Nov. 1956	
	FSF	14:113	May 1958	Anthony Boucher
	VEN	2:57	May 1958	Theodore Sturgeon
	SFA	2:92-93	June 1958	Calvin M. Knox
	PW	190:64	1 Aug. 1966	B.A. Bannon
	NYTBR	p. 33	7 May 1967	Martin Levin
	PL	14:34	July 1967	
	Punch	256:35	1 Jan. 1969	B.A. Young

E12	The Coast of Coral			
	KR	24:201	1 Mar. 1956	
	BL	52:301	1 Apr. 1956	
	NWB	17:126-27	Sept. 1956	Leslie Flood
	NYT	p. 5	3 May 1956	Archie Carr
	SFC	p. 25	14 May 1956	William Hogan
	CST	p. 6	27 May 1956	Fritz Leiber
	BM	15:209	June 1956	
	BL	52:404	1 June 1956	
	LJ	81:1515	1 June 1956	E.M. Cole
	WLB	52:171	1 June 1956	
	SR	39:29	2 June 1956	Eugenia Clark
	HB	32:280	Aug. 1956	Margaret C. Scoggin
	NSN	52:430	6 Oct. 1956	Richard Garnett
	TLS	p. 620	19 Oct. 1956	
	AUT	no. 75:154	Dec. 1956	
	GAL	13:86	Dec. 1956	Floyd C. Gale
	SciBks	1:213	Mar. 1966	
	PW	194:65	22 July 1968	
	SR	51:39	28 Sept. 1968	Rollene W. Saal

E13	The Coming of the Space Age			
	KR	35:233	15 Feb. 1967	
	LJ	92:1022	1 Mar. 1967	Richard S. Potts
	PL	14:34	July 1967	
	TLS	p. 778	31 Aug. 1967	
	SciBks	3:159	Sept. 1967	
	BL	64:28	1 Sept. 1967	
	Punch	253:485	27 Sept. 1967	B.A. Young
	Times	p. 8	5 Oct. 1967	A.W. Haslett
	FSF	34:39-41	Mar. 1968	Judith Merril

	JAS	15:153	May–June 1968	James G. Allen
	*VOT	1:29–30	June 1970	Walter Gillings
E14	The Deep Range			
	KR	25:49	15 Jan. 1957	
	LJ	82:750	15 Mar. 1957	
	SFC	p. 23	20 Mar. 1957	William Hogan
	SMR	p. 8C	31 Mar. 1957	R[ichard] F. H[usband]
	WSJ	p. 12	2 Apr. 1957	John F. Bridge
	CSM	p. 13	11 Apr. 1957	Stanley B. Hall
	NYHTBR	p. 36	12 May 1957	H.H. Holmes
	BL	53:478	15 May 1957	
	LJ	82:1365	15 May 1957	
	FSF	12:1100–01	8 June 1957	Anthony Boucher
	SR	51:17	8 June 1957	Daniel B. Dodson
	NEB	no. 22:103	July 1957	Kenneth F. Slater
	VEN	1:79	July 1957	Theodore Sturgeon
	FAU	8:112–13	Aug. 1957	Hans Stefan Santesson
	ASF	60:144–45	Sept. 1957	P. Schuyler Miller
	INF	2:99–100	Sept. 1957	Damon Knight
	Spec	p. 376	20 Sept. 1957	Robert Conquest
	GAL	14:122	Oct. 1957	Floyd C. Gale
	NWB	22:123–24	Nov. 1957	Leslie Flood
	ISF	9:123	Feb. 1958	Henry Bott
	BB	13:35–36	June 1968	Leo Harris
	NWB	no. 186:		
		60–61	Jan. 1969	James Cawthorn
E15	Dolphin Island: A Story of the People of the Sea			
	LJ	88:2152	15 May 1963	
	NYTBR	p. 38	9 June 1963	Robert Berkvist
	ASF	72:90–91	Oct. 1963	P. Schuyler Miller
	NWB	46:128	Jan. 1964	Leslie Flood
	PW	192:44	27 Nov. 1967	
	TLS	p. 377	7 Apr. 1978	Sarah Hayes
	SL	26:169	June 1978	N. Culpan
E16	"The Dynamics of Space Flight"			
	JBAA	61:136–37	Apr. 1957	M[artin] Davidson
E17	Earthlight			
	NYHTBR	p. 14	27 Mar. 1955	[H.H. Holmes]
	BL	51:344	15 Apr. 1955	
	FSF	8:71	May 1955	Anthony Boucher
	ASF	55:160	June 1955	P. Schuyler Miller
	GAL	10:117	June 1955	Groff Conklin
	NSN	49:854	18 June 1955	Edmund Crispin
	NYTBR	p. 18	19 June 1955	J. Francis McComas
	AMZ	29:95–96	July 1955	Villiers Gerson
	OSFS	6:107	July 1955	Damon Knight
	NWB	13:127–28	July 1955	Leslie Flood

AUT	no. 62:153	Oct. 1955	
FAU	4:127–28	Dec. 1955	Hans Stefan Santesson
FSF	14:113	May 1958	Anthony Boucher
GAL	17:74	Nov. 1958	Floyd C. Gale
PW	201:59	12 June 1972	
KR	40:697	15 June 1972	
PL	19:26, 29	Sept. 1972	
BB	18:122	May 1973	Trevor Allen
ST	p. 38	6 May 1973	Edmund Cooper
DSFR	3:31–32	June 1977	Robert Chilson
ASF	98:172	July 1978	Lester del Rey

*E18   "Electronics and Space Flight"
RB	pp. 15–16	Jan. 1948

E19   Expedition to Earth
KR	21:721	1 Nov. 1953	
NYHTBR	p. 9	20 Dec. 1953	H.H. Holmes
CSM	p. 11	24 Dec. 1953	Peter J. Henniker-Heaton
NYTBR	p. 24	14 Feb. 1954	J. Francis McComas
BL	50:280	15 Mar. 1954	
FSF	6:73	Apr. 1954	Anthony Boucher and J. Francis McComas
GAL	8:132	May 1954	Groff Conklin
SFCTW	p. 19	13 June 1954	Don Fabun
ASF	54:150–51	Nov. 1954	P. Schuyler Miller
AUT	no. 53:125	Jan. 1955	
NWB	11:117–18	Feb. 1955	Leslie Flood
Obs	p. 22	23 Jan. 1966	
BB	11:65	Mar. 1966	Tom Boardman
ASF	86:169	Feb. 1971	P. Schuyler Miller

E20   The Exploration of the Moon
JBAA	65:120	Feb. 1955	Patrick Moore
LJ	80:880	15 Apr. 1955	J.E. Brown
NYTBR	p. 14	24 Apr. 1955	J. Francis McComas
BL	51:358	1 May 1955	
SFCTW	p. 17	24 July 1955	Don Fabun
FSF	9:95	Aug. 1955	Anthony Boucher
ASF	56:147–48	Sept. 1955	P. Schuyler Miller

E21   The Exploration of Space
DMr		25 Sept. 1951	Ronald Bedford
Picture Post			
	pp. 36–37	29 Sept. 1951	Derek Wragge Morley and Kenneth Allsop
TLS	p. 633	5 Oct. 1951	
Obs		7 Oct. 1951	Charles Davy
Aerop	82:507	12 Oct. 1951	J.L.P.
SM1		14 Oct. 1951	Robin Wise
Times		17 Oct. 1951	

ST	p. 3	21 Oct. 1951	Fred Hoyle
Aeron	22:56	Nov. 1951	A.F.
UNC	4:10	Nov. 1951	Maurice Goldsmith
AUT	no. 16:111	Dec. 1951	
Heiress		Dec. 1951	
JBAA	62:49-50	Dec. 1951	F.J. Sellers
JRAS	55:806-7	Dec. 1951	
SFaN		2 Dec. 1951	H[annes] K. B[ok]
NWB	4:93	Winter 1951	John Carnell
JBIS	11:53-54	Jan. 1952	L.R. Shepherd
NYT	p. 13	21 June 1952	Charles Poore
NYTBR	p. 1	22 June 1952	Willy Ley
SFCTW	p. 16	22 June 1952	Don Fabun
WP	p. 6B	22 June 1952	Sterling North
NYP	p. 12M	29 June 1952	Gilbert Cant
Atl	190:83	July 1952	
CSM	p. 13	3 July 1952	Robert C. Cowen
SR	35:13	3 July 1952	Fred L. Whipple
CST	p. 5	13 July 1952	Roy Gibbons
NYHTBR	p. 5	13 July 1952	H.H. Holmes
NYkr	28:76	19 July 1952	
Minneapolis Tribune			
	sec. E, p. 6	27 July 1952	Clifford D. Simak
JARS	22:227	July-Aug. 1952	Frederic C. Durant III
SMR	p. 4C	31 Aug. 1952	Ethel Dexter
WLB	48:212	Sept. 1952	
BL	49:6	1 Sept. 1952	
LJ	77:1515	15 Sept. 1952	R.R. Hawkins
ASF	59:162-63	Oct. 1952	P. Schuyler Miller
BM	12:4	Oct. 1952	Florence Boochever
GAL	5:121-22	Oct. 1952	Groff Conklin
HB	28:343	Oct. 1952	Margaret C. Scoggin
ME	74:1035-36	Dec. 1952	G. Edward Pendray
*STL	28:145-46	Jan. 1953	
SFA	1:68-70	Mar. 1953	Lester del Rey
SF+	1:60	Mar. 1953	Sam Moskowitz
AUT	no. 65:154	Jan. 1956	
LJ	84:2514	1 Sept. 1959	Milton B. Wenger
BL	56:121	15 Oct. 1959	
GAL	18:145	Apr. 1960	Floyd C. Gale
BS	24:67	1 Mar. 1964	

E22	A Fall of Moondust			
	Punch	p. 627	19 Apr. 1961	B.A. Young
	KR	29:568	1 July 1961	
	LJ	86:2815	1 Sept. 1961	J.E. Halzour
	CSM	p. 7	14 Sept. 1961	Peter J. Henniker-Heaton
	BS	21:226	15 Sept. 1961	James Ball
	NYTBR	p. 42	17 Sept. 1961	Jonathan N. Leonard

GDN	p. 42	22 Sept. 1961	Andrew Leslie
SMR	p. 4D	24 Sept. 1961	L.H.S. [Horace B. Hill]
PL	8:53–54	Oct. 1961	
TLS	p. 679	13 Oct. 1961	
NRP	145:25	23 Oct. 1961	Asher Byrnes
Spec	p. 600	27 Oct. 1961	Alan Brien
NWB	38:122	Nov. 1961	Leslie Flood
NR	p. 421	16 Nov. 1961	Theodore Sturgeon
BL	58:227	1 Dec. 1961	
FSF	22:86	Jan. 1962	Alfred Bester
ASF	68:163–64	Feb. 1962	P. Schuyler Miller
BM	21:157	Mar. 1962	Esther Helfand
GAL	20:192–93	June 1962	Floyd C. Gale
NWB	45:127	Aug. 1963	John Carnell
HR	16:478, 480	Autumn 1963	Roger Sale

E23   The First Five Fathoms

SFCTW	p. 37	8 May 1960	
CSM	p. 6B	12 May 1960	Robert C. Cowen
LJ	85:2047	15 May 1960	Jane Manthorne
CMWL	72:236	27 May 1960	Claire H. Bishop
HB	36:226	June 1960	Virginia Haviland
BL	56:608	1 June 1960	
SR	43:38	16 July 1960	Betty Miles

E24   First on the Moon

KR	38:351	15 Mar. 1970	
PW	197:48	16 Mar. 1970	
KR	38:397	1 Apr. 1970	
NYT	p. 37	20 Apr. 1970	Christopher Lehmann-Haupt
NO	9:19	18 May 1970	Patrick Young
BWd	4:10	31 May 1970	Thomas O'Toole
LJ	95:2171	1 June 1970	R.L. Hough
LJ	95:2546	July 1970	Jeanne Cavallini
Spec	225:187	18 Aug. 1970	Edmund Crispin
NS	80:245	28 Aug. 1970	Jonathan Raban
Econ	236:40	29 Aug. 1970	
TLS	p. 1006	11 Sept. 1970	
Choice	7:1070	Oct. 1970	
BL	223:124	Dec. 1970	Philip and Phylis Morrison

E25   The Fountains of Paradise

KR	46:1329	1 Dec. 1978	
PW	214:59	11 Dec. 1978	
LJ	104:212	15 Jan. 1979	Rosemary Herbert
NST	181:190	18 Jan. 1979	David Austin
DM1		25 Jan. 1979	Angus MacPherson
NS	97:119–20	26 Jan. 1979	Kingsley Amis

```
*TS              p. 12       28 Jan. 1979
GDN              p. 10       1 Feb. 1979    Tom Shippey
Los Angeles Herald-Examiner
                 p. B5       10 Feb. 1979   Joseph Claussen
ES                           27 Feb. 1979
SFR              no. 30:58   Mar. 1979      Steve Brown
BL               75:1037     1 Mar. 1979    Algis Budrys
Obs              p. 37       4 Mar. 1979    Nick Totton
NYTBR            pp. 13, 25  18 Mar. 1979   Gerald Jonas
NRP              180:40      24 Mar. 1979   Tim Myers
*Vector          no. 92:21-  Mar.-Apr.
   [f]              23       1979           Paul Kincaid
IASFM            3:13        Apr. 1979      Charles N. Brown
Baltimore Sun
                 p. D5       1 Apr. 1979    Joseph Franzone, Jr.
CSM              p. 22       4 Apr. 1979    Douglas Stair
LATBR            p. 18       22 Apr. 1979   Charles Solomon
SFRSL            2:102       May 1979       R.J. Faulder
BS               39:50       9 May 1979     Paul Granahan
HCt              p. 8G       20 May 1979    George W. Earley
St. Louis Post-Dispatch
                 p. 4C       27 May 1979    Robert La Rouche
DT               p. 15       28 June 1979   Michael Maxwell Scott
*SFFBR           1:69-70     July 1979      D. Mackey
AMZ              52:10-11    Aug. 1979      Tom Staicar
VYA              2:52        Aug. 1979      Mary K. Chelton
FSF              57:24-26    Sept. 1979     Algis Budrys
FOU              no. 17:75-
                    77       Sept. 1979     Ian Watson
PH               11:50       Sept. 1979     Gerald Jonas
SLJ              26:166      Sept. 1979     J.R. Brown
GLO              no. 15:84   Nov. 1979      Floyd Kemske
Times            p. 15       29 Nov. 1979   Tom Hutchinson
SFRSL            2:191-93    Dec. 1979      R.J. Faulder
PW               217:87      11 Jan. 1980
NYTBR            p. 35       27 Jan. 1980
KPG              14:14       Spring 1980    John J. Adams
Arena [f]        no. 11:14-
                    16       Nov. 1980      Barry Bayley
Questar          3:17-18     Dec. 1980      C.J. Henderson

E26   From the Ocean, From the Stars
PL               9:14        Mar. 1962
LJ               87:1706     15 Apr. 1962
ASF              69:159-60   June 1962      P. Schuyler Miller
FSF              23:109      July 1962      Alfred Bester
GAL              21:142-43   Feb. 1963      Floyd C. Gale
FSF              25:78       Dec. 1963      Avram Davidson
```

E27   Glide Path
      NYTBR   p. 44   8 Sept. 1963   Martin Levin
      PL   10:44   Oct. 1963
      NYkr   39:188-89   5 Oct. 1963
      NYHTBR   p. 16   17 Nov. 1963   Taliaferro Boatwright
      CST   p. 8   22 Dec. 1963   Gene Graff
      HR   16:604   Winter 1963-
                               1964   Roger Sale

E28   Going Into Space (aka Into Space, The Scottie Book of Space
         Travel, The Young Traveller in Space)
      KR   22:490   1 Aug. 1954
      LJ   79:1941   15 Oct. 1954   Learned T. Bulman
      LJ   79:2020   15 Oct. 1954   Dorothy Schumaker
      JBIS   13:359-60   Nov. 1954   E.J. Cole
      NWB   10:122   Nov. 1954   John Carnell
      CST (Section 2, "Books for Boys and Girls")
                 p. 45   14 Nov. 1954   John Lewellen
      BL   51:137   15 Nov. 1954
      CMWL   61:200   19 Nov. 1954
      NYkr   30:219   27 Nov. 1954   K.T. Kinkead
      NYHTBR   p. 16   28 Nov. 1954   H.H. Holmes
      Atl   194:97   Dec. 1954   Margaret F. Kiernan
      AUT   no. 52:131   Dec. 1954
      COS   p. 37   Dec. 1954
      NEB   no. 11:118   Dec. 1954   Kenneth F. Slater
      NYTBR   p. 28   12 Dec. 1954   Jonathan N. Leonard
      FSF   8:96   Jan. 1955   Anthony Boucher
      KR   39:1088   1 Oct. 1971
      LJ   96:3473   15 Oct. 1971   P.M. Mitchell
      BL   68:335   1 Dec. 1971
      BS   31:432   15 Dec. 1971   F.C. Carmody
      GT   89:86   Jan. 1972
      SciBks   7:238   Mar. 1972

E29   Imperial Earth
      KR   43:1306   15 Nov. 1975
      Obs   p. 30   16 Nov. 1975   Martin Amis
      PW   208:96   17 Nov. 1975
      TLS   p. 1438   5 Dec. 1975   Thomas A. Shippey
      KR   43:1387   15 Dec. 1975
      *SFO   3:17   Jan. 1976   Peter Weston
      Salt Lake Tribune
                 p. 2E   11 Jan. 1976   Gordon Harman
      ST   p. 39   11 Jan. 1976   Edmund Cooper
      HCt   p. 43   15 Jan. 1976   Ken Cruickshank
      LJ   101:362   15 Jan. 1976   Robert Molyneux
      NYTBR   p. 20   18 Jan. 1976   Gerald Jonas
      Albany (N.Y.) Times-Union
                 p. E5   25 Jan. 1976   Fred Le Brun
      Memphis Commercial-Appeal
                 p. G6   25 Jan. 1976   Dan Henderson

BL	72:756	1 Feb. 1976	Dan Miller
BL	72:759	1 Feb. 1976	
Sacramento Bee ("Forum")			
	p. 8	1 Feb. 1976	Stanley Gilliam
America	134:106	7 Feb. 1976	John B. Breslin
Milwaukee Journal			
	pt. 5, p. 4	8 Feb. 1976	Gene De Weese
Boston Globe			
	p. 23	13 Feb. 1976	Christina Robb
LM	no. 63:14-		
	15	Mar. 1976	Paul Walker
NRP	174:28	20 Mar. 1976	Mark Rose
Houston Post ("Spotlight")			
	p. 10	21 Mar. 1976	Eric Gerber
South Bend Tribune ("Michigan" magazine)			
	p. 18	21 Mar. 1976	K.M. Jun
VQR	52:56	Spring 1976	
Buffalo Evening News			
	p. C12	27 Mar. 1976	Mike Vogel
CDN	p. 11	27 Mar. 1976	Dan Miller
San Diego Union			
	p. E6	28 Mar. 1976	Mike Curtis
DSFR	2:7	Apr. 1976	Jay Rich
Seattle Times ("Magazine")			
	p. 14	4 Apr. 1976	Barbara Kahn
St. Louis Globe-Democrat			
	p. 4F	24-25 Apr.	
		1976	Jonathan Megibow
BS	36:36	May 1976	Lew Wolkoff
PH	7:50	May 1976	Gerald Jonas
SLJ	22:119	May 1976	Regina Minudri
SFR	no. 17:45	May 1976	Richard E. Geis
NR	28:519	14 May 1976	Steve Ownsberg
Tallahassee Democrat			
	p. 12E	16 May 1976	Brenda Jones
ASF	96:168-70	June 1976	Lester del Rey
FOU	10:87-90	June 1976	Hilary Bailey
Futures	8:277-78	June 1976	Dennis Livingston
Algol [f]	no. 26:38-		
	39	Summer 1976	Richard Lupoff
Locus [f]	no. 190:		
	3-4	30 June 1976	Charles N. Brown
SFBL	no. 10:16	July-Aug.	
		1976	R. Laurraine Tutihasi
SFBL	no. 10:16-	July-Aug.	
	17	1976	A.K. Molnar
PS	50:270-71	Fall 1976	L. David Allen
*Oui	5:32+	Nov. 1976	Bury St. Edmund
STM	p. 17	24 July 1977	Alan Brien

E30 Indian Ocean Adventure
     KR   29:684   1 Aug. 1961
     LJ   86:3072   15 Sept. 1961 Jane Manthorne
     NYHTB ("Children's Books" section)
               p. 12   12 Nov. 1961   Margaret S. Libby
     BL   58:200   15 Nov. 1961
     CSM   p. 8B   16 Nov. 1961   Robert C. Cowen
     NYTBR   p. 32   7 Jan. 1962   Robert Hood
     HB   38:64   Feb. 1962   Virginia Haviland
     SR   45:33   17 Feb. 1962   Alice Dalgleish
     SeaF   8:188   Aug. 1962   J.G.
     Times   p. 13   30 Aug. 1962

E31 Indian Ocean Treasure
     BS   24:233   15 Sept. 1964
     NYTBR   p. 30   11 Oct. 1964   F.W. Foley
     CSM   p. 9B   5 Nov. 1964   Robert C. Cowen
     LJ   89:4637   15 Nov. 1964   T.E. Tyler
     HB   40:626   Dec. 1964   Jane Manthorne
     YRR   1:10   Mar. 1965   P. Cohen
     CCB   19:5   Sept. 1965

E32 Interplanetary Flight
     Aerop   78:596   19 May 1950   A.R. Weyl
     TLS   p. 376   16 June 1950
     Times   28 June 1950
     NWB   3:79   Summer 1950   [John Carnell]
     SCF   1:29   Summer 1950   Geoffrey Giles
     JBAA   60:204-5   July 1950   M[artin] Davidson
     AER   9:77   Sept. 1950   Alfred Africano
     JBIS   9:253-54   Sept. 1950   M[ichael] W. Ovenden
     Econ   159:510   23 Sept. 1950
     Observatory
               70:195   Oct. 1950   P.J.T.
     SciProg   38:764   Oct. 1950   E.G.R.
     Disc   Nov. 1950   D.S. Evans
     JRAS   54:716-17   Nov. 1950   A.V. C[leaver]
     SFF   no. 5:126   1 Mar. 1951
     SNL   59:411   30 June 1951
     SR   34:29   7 July 1951   Myron Weiss
     BL   47:358   15 July 1951
     GAL   2:101   Aug. 1951   Willy Ley
     Denver Post   2 Sept. 1951   Gene Lindberg
     SFCTW   p. 23   30 Sept. 1951 Don Fabun
     FSF   2:60   Oct. 1951   Anthony Boucher and J.
                                             Francis McComas
     ASF   48:116   Nov. 1951   P. Schuyler Miller
     TWS   39:141   Dec. 1951   [Samuel Mines]
     Sky   11:63   Jan. 1952   H.R.J. Grosch
     JARS   22:48   Jan.-Feb.
                              1952   Frederick C. Durant III

E33   Islands in the Sky
       KR   20:561   1 Sept. 1952
       NYHTBR   p. 10   26 Oct. 1952   H.H. Holmes
       NWB   6:96   Nov. 1952   Leslie Flood
       CST   p. 5   16 Nov. 1952   Mark Reinsberg
       NYTBR   pt. 2,
                   p. 28   16 Nov. 1952   Villiers Gerson
       SFCTW   p. 12   16 Nov. 1952   Don Fabun
       FSF   4:89   Jan. 1953   Anthony Boucher and J.
                                                       Francis McComas
       BL   49:192   1 Feb. 1953
       GAL   5:111   Mar. 1953   Groff Conklin
       SPS   2:128   Apr. 1953
       BM   12:210   June 1953   Florence Boocheever
       SSM   2:92   July 1953   George O. Smith
       ASF   51:144-45   Aug. 1953   P. Schuyler Miller
       SF+   1:27   Aug. 1953   Sam Moskowitz
       WIF   10:87   Sept. 1960   Frederik Pohl
       NS   81:777   4 June 1971   Catherine Starr
       *Cypher
        [f]   5:36   July 1971   R. Waddington
       SWSFAJ   no. 129:5   Feb. 1974   Ken Ozanne
       SFFBR   1:43   Nov. 1979   Wain Saeger

E34   "Kalinga Award Speech"
       NST   16:11   4 Oct. 1962

E35   The Lion of Comarre and Against the Fall of Night
       PW   194:78   19 Aug. 1968
       KR   36:1068   15 Sept. 1968
       LJ   93:4577   1 Dec. 1968   Mary Kent Grant
       LJ   94:891   15 Feb. 1969   Alberta L. Hankenson
       ASF   84:169   Nov. 1969   P. Schuyler Miller
       FSF   37:49   Nov. 1969   Alexei Panshin
       *SFO   no. 22:15-
                   17   July 1971   D. Boutland

E36   The Lost Worlds of "2001"
       BS   32:263   1 Sept. 1972   Lewis H. Wolkoff
       Obs   p. 37   12 Nov. 1972   Henry Tilney
       LM   no. 43:30   Dec. 1972   Greg Bear
       BB   18:125   Jan. 1973   Trevor Allen
       SFST   7:319-22   Nov. 1980   Frederic Jameson

E37   The Making of a Moon
       KR   25:406   1 June 1957
       BL   53:549   1 July 1957
       CST   p. 3   28 July 1957   Fritz Leiber
       NYTBR   p. 10   28 July 1957   John Pfeiffer
       SFC   p. 17   2 Aug. 1957   William Hogan
       WLB   53:512   Sept. 1957

	BL	54:12	1 Sept. 1957	
	CSM	p. 11	10 Oct. 1957	Robert C. Cowen
	FSF	13:118–19	Nov. 1957	Anthony Boucher
	NWB	22:125–26	Nov. 1957	Leslie Flood
	JBIS	16:322	Jan.–Feb. 1958	S.W. Greenwood
	GAL	15:121	Mar. 1958	Floyd C. Gale
	ASF	61:141	Apr. 1958	P. Schuyler Miller
	FSF	14:113	May 1958	Anthony Boucher

E38   Man and Space

	FSF	29:83	July 1965	Judith Merril
	SFP	8:148–49	Apr. 1966	N.H. Langton
	TLS	p. 373	28 Apr. 1966	

E39   Mars and the Mind of Man

	KR	41:582	15 May 1973	
	PW	203:38	28 May 1973	
	KR	41:613	1 June 1973	
	BWd	7:15	22 July 1973	
	WSJ	p. 8	29 Aug. 1973	Edmund Fuller
	SciAm	229:127	Oct. 1973	Philip Morrison
	BL	70:142	1 Oct. 1973	
	LATC	p. 64	14 Oct. 1973	Ralph E. Hone
	BL	70:222	15 Oct. 1973	
	CSM	p. 9	24 Oct. 1973	David Salisbury
	LJ	98:3384	15 Nov. 1973	R.L. Hough
	Choice	10:1575	Dec. 1973	
	LJ	99:619	1 Mar. 1974	Edith S. Crockett or Ellis Mount
	Science	184:663	10 May 1974	William K. Hartmann

E40   "Meteors as a Danger to Space Flight"

	Aerop	77:649	11 Nov. 1949	F.T. Meacock

E41   The Nine Billion Names of God

	PW	191:102	27 Feb. 1967	
	KR	35:301	1 Mar. 1967	
	LJ	92:1509	1 Apr. 1967	Larry Earl Bone
	LJ	92:2467	15 June 1967	
	PL	14:34	July 1967	
	KPG	8:24	Nov. 1974	

E42   Of Time and Stars

	Obs	p. 37	24 Sept. 1972	Naomi Lewis
	Obs	p. 37	12 Nov. 1972	Henry Tilney
	Obs	p. 25	8 Dec. 1972	

E43   The Other Side of the Sky

	KR	25:916	15 Dec. 1957	
	DSM	p. 11	13 Feb. 1958	Robert C. Cowen

	CST	p. 7	16 Feb. 1958	Fritz Leiber
	SMR	p. 8C	16 Feb. 1958	H[orace] B. H[ill]
	Time	71:108	17 Feb. 1958	
	NYHTBR	p. 6	2 Mar. 1958	H.H. Holmes
	LJ	83:973	15 Mar. 1958	
	BL	54:445	1 Apr. 1958	
	SFCTW	p. 25	20 Apr. 1958	Robert McCary
	FSF	14:112-13	May 1958	Anthony Boucher
	AMZ	32:85	June 1958	S.E. Cotts
	FAU	9:114-15	June 1958	Hans Stefan Santesson
	HB	34:220	June 1958	Margaret C. Scoggins
	SR	41:17	7 June 1958	Siegfried Mandel
	ASF	61:142-43	Aug. 1958	P. Schuyler Miller
	GAL	16:132	Oct. 1958	Floyd C. Gale
	WIF	9:111	Dec. 1958	Damon Knight
	Punch	240:627	9 Apr. 1961	
	NWB	37:128	Aug. 1961	Leslie Flood
	PL	15:20-21	Aug. 1968	
	Obs	p. 27	7 Dec. 1969	
	SWSFAJ	no. 125:5	Feb. 1974	Ken Ozanne

E44   **Prelude to Mars**

	KR	33:508	15 May 1965	
	KR	33:534	1 June 1965	
	NYHT	p. 17	25 June 1965	Maurice Dolbier
	BWk	2:4, 23	27 June 1965	Martin Green
	NO	4:21	12 July 1965	R. Ostermann
	*CLW	37:202	Nov. 1965	Mary Eutropia
	FSF	30:45	Feb. 1966	Judith Merril
	ASF	77:152	Mar. 1966	P. Schuyler Miller

E45   **Prelude to Space** (aka "The Space Dreamers," "Master of Space")

	GAL	2:61	Apr. 1951	Groff Conklin
	FSF	2:83	Aug. 1951	Anthony Boucher and J. Francis McComas
	JBIS	10:230-33	Sept. 1951	A. Valentine Cleaver
	NWB	7:122-23	June 1953	Leslie Flood
	JBAA	63:284	July 1953	Patrick Moore
	KR	22:84	1 Feb. 1954	
	NYHTBR	p. 13	21 Mar. 1954	H.H. Holmes
	NYTBR	p. 21	28 Mar. 1954	Villiers Gerson
	BL	50:322	15 Apr. 1954	
	FSF	6:70	June 1954	Anthony Boucher and J. Francis McComas
	GAL	8:96-97	July 1954	Groff Conklin
	ASF	54:151-52	Nov. 1954	P. Schuyler Miller
	ASF	85:170	Apr. 1970	P. Schuyler Miller
	ASF	86:169	Feb. 1971	P. Schuyler Miller
	*SFO	no. 22:17-18, 26	July 1971	D. Boutland
	Futures	8:549-51	Dec. 1976	Dennis Livingston

E46	Profiles of the Future			
	ES		20 Nov. 1962	Peter Fairley
	Oxford Mail		22 Nov. 1962	Brian W. Aldiss
	Times	p. 18	6 Dec. 1962	
	Topic	p. 39	8 Dec. 1962	Michael Denny
	LJ	88:568	1 Feb. 1963	J.K. Lucker
	CSM	p. 9	26 Feb. 1963	Robert C. Cowen
	LJ	88:1382	15 Mar. 1963	
	Atl	211:152	Apr. 1963	William Barrett
	HB	39:195	Apr. 1963	Margaret C. Scoggin
	NR	14:289	9 Apr. 1963	Fritz Leiber
	NYTBR	p. 22	14 Apr. 1963	Isaac Asimov
	IndRsch	p. 41	May 1963	
	PL	10:40	May 1963	
	SR	46:30	4 May 1963	Edwin Diamond
	JAS	10:61-62	Summer 1963	David E. Anderson
	ASF	71:89	July 1963	P. Schuyler Miller
	NWB	16:82	July-Aug. 1964	James Colvin
	BB	10:33	Jan. 1965	Alex Hamilton
	BS	27:43	15 Apr. 1967	
	SPF	13:40	Jan. 1971	I. Graham
	LJ	98:858	15 Mar. 1973	
	BB	19:141	Oct. 1973	Trevor Allen
	LM	no. 53:23	Aug. 1974	Samuel Mines
E47	The Promise of Space			
	KR	36:220	15 Feb. 1968	
	KR	36:280	1 Mar. 1968	
	PW	193:57	27 May 1968	
	NYT	p. 37	29 May 1968	Eliot Fremont-Smith
	BWd	2:1, 3	30 June 1968	Robert Jastrow
	America	119:48-49	20 July 1968	Robert H. Goldsmith
	NYkr	44:88	27 July 1968	
	LJ	93:2888	Aug. 1968	Richard S. Potts
	NYTBR	p. 10	25 Aug. 1968	Willy Ley
	PL	15:20-21	Aug. 1968	
	Science	161:874-75	30 Aug. 1968	Eugene W. Emme
	SciBks	4:149	Sept. 1968	
	BL	65:80	15 Sept. 1968	
	LJ	93:3337	15 Sept. 1968	Collin Clark
	BE	6:31	Nov. 1968	David Videan
	NST	40:578	5 Dec. 1968	Colin Ronan
	LJ	93:4699	15 Dec. 1968	
	NS	76:877	20 Dec. 1968	Brenda Maddox
	Times	p. 17	28 Dec. 1968	Dennis Potter
	NR	20:1332	31 Dec. 1968	Thomas H. Jukes
	Econ	230:35	4 Jan. 1969	
	Choice	5:1598	Feb. 1969	
	NWB	no. 187:62	Feb. 1969	Charles Platt
	LJ	94:950	1 Mar. 1969	Daniel R. Pfoutz

BAS	23:56	May 1969	James E. Lamport
JBAA	79:409-10	Aug. 1969	Howard Miles
PW	196:37	15 Dec. 1969	
SPF	11:448	Dec. 1969	J.C. Gilbert
CSM	p. 6	2 Apr. 1970	
Obs	p. 26	27 Sept. 1970	

E48 **Reach for Tomorrow**

KR	24:141	15 Feb. 1956	
FAU	5:125-26	July 1956	Hans Stefan Santesson
FSF	11:94	July 1956	Anthony Boucher
NYTBR	p. 20	15 July 1956	Basil Davenport
ASF	58:153-54	Sept. 1956	P. Schuyler Miller
GAL	12:110	Sept. 1956	Floyd C. Gale
NYHTBR	p. 10	11 Nov. 1956	H.H. Holmes
Punch	p. 843	30 May 1962	B.A. Young
NWB	40:127	June 1962	Leslie Flood
ASF	86:169	Feb. 1971	P. Schuyler Miller

E49 **The Reefs of Taprobane**

KR	25:133	1 Feb. 1957	
CST	p. 5	5 Mar. 1957	Fritz Leiber
BL	53:374	15 Mar. 1957	
CSM	p. 13	11 Apr. 1957	Stanley B. Hall
BL	53:420	15 Apr. 1957	
LJ	82:1049	15 Apr. 1957	R.W. Henderson
NYTBR	p. 16	28 Apr. 1957	E.B. Garside
BM	16:186	May 1957	Florence Boochever
WLB	53:399	May 1957	
SR	40:32	6 July 1957	Thomas E. Cooney
NYHTBR	p. 6	7 July 1957	Eugenia Clark
SFCTW	p. 26	14 July 1957	James Benet
GAL	14:123	Oct. 1957	Floyd C. Gale
PW	190:64	1 Aug. 1966	B.A. Bannon

E50 **Rendezvous with Rama**

PW	203:70	25 June 1973	
KR	41:714	1 July 1973	
NST	59:161	19 July 1973	Michael Kenward
ST	p. 40	22 July 1973	Edmund Cooper
LJ	98:2339	Aug. 1973	Robert Molyneux
Spec	231:153	4 Aug. 1973	Kingsley Amis
CSM	p. 9	8 Aug. 1973	Stanley B. Hall
NYT	p. 35	22 Aug. 1973	Jonathan N. Leonard
VAR	5:40	Sept. 1973	Robert E. Briney
Obs	p. 35	2 Sept. 1973	Henry Tilney
NO	12:23	22 Sept. 1973	Patrick Young
NYTBR	p. 38	23 Sept. 1973	Theodore Sturgeon
Time	102:125	24 Sept. 1973	R.Z. Sheppard
SWSFAJ	111:3	Oct. 1973	Don D'Ammassa
SWSFAJ	111:3	Oct. 1973	Barry Gillam

SWSFAJ	111:3	Oct. 1973	David Stever
BS	33:291	1 Oct. 1973	Melody Hardy
LATC	p. 57	4 Nov. 1973	Edward M. White
TLS	p. 1377	9 Nov. 1973	
BL	70:319	15 Nov. 1973	
LJ	98:3474	15 Nov. 1973	Carol Starr
Choice	10:1547	Dec. 1973	
CDN	p. 10	1-2 Dec. 1973	Beverly Friend
LATC	p. 40	30 Dec. 1973	Harlan Ellison
VQR	50:R8	Winter 1974	
FOU	no. 5:91-		
	94	Jan. 1974	Christopher Priest
TAC	no. 8:21	Feb. 1974	Richard E. Geis
Vertex	1:12-13	Feb. 1974	James Sutherland
ASF	93:169	Mar. 1974	P. Schuyler Miller
NRV	1:70-72	June 1974	Brian Aldiss
SWSFAJ	146-47:7	June 1974	David Weems
SWSFAJ	153-54:4	July 1974	David Weems
PW	206:60	29 July 1974	
*Vector	no. 66:34-	July-Aug.	
[f]	36	1974	Malcolm Edwards
Algol [f]	no. 23:31-		
	32	Nov. 1974	Richard Lupoff
BWd	9:4	17 Nov. 1974	Joseph McLellan
KPG	9:76	Feb. 1975	Dorothy M. Barnett
Vertex	2:9	Feb. 1975	
WSFAJ	85:R12	Aug. 1975	Stan Burns
LM	no. 59:17-		
	18	Nov. 1975	Paul Walker

E51 Report on Planet Three and Other Speculations

KR	39:1185	1 Nov. 1971	
PW	200:44	8 Nov. 1971	
LJ	96:4013	1 Dec. 1971	Hal W. Hall
BWd	5:6	19 Dec. 1971	Diane Ackerman
PL	19:28	Feb. 1972	
WSJ	179:14	9 Feb. 1972	Edmund Fuller
CSM	p. 10	10 Feb. 1972	Peter J. Henniker-Heaton
Sky	43:182	Mar. 1972	
LJ	97:1628	15 Apr. 1972	Regina Minudri
Choice	9:388	May 1972	
BL	68:784	15 May 1972	
GAL	33:88	Sept. 1972	Theodore Sturgeon
LJ	98:692	1 Mar. 1973	Daniel R. Pfoutz

E52 The Sands of Mars

Star		29 Oct. 1951	Joseph Taggart
Obs		2 Dec. 1951	
SFaN		2 Dec. 1951	A. V[alentine] C[leaver]
NWB	4:93-94	Winter 1951	John Carnell
AUT	no. 17:112	Jan. 1952	

SFAd	5:13-14	Jan. 1952	Clyde Beck
JBAA	62:119-20	Feb. 1952	F.J. Sellers
Aerop	82:130	1 Feb. 1952	J.L.P.
KR	20:238	1 Apr. 1952	
NYHTBR	p. 12	15 June 1952	H.H. Holmes
FSF	3:43	Sept. 1952	Anthony Boucher and J. Francis McComas
CST	p. 6	7 Sept. 1952	Mark Reinsberg
NYTBR	p. 33	14 Sept. 1952	J. Francis McComas
ASF	50:167-68	Oct. 1952	P. Schuyler Miller
GAL	5:121-22	Oct. 1952	Groff Conklin
BM	12:57	Dec. 1952	Florence Boochever
*STL	28:145-46	Jan. 1953	
SPM	1:98-99	Feb. 1953	George O. Smith
PL	14:34	July 1967	
KPG	6:20	Sept. 1972	

E53   Tales from the White Hart

FAU	7:108	Apr. 1957	Hans Stefan Santesson
FSF	12:84	Apr. 1957	Anthony Boucher
ASF	59:145-46	June 1957	P. Schuyler Miller
GAL	14:108-9	June 1957	Floyd C. Gale
INF	2:98-99	July 1957	Damon Knight
ASF	86:169	Feb. 1973	P. Schuyler Miller
BB	18:125	Feb. 1973	
SWSFAJ	no. 130:3	Mar. 1974	Ken Ozanne
GAL	37:133	Oct. 1976	Spider Robinson

E54   Tales of Ten Worlds

CST	p. 6	23 Sept. 1962	Dan Q. Posin
PL	9:40	Oct. 1962	
BS	22:262	1 Oct. 1962	Vincent J. Colimore
SFCTW	p. 33	4 Nov. 1962	Jim Estes
LJ	87:4294	15 Nov. 1962	
NR	p. 403	20 Nov. 1962	Theodore Sturgeon
WP	p. G9	16 Dec. 1962	Richard Wathen
ASF	70:170-73	Jan. 1963	P. Schuyler Miller
NYkr	38:94, 96-97	5 Jan. 1963	Jeremy Bernstein
AMZ	37:126	Mar. 1963	S.E. Cotts
Punch	p. 831	5 June 1963	B.A. Young
NWB	45:124-25	Aug. 1963	Leslie Flood
TLS	p. 589	2 Aug. 1963	
FSF	25:22	Oct. 1963	Avram Davidson
*KPG	7:23	Nov. 1973	
SWSFAJ	121:4-5	Jan. 1974	Ken Ozanne

E55   Technology and the Frontiers of Knowledge

KR	42:1328	15 Dec. 1974	
BL	71:885	1 May 1975	
LJ	10:1562	1 Sept. 1975	Michael S. Fetta

Int	104:200	Nov. 1975	James A. Goldman
LJ	101:667	1 Mar. 1976	Edith S. Crockett or Ellis Mount

E56 Time Probe: The Sciences in Science Fiction

KR	34:331	15 Mar. 1966	
KR	34:382	1 Apr. 1966	
LJ	91:2358	1 May 1966	Milton B. Wenger
NYTBR	p. 34	26 June 1966	Martin Levin
PL	13:29	July 1966	
LJ	91:3555	1 July 1966	
HB	42:733	Dec. 1966	Margaret C. Scoggin
FSF	32:68	Jan. 1967	Judith Merril
PW	191:262	23 Jan. 1967	
BT	4:11	19 Mar. 1967	Clarence Petersen
ASF	80:168-69	Feb. 1968	P. Schuyler Miller

E57 The Treasure of the Great Reef

Times	p. 15	5 Mar. 1964	
LJ	89:1608	1 Apr. 1964	W. Necker
LJ	89:2242	15 May 1964	
TIS	p. 558	June 1964	
ASF	73:91	July 1964	P. Schuyler Miller
FSF	27:23	Aug. 1964	Avram Davidson
NH	73:13	Aug. 1964	W.N. Travolga
BWk	1:13	6 Sept. 1964	Taliaferro Boatwright

E58 2001: A Space Odyssey

Cøsign [f]	no. 16:24-25	June 1968	Ron Miller
NYT	p. 23	5 July 1968	Eliot Fremont-Smith
LJ	93:2897	Aug. 1968	M.S. Cross
PL	15:20-21	Aug. 1968	
Obs	p. 23	4 Aug. 1968	Benedict Nightingale
TLS	p. 865	15 Aug. 1968	
Cleveland Press ("showtime")	p. 16	16 Aug. 1968	Don Thompson
BB	13:44	Sept. 1968	Tom Boardman
SN	83:33	Sept. 1968	
BWd	2:13	1 Sept. 1968	Clarence Petersen
New York Daily News	p. 33	9 Sept. 1968	[editorial]
LJ	93:3335	15 Sept. 1968	Collin Clark
SciRsch	3:38-39	16 Sept. 1968	Roger P. Smith
NYkr	44:180	21 Sept. 1968	Jeremy Bernstein
NWB	no. 183:62	Oct. 1968	W.E.B.
FSF	35:42-43	Nov. 1968	Judith Merril
MM	5:53, 61	Nov. 1968	
NWB	no. 184:61	Nov. 1968	R.G. Meadley and M. John Harrison

<u>Yandro</u>	no. 185:6-		
[f]	8	Dec. 1968	Michael Viggiano
NS	76:877	20 Dec. 1968	Brenda Maddox
AMZ	42:140-		
	42	Jan. 1969	William Atheling, Jr.
ASF	82:166-67	Jan. 1969	G. Harry Stine
SFO [f]	no. 1:55-		
	56	Jan. 1969	George Turner
TON	25:207	6 Jan. 1969	George Turner
Enc	32:48-50	June 1969	Robert Conquest
SWSFAJ	33:6	Sept. 1971	Yngvi
BB	18:138	Apr. 1973	Trevor Allen
<u>Cresset</u>	41:24-25	Oct. 1978	Ronald J. Sommer
JR	22:126	Nov. 1978	

E59 The View from Serendip

PW	212:59	8 Aug. 1977	
KR	45:892-93	15 Aug. 1977	
KR	45:941-42		
BL	74:128	15 Sept. 1977	
LJ	102:2054	1 Oct. 1977	R.W. Ryan
NYTBR	p. 12	30 Oct. 1977	Gerald Jonas
EN		9 Jan. 1978	Colin Wilson
LATBR	p. 4	29 Jan. 1978	Don Strachan
GAL	39:130-33	Mar. 1978	Paul Walker
Florida Times-Union (Jacksonville)			
	p. I3	5 Mar. 1978	Judy Wells Martin
<u>Choice</u>	15:253	Apr. 1978	
NST	78:692	8 June 1978	Ian Ridpath
<u>Future</u>	3:56	July 1978	Howard Zimmerman
<u>Vector</u>	no. 90:56-	Nov.-Dec.	
[f]	57	1978	Bob Shaw
WSFB	13:47	Jan.-Feb.	
		1979	
SFST	6:230-31	July 1979	Donald F. Theall and
			Jane Benedict

E60 Voice Across the Sea

KR	26:437	15 June 1958	
LJ	83:2156	Aug. 1958	Milton B. Wenger
NYHTBR	p. 6	24 Aug. 1958	Harry W. Baehr
SFC	p. 25	29 Aug. 1958	William Hogan
BL	55:12	1 Sept. 1958	
CSM	p. 9	2 Sept. 1958	Robert C. Cowen
NYTBR	p. 37	7 Sept. 1958	Jonathan N. Leonard
SMR	p. 4D	28 Sept. 1958	Donald B. Bagg
BM	18:8	Oct. 1958	Florence Boochever
SR	41:56	1 Nov. 1958	Elaine Simpson
BL	71:861	15 Apr. 1975	

E61	Voices from the Sky			
	KR	33:607	15 June 1965	
	KR	33:638	1 July 1965	
	BWk	pp. 12, 14	31 Oct. 1965	A.G.W. Cameron
	BL	62:388	15 Dec. 1965	
	LJ	90:5406	15 Dec. 1965	Richard S. Potts
	NYkr	41:202	18 Dec. 1965	
	NYTBR	p. 7	19 Dec. 1965	Jonathan N. Leonard
	Choice	2:786	Jan. 1966	
	NYT	p. 19	12 Jan. 1966	Harry Schwartz
	Times	p. 13	13 Jan. 1966	
	LJ	91:445	15 Jan. 1966	
	GDN	94:11	20 Jan. 1966	Anthony Tucker
	Obs	p. 26	13 Feb. 1966	Marghanita Laski
	DT		14 Feb. 1966	Michael Maxwell Scott
	Punch	p. 365	9 Mar. 1966	B.A. Young
	TLS	p. 266	31 Mar. 1966	
	NWB	49:156-59	Apr. 1966	Langdon Jones
	PL	12:32	Apr. 1966	
	Spec	p. 504	22 Apr. 1966	Lyman Andrews
	ASF	77:164-65	Aug. 1966	P. Schuyler Miller
	SPF	9:35	Jan. 1967	P. Brunt
	IntRel	3:250	Apr. 1967	
	KPG	14:24	Spring 1980	Valentin R. Livada

E62	The Wind from the Sun			
	PW	201:68	14 Feb. 1972	
	KR	40:223	15 Feb. 1972	
	LJ	97:1462	15 Apr. 1972	J. Post
	LM	no. 37:31	June 1972	J.B. Post
	LJ	97:2493	July 1972	G. Merrill
	BL	68:976	15 July 1972	
	CCB	26:3-4	Sept. 1972	
	GAL	33:88	Sept. 1972	Theodore Sturgeon
	TLS	p. 1235	13 Oct. 1972	
	AMZ	46:119-20	Nov. 1972	Thomas F. Monteleone
	ASF	90:167-68	Nov. 1972	P. Schuyler Miller
	Obs	p. 37	12 Nov. 1972	Henry Tilney
	BB	18:73	Dec. 1972	Brian Patten
	SWSFAJ	74:10	Dec. 1972	James R. Newton
	ST	p. 31	14 Jan. 1973	Edmund Cooper
	KPG	7:22	Nov. 1973	
	SFO	no. 47:30-32	Aug. 1976	V. Ikin

Appendix 1: Manuscripts in Collections

The most accessible collections of Clarke manuscripts and type-scripts are in Boston, Massachusetts, and Taunton, Somerset, England. Boston University's Mugar Memorial Library holds a 1969 gift and two small additions from 1970 and 1976. The "Clarkives" at Dene Court, where Fred Clarke runs the Rocket Publishing Company, are eventually to be augmented by Arthur's papers from Sri Lanka.

Information from Boston was supplied by the library. Most papers in Taunton were personally inspected: information includes file numbers (in parentheses), which apparently indicate composition date. Information for titles asterisked comes from Fred Clarke. Both lists are in alphabetical order (with miscellaneous items at the end) and cross-referenced to Section A-C where identity could be confirmed.

Mugar Memorial Library, Department of Special Collections, Boston University, 771 Commonwealth Avenue, Boston, Massachusetts, 02215.

"All the Time in the World." 19-page carbon. A53
"Apollo." Screenplay. 34-page corrected typescript. B20
"Apollo and Beyond." 3-page corrected typescript. C522
"Apollo and Beyond." 3-page carbon. C522
"Beyond Babel: The Century of the Communications Satellite." 11-page corrected typescript dated 10 November 1969. C528
"Beyond the Moon." 7-page corrected typescript. C524
The Challenge of the Sea. 133-page corrected typescript. C330
"The Communications in the Second Century of the Telephone." 24-page corrected typescript. C623
"The Deep Range." 17-page carbon. A69
"The Defenestration of Ermintrude Inch." 11-page carbon. A108
Dolphin Island. 192-page corrected typescript. A168
Dolphin Island. 200-page corrected typescript. A168
"The First Men on the Moon." 21-page corrected typescript identified as new chapter(s) for Man and Space. C436
Glide Path. 273-page corrected typescript. A171
Glide Path. 276-page corrected carbon. A171
"The Men on the Moon." 22-page typescript. C291

"Post-Apollo Preface" to <u>Prelude to Space</u>. 5-page corrected type-
    script. C536
<u>The Promise of Space</u>. 238-page corrected original typescript. C505
<u>The Promise of Space</u>. 437-page corrected carbon. C505
<u>The Promise of Space</u>. 350-page corrected carbon. C505
<u>The Reefs of Taprobane</u>. 186-page corrected typescript. C240
"Report on Planet Three." 13-page typescript. C313
"The Satellite Instructional Television Experiment (SITE)." 1-page
    mimeo [typescript] from Clarke's secretary.
"Space, the Unconquerable." 11-page carbon. C392
"Standing Room Only." 8-page carbon. C265
<u>The Treasure of the Great Reef</u>. 221-page corrected typescript. C429
Correspondence: form letter response to general fan letters. 4-page
    mimeo typescript. C691
Correspondence: 16 letters between Clarke and C[live] S[taples]
    Lewis, 1943-1954 (photocopies).
Handwritten notebook, 1930.

Dene Court, Bishop's Lydeard, Taunton, Somerset, England, TA4 3LT.

"Across the Sea of Stars." 2250 words (#280a/57). C311
"Address to World SF Convention." Dated 2 September 1956.
*"Against the Fall of Night." 58-page typescript, "second fair
    copy." A25
"Astronautics." Page proofs, 750 words. C123
*["At the Interface."] Transcript of Clarke/Watts "interview" for
    <u>Playboy</u>. C548
"The Beautiful and Deadly." 1800 words. C235
"Beneath the Seas of Ceylon." 1000 words (#279). C245
*<u>The Best of Arthur C. Clarke</u>. Galley proofs. A209
*["Beyond Apollo."] <u>First on the Moon</u>. 116-page carbon. C541
"Beyond the Mountains of the Moon." <u>Public Opinion</u>. C140
"Beyond the Satellite." 5000 words (#285).
"The Billion Dollar Moon." 3000 words (#238).
"Britain and the Space Age." 1250 words (#286).
"Broken Circuit." 750 words (#108). A50
"Candid Camera." 2200 words (#124).
*<u>The Challenge of the Sea</u>. Corrected typescript. C330
*<u>The City and the Stars</u>. 293-page corrected typescript. A81
"Dunsany--Lord of Fantasy." C48
*<u>Earthlight</u>. 218-page corrected typescript. A76
*<u>The Exploration of Space</u>. 328-page original manuscript with com-
    ments by A.V. Cleaver. C150
*<u>The Exploration of Space</u>. 244-page corrected typescript set out for
    typesetting. C150
"Explorers of Space." <u>Illustrated</u>.
"Explorers of Space." <u>Natural History</u>.
"Explorers of Space." <u>Tuck Annual</u> (#114).
"Fiction and the Future." 2000 words (#300/57).
"Fiction of the Future." <u>Smith's Trade Circular</u>, dated 19 October

1951 (#130). C151
"First Step, the Moon" (#304). C269
"Flying Saucers--Ours or Theirs?" Answers. C129
"Foam." 400 words (#148).
"The Fourth Dimension." 2750 words (#134). C699
*Glide Path. 276-page carbon. A171
"The Greatest Show off Earth." 4500 words (#181). C218.
"Holiday on the Moon." 14,000 words (#94). A40
"Housekeeping Without Gravity." Seventeen. C247
*Imperial Earth. 135 pages, page proofs. A216
"Interplanetary Travel." 300 words. Fortnightly.
"Into the Abyss" (#197). C219
"Into the Sea" (#235).
"Into Space." Sunday Times (#128).
"Introduction" to Space Research and Exploration (#228). C242
*Islands in the Sky. 247-page original manuscript with letter of
    impressions from A.V. Cleaver. A54
"The Last Voyage of Mary Watson." 5000 words (#219).
"Liners of Space." 1100 words. Picture Post (#135). C157
*The Lost Worlds of 2001. Corrected typescript. A199
"Love and Electronics" (#198). C216
"Man and Space." 3500 words (#270).
"Man vs. Machine" (#195). C215
"Meteors." 4000 words (#243). C307
"The Mind of the Machine." Public Opinion. C128
"The Mobile Home" (#213).
"The Nature of the Universe." C125
"No Place Like Earth." C147
"On the Threshold of Space." 2000 words, "for revision" (#217).
"On the Threshold of Space." 2000 words (#267).
"The Perfect Pet" (#196). C217
*Prelude to Space. 5 original manuscript notebooks, dated 9 July
    1947. A41
"Ray Bradbury." Science Fiction Book Club News (#155). C182
"Refutation." 1000 words (#112).
*Rendezvous with Rama. 392-page carbon. A207
*Report on Planet Three. 430-page corrected typescript. C565
"Richard Jeffries." 2000 words. C86
*"The Road Between the Worlds." Screenplay, 50-page typescript. B67
"The Road to Space." 1500 words. Lion. C238
"The Road to Space." 1000 words. Star (#90).
"The Robot and the Child." 750 words (#288b/57). C274
"Rockets to Other Worlds." Public Opinion. C121
*The Sands of Mars. 356-page original manuscript, dated 1 August
    1950. A51
"Science-Fiction." 1500 words (#165).
"Science Fiction and the Age of Space." 500 words "for Library
    Association" (#298).
"Science Fiction and Space Flight" (#170). C210
"The Shape of Ships to Come." 1750 words. C99
"Signals from the Stars." Radar Bulletin (#107). C143

"Sleep No More." 750 words (#241). C259
"Society and the Satellites." 2500 words (#282).
*"The Space Elevator." 32-page typescript, dated September 1979.
"The Space Elevator." 32-page carbon, dated September 1979.
"Space-Suits Will Be Worn." 1200 words. C146
"Spaceships." Children's Britannica (#119).
"Standing Room Only." 2500 words (#265). C265
"The Stay-at-Homes" (#214).
"Tales from the White Hart" ("Preface"). C236
"Through Other Eyes" (#299/57).
*2001: A Space Odyssey. Corrected typescript. A188
"The Ultimate Camera." 3000 words.
"Underwater Ceylon." 4500 words. C245
*Voice Across the Sea. Corrected typescript. C273
"A Voice Beneath the Sea." 3750 words (#260).
"Washing Day--2000 A.D." (#212).
"Whacky." Dedicated "to Lee Jacobs." A17
"What Can We Do About the Weather?" 3500 words. C310
*The Wind from the Sun. Carbon. A201
"Yo Ho Ho and A Bottle of Air." 2500 words (#175). C208
"You're on the Glide Path . . . I Think." 3500 words "by Harry
    Spanner." C105
Untitled item for Star. "John Hunter" series (#161).
*Untitled underwater manuscript.
"Books Read and Acquired." Notebook, 1933-1937.
"A Fall of Moondust." Screenplay by Robert Temple. 2 vols. 37-page
    typescript. B36
"The Songs of Distant Earth." Screenplay by Robert Temple. 57-page
    typescript. B18

Appendix 2: Resources—People, Institutions, Publications

The initials following some entries are those used in the bibliography to identify sources of data about items not examined firsthand.

People

Forrest J. Ackerman (Los Angeles)
Arthur C. Clarke (Colombo, Sri Lanka) [ACC]
Fred Clarke (London and Taunton, England) [FC]
Patrick Codd (London) [PC]
William G. Contento (Livermore, Calif.) [BC]
Alex Eisenstein (Chicago)
Elmer Gertz (Chicago)
Hal Hall (Bryan, Tex.)
Bruce Pelz (Los Angeles)
Arnold Post (New York)
Eric S. Rabkin (Ann Arbor, Mich.)
Leslie Kay Swigart (Long Beach, Calif.)
Marshall B. Tymn (Ann Arbor, Mich.) [MT]
Lois Weisberg (Chicago)

Companies and Agencies
British Airways (Hounslow, England)
British Sub-Aqua Club (London)
British Interplanetary Society (London)
Comsat General Corporation (Washington)
Tom Craven Film Co. (New York) [TC]
David Higham Associates (London) [DH]
Scott Meredith Literary Agency (New York)
Minnesota Mining and Manufacturing Co. (St. Paul)
The Open University (Milton Keynes, England)
Postal Training Institute (Colombo, Sri Lanka)
W.H. Smith & Sons Ltd. (London)
United Nations Educational, Scientific and Cultural Organization
    (Paris)

United States Department of Energy (Washington)
United States International Communication Agency (Washington)

Libraries

The Associated Newspapers of Ceylon Ltd. (Colombo)
Braille Institute (Los Angeles)
British Library (London)
British Newspaper Library (Colindale, London)
California State University, Fullerton
California State University, Long Beach
Department of National Museums (Colombo, Sri Lanka)
Margaret Herrick Library, Academy of Motion Picture Arts and Sciences
    (Beverly Hills, Calif.)
University of California, Irvine
University of California, Los Angeles
University of Kelaniya (Sri Lanka)
University of Massachusetts (Amherst)

Publications (alphabetical by title)

[N.B. Information about and actual copies of numerous publications
    were obtained from the publishers themselves; additional refer-
    ence books are listed in Section E.]

Access: The Supplementary Index to Periodicals and Professional
    Publications (1975-1980). Syracuse, N.Y. and Stockton, Calif.
Alternative Press Index (1969-1980). Northfield, Minn.: Radical
    Research Center
Arts and Humanities Citation Index (1977-1980). Philadelphia:
    Institute for Scientific Information.
Book Review Digest (1951-1980). New York: H.W. Wilson.
Book Review Index (1965-1980). Detroit: Gale Research.
British National Bibliography (1950-1980). London: Council of the
    British National Bibliography (1950-1973), British Library (1974-
    1980).
California Academic Libraries List of Serials [microfiche] (1981-
    1983). Berkeley: University of California.
The Checklist of Fantastic Literature in Paperbound Books, by Bradford
    M. Day. New York: Arno, 1975,[reprint--orig. publ. 1965].
A Checklist of Science Fiction Anthologies, by W.R. Cole. [Brooklyn:
    W.R. Cole], 1964.
"The Complete Checklist of Science Fiction Magazines" (pamphlet), by
    Bradford M. Day. New York: Science-Fiction and Fantasy Pub-
    lications, 1961.
Cumulative Book Index (1950-1980). New York: H.W. Wilson.
Cumulative Book Review Index (1905-1974). Princeton, N.J.: National
    Library Service, 1975.
Cumulative Paperback Index 1939-1959: A Comprehensive Guide to

14,000 Mass-market Paperback Books of 33 Publishers Issued under
69 Imprints, by "R. Reginald" and M.R. Burgess. Detroit: Gale
Research, 1973.
Current Book Review Citations (1976-1980). New York: H.W. Wilson.
The Encyclopedia of Science Fiction and Fantasy: A Bibliographical
Survey of the Fields of Science Fiction, Fantasy and Wierd Fic-
tion through 1968. 3 vols, by Donald H. Tuck. Chicago: Advent,
1974-1982. [D8: DT]
English Catalogue of Books (1952-1968). London: Publishers'
Circular.
English Language Books by Title (1969-1971). Detroit: Gale Research.
Film Literature Index (1973-1979). Albany: State University of New
York.
Humanities Index (1975-1980). New York: H.W. Wilson.
The Index of Science Fiction Magazines 1951-1955, by Norman Metcalf.
El Cerrito, Calif.: J. Ben Stark, 1968.
An Index to Book Reviews in the Humanities (1960-1980). Detroit and
Williamston, Mich.: Philip Thomson.
Index to Critical Film Reviews in British and American Film Periodi-
cals, by Stephen E. Bowles. New York: Burt Franklin, 1974-1975.
Index to Science Fiction Anthologies and Collections by William G.
Contento. Boston: G.K. Hall, 1978.
Index to the Science Fiction Magazines 1926-1950, by Donald B. Day
Portland, Ore.: Perri Press, 1952.
Index to the Science Fiction Magazines 1966-1970. Cambridge, Mass.:
New England Science Fiction Association, 1971. Annual supple-
ments: The NESFA Index [to the] Science Fiction Magazines [and
Original Anthologies] (1970-1980).
International Bibliography of Books and Articles in the Modern Lan-
guages and Literatures (1952-1980). New York: Modern Language
Association.
International Index to Periodicals (1946-1965). New York: H.W.
Wilson.
Los Angeles Times Index [aka Index to the Los Angeles Times] (1972-
1980). Wooster, Ohio: Bell & Howell.
The M.I.T. Science Fiction Society's Index to the S-F Magazines 1951-
1965, by Erwin S. Strauss. [Cambridge, Mass.: M.I.T. Science
Fiction Society], 1966. [ES]
The New Film: A Bibliography of Magazine Articles in English, by
Richard Dyer McCann and Edward S. Perry. New York: E.P. Dutton,
1975.
New Serial Titles (1950-1980). New York: R.R. Bowker.
New York Times Index: A Book of Record (1950-1980). New York: New
York Times.
Newsbank Review of the Arts: Literature (1975-1980). Greenwich,
Conn.: Newsbank (loose-leaf).
On Line Computer Library Center (1979-1981). Columbus, Ohio.
Popular Periodicals Index (1974-1980). Camden, N.J.: Robert M.
Bottorff.
Reader's Guide to Periodical Literature (1945-1980). New York: H.W.
Wilson.

Retrospective Index to Film Periodicals 1930-1971, by Linda Blatty.
  New York and London: R.R. Bowker, 1975.
Science Citation Index: An International Interdisciplinary Index to
  the Literature of Science, Medicine, Agriculture, Technology and
  Behavioral and Social Sciences (1965-1980). Philadelphia: In-
  stitute for Scientific Information.
Science Fiction and Fantasy Authors: A Bibliography of First Printings
  of their Fiction and Selected Non-Fiction, by L[loyd] W. Currey.
  Boston: G.K. Hall, 1979.
Science Fiction and Fantasy Literature: A Checklist, 1700-1974, with
  Contemporary Science Fiction Authors II. 2 vols. Detroit: Gale
  Research, 1979. [D105: RR]
Science Fiction Book Review Index 1923-1973, by H[albert] W. Hall.
  Annual supplements--Bryan, Tex.: Science Fiction Book Review
  Index.
Science Fiction Criticism: An Annotated Checklist, by Thomas D.
  Clareson. Kent, Ohio: Kent State University Press, 1972. Ir-
  regular supplements in the magazine Extrapolation: "The Year's
  Guide to Science Fiction and Fantasy Scholarship," by Roger C.
  Schlobin and Marshall B. Tymn.
Science Fiction Index--Criticism: An Index to English Language
  Books and Articles about Science Fiction and Fantasy [microfiche],
  by H[albert] W. Hall. Bryan, Tex.: Science Fiction Book Review
  Index, 1980.
Science Fiction Short Story Index 1950-1968, Frederick Siemon.
  Chicago: American Library Association, 1971. Revised 1981 as
  Science Fiction Story Index, 1959-1970, by Marilyn Fletcher.
Seekers of Tomorrow: Modern Masters of Science Fiction, by Sam
  Moskowitz. Cleveland and New York: World, 1966. [D34: SM]
Social Science Index (1975-1980). New York: H.W. Wilson.
Social Science Citation Index: An International Multidisciplinary
  Index to the Literature of the Social, Behavioral and Religious
  Sciences. Philadelphia: Institute for Scientific Information.
Stanley Kubrick: A Guide to References and Resources, by Wallace
  Coyle. Boston: G.K. Hall, 1980. [D267: WC]
Talking Book Topics (1965-1980). Washington, D.C.: Division for the
  Blind and Physically Handicapped, Library of Congress [compila-
  tions also available for Science and for Science Fiction and
  Fantasy] [LC]
Television Drama Series Programming: A Comprehensive Chronicle,
  1947-1959, by Larry James Gianakos. Metuchen, N.J. and London:
  Scarecrow Press, 1980.
The Times Index (1973-1980) and Index to the Times (1972). Reading,
  England: Newspaper Archive Developments. Index to the Times
  (1963-1971). London: Times. Index to the Times (1957-1962)
  and The Official Index to the Times (1947-1956). Nendeln/
  Liechtnstein: Kraus-Thomson.
Union List of Serials (1927-1960). New York: H.W. Wilson.
Union List of Serials [microfiche] (1978-1981). Berkeley: Univer-
  sity of California.
Whitaker's Cumulative Book List (1948-1980). London: Whitaker.

Appendix 3: Honors and Awards

1952   International Fantasy Award (<u>The Exploration of Space</u>)

1956   World Science Fiction Convention, Hugo Award ("The Star")

1961   United Nations Educational Social and Cultural Organization, Kalinga Prize for science writing

1963   Franklin Institute, Stuart Ballantine Gold Medal

1965   Space-Writers' Association, Robert Bell Award

1969   American Association for the Advancement of Science, Westinghouse Science Writing Prize

1969   Academy of Motion Picture Arts and Sciences, Oscar Nomination (<u>2001: A Space Odyssey</u> screenplay, co-authored with Stanley Kubrick)

1971   Playboy Editorial Award

1971   Beaver College (Jenkintown, Pennsylvania), Honorary D.Sc.

1971   Franklin Institute, Fellow

1973   Science Fiction Writers of America, Nebula Award ("A Meeting with Medusa")

1974   American Institute for Astronautics and Aeronautics, Aerospace Communications Award

1974   John W. Campbell Award (<u>Rendezvous With Rama</u>)

1974   Science Fiction Writers of America, Nebula Award (<u>Rendezvous With Rama</u>)

1974   World Science Fiction Convention, Hugo Award (<u>Rendezvous With Rama</u>)

1977   Boston Museum of Science, Bradford Washington Award

1979   Science Fiction Writers of America, Nebula Award (<u>The Fountains of Paradise</u>)

1979   University of Moratuwa, Sri Lanka, Honorary D.Sc.

1980   Vikram Sarabhai Professor, Physical Research Laboratory, Ahmedabad, India

1980   Chancellor, University of Moratuwa, Sri Lanka

Appendix 4: Radio and Television Broadcasts

   Long before the American Apollo program, during which Clarke was
a frequent commentator with CBS and Walter Cronkite, he made regular
broadcast appearances on behalf of space travel, science fiction, his
books, and his own reputation as a maverick scientist. Time did not
permit a thorough search of American network programming via TV Guide
and other trade publications, followed up by correspondence. Records
of Clarke's English agent, David Higham, and his brother Fred Clarke,
have been supplemented by helpful personnel at the British Broadcasting Corporation. Known appearances from 1950 to 1977 are listed
here, but very little information is available about them; their
chief function is to demonstrate a continuing record of activity.
The list is arranged by date of broadcast, where known. Brackets
indicate confirmation by [B] BBC or [FC] tape recording. None of
these broadcasts has been heard or seen by me personally, although
Fred Clarke has a few on audio-tape at his home.

1950

4 May. BBC-TV. "The Fourth Dimension."
23 May. BBC-TV. "Space Flight."
27 July. BBC-TV. "Asking for the Moon."
7 December [date paid]. BBC-TV. "Voyage to the Moon."
12 December [date paid]. BBC. "Astronautics in Great Britain."

1952

9 January. BBC. "The Younger Generation" ("Space Travel").
9 September. BBC. "Asian Club" (speaker).

1953

11 February. BBC. "Press Conference."
19 March. BBC. "General Science."
3 July. BBC. "Through the Air and Beyond."

10 December. BBC. "Flying Saucers."
15 December. BBC. "Conquest of the Air."

1954

2 January. BBC. "What Do You Know?"
4 October. BBC-TV. "This Was News."
26 October. BBC. "Talking About Science."

1957

16 September [date paid]. Associated Rediffusion. "This Week."

1960

27 August. BBC. "Radio Newsreel."
1 September. BBC. "Eye Witness."
11 September. BBC. "Assignment."
11 September. BBC. "Interview with P. Munn."
21 September. BBC. "Today." [B]
27 September. BBC. "Today" ("Synchronous Satellites"). [B]

1963

10 September. BBC. "The Sky at Night." [B]
27 September. "BBC Magazine."
7 October. BBC. "This is Britain."

1964

13 August. BBX-TV. "The Knowledge Explosion."
15 October. BBC. "Fantasies of the Future." [See C407]

1966

12 January. BBC-TV. "Horizon."
21 January. BBC. "The World of Books" (interview concerning <u>Voices from the Sky</u>).
8 February. BBC. "The World of Books" ("Discussion with One Other").
6 March. BBC-TV. "People to Watch" ("Talking of Things to Come").
30 March. BBC. "Midday Story."
31 July. BBC-TV. "Twenty-Four Hours." [B]

1967

2 October. BBC. "Dateline London."
2 October. BBC 4. "The World at One." [B]
18 October. BBC. "Towards Tomorrow."
16 December. BBC-TV. "Line Up."
22 December. BBC-TV. "Twenty-Four Hours." [B]

1968

29 April. BBC-TV. "Twenty-Four Hours." [B]
29 November. London Weekend TV. "Frost on Friday."
30 November. BBC. "Towards Tomorrow" ("Think Tanks").
5 December. BBC 4. "The World this Weekend." [B]
6 December. BBC-TV. "Twenty-Four Hours." [B]
6 December. BBC. "The World of Books."

1970

29 September. BBC 4. "PM." [B]
31 [30?] November. BBC 4. "New Worlds" (interview). [B]

1971

7 January. BBC. "These Exciting Times" ("A Look Ahead").
12 May. BBC. "A Look Ahead."
19 July. Thames TV. "Today."
27 September. BBC. "Late Night Line Up" (interview on The Promise of Space). [B]
20 October. BBC World. "Discovery 25." [B]
18 November. BBC. "New Worlds."

1972

8 August. BBC 4. "This World." [B]
17 August [date paid]. Thames TV. "Today."
17 October. BBC. "The Future of Communications."

1973

27 May. BBC 4. "The World this Weekend" (interview). [B]
3 August. BBC 4. "The World at One." [B]
8 August. BBC. "The World of Books."
31 August [date paid]. Thames TV. "Today."
3 September. BBC. "Your World."
10 October. BBC. "Science in Action."

12 October. BBC-TV. "Nationwide" (interview). [B]
23 October. BBC 4. "It's Your Line." [B]
23 October. BBC 4. "Kaleidoscope." [B]
29 November [date paid]. Westward TV. "Westward Report."

1974

14 June. BBC 4. "PM Reports" (interview). [B]
15 July [date paid]. BBC. "Newsreel."
2, 3, 5 September. BBC 4. "The Real Future Will be Rather Dull"
    (interview--4 broadcasts). [B/FC]
27 October. BBC African English [sender?]. "Africa's Sunday People"
    (interview).
21 November [date paid]. BBC. Interview on "Profiles of the Future."

1975

16 January [date paid]. London Broadcasting Corporation. "Jelly-
    bone."
14 March. BBC 1. "Newsbeat."

1977

20 April. BBC-TV. "Horizon" ("Ancient Astronauts," interview). [B]
21 April [recording date--paid 1 May]. BBC 4. "Forty Years of
    Space" (scripted talk). [B]
25 July. BBC 4. "Desert Island Discs." [B/FC]
1 November. BBC. "Our Changing World" (interview). [B]
23 November. BBC. "World Service" ("TV by Satellite" interview).
    [B]
16 December. BBC-TV. "The Sky at Night." [B/FC]

    Fred Clarke also has undated home recordings (audio-cassettes)
of Arthur C. Clarke broadcasts which may duplicate some of the above:
two are interviews concerning Rendezvous with Rama (published 1973);
one is an interview by Sharmini Tiruchelvam; one is an interview by
Cynthia Hamilton.

Index 1: Works by Arthur C. Clarke

"Between Two Worlds" [Part 8, "Journey to Jupiter"], A212.
"Beyond Apollo" [epilogue to First on the Moon], C541.
"Beyond Babel," C528.
"Beyond Centaurus," C441.
"Beyond Gravity," C389.
"Beyond Infinity with Arthur C. Clarke" [interview by Jeffrey Shane], C664.
"Beyond Jupiter," C591.
Beyond Jupiter: The Worlds of Tomorrow [co-authored], C591.
"Beyond the Moon: No End," C524.
"Beyond the Moon's Horizon," C525.
"Beyond the Mountains of the Moon" [review of The Conquest of Space], C140.
"Beyond the Stars" [interview by Jeremy Bernstein], C443.
"Bibliographical Note," The Other Side of the Sky, C263.
"Bicarbonate for Eric," C45.
"Big Game Hunt," A100.
"The Birth of Hal," C561.
"Blacking Out the Sun: The Risks are Slight," C367.
"Booty at the Bottom of the Sea" [review of Sea Diver], C297.
Boy Beneath the Sea [co-authored], C281.
"Brain and Body," C399.
"Bread from the Waters," C220.
"Breaking Strain," A55.
"A Breath of Fresh Vacuum" [letter], C469.
"Brendon" [co-authored], C17.
"Brendon House" [co-authored], C10-11, C13.
"The British Fan, #7, William F. Temple," C35.
"Broadway and the Satellites," C455.
"Broken Circuit," A50.
"Building a City on the Moon" [Part 14, The Exploration of Space serialized], C150.
"Building Living Areas in Space" [Part 21, The Exploration of Space serialized], C150.

Bulletin of the British Interplanetary Society, Editor, C32.
"Buried Alive on the Moon," A151.
"By Rocket to the Moon," C63.

"A Cable Car to Outer Space," C687.
"Call it Sri Lanka or Ceylon," C593.
"The Call of the Stars," A121
"Captain Wyxtpthll's Flying Saucer," A45.
The Case for Going to the Moon by Neil P. Ruzic, "Foreword," C445.
"A Case of Sunstroke," A140.
"The Case of the Snoring Heir," A113.
"Castaway" [originally by "Charles Willis"], A21.
"Ceylon: An Adventurer's Retreat," C575.
"Ceylon's Fortress in the Sky," C344.
"Chairman's Address" [1947], C79.
"Chairman's Address" [1951], C149.
"Chairman's Address" [1952], C164.
"Chairman's Address" [1953], C188.
"The Challenge of Change", C659.
"The Challenge of the Planets," C209.
The Challenge of the Sea, C330.
"The Challenge of the Spaceship," C64.
The Challenge of the Spaceship: Previews of Tomorrow's World, C302.
Challenge of the Stars by Patrick Moore and David A. Hardy, "Foreword," C577.
"Champion of Space-Flight" [interview by "Thomas Sheridan"], C74.
"Change Your Body, Sir?" C289.
"Chart of the Future," C402.
Childhood's End, A64.
Childhood's End [recordings], B32, B51-52.
"Childhood's End" Excerpts Read by the Author, Arthur C. Clarke, B51.

The Deep Range [recording], B63.
"'Deep Space' Ships with Atomic
Engines" [preview title,
Part 7, The Exploration of
Space serialized], C150.
"The Defenestration of Ermintrude
Inch," A108.
"Departure Time Must Be Exact for
Journey Between Planets"
[Part 4, The Exploration of
Space serialized], C150.
Destination Moon by George Pal,
review, C138.
"Destination 2001: Kubrick at
the Controls," C497.
"The Destruction of Sri Lanka,"
C662.
"The Determination of Meteor
Orbits by Radar" [review of
"Determination of the Ele-
ments of Meteor Paths from
Radar Observations"], C112.
"Determination of the Elements of
Meteor Paths from Radar Ob-
servations" by D.W.R.
McKinley and P[eter] M.
Millman, review, C112.
"Devil on the Reef," C221.
"Dial 'F' for Frankenstein," A177.
"Dial 'F' for Frankenstein" [re-
cording], B15.
"Dial World--Via a Radio Station
on Your Wrist," C383.
"Diamonds! . . . and then
Divorce," A87.
"Did the Whale Really Swallow
Jonah?" C355.
"Discoverer of Radium," C163.
"Disney on the Screen," [review
of "Rite of Spring" segment
from Fantasia], C44.
"The Distant Worlds of Arthur C.
Clarke" [interview by Martin
Walker], C670.
"Diurnal Variations of Meteor
Trails" by Charles A. Little,
review, C96.
"Does the Star of Bethlehem
Still Shine?" C211.
"Dog Star," A166.
Dolphin Island: A Story of the

People of the Sea, A169.
"Double-Crossed in Outer Space,"
A84.
"Down to Earth Survey of Space,"
C346.
"Dunsany--Lord of Fantasy," C48.
"The Dynamics of Space-Flight,"
C97.

"An 'Earth' in Outer Space in 50
Years" [interview by H.P.
Mama], C636.
"Earthlight," A46.
Earthlight, A76.
Earthlight [recordings], B34, B53.
"Earth's Atmosphere to Aid in
Planet-Ship Return" [Part 6,
The Exploration of Space
serialized], C150.
"Eclipses of the Sun," C333.
"Editorial," C412.
"'Ego' Visits America," C172.
"Ego's Review," A13.
"Einstein and Science Fiction,"
C697.
"Electromagnetic Launching as a
Major Contribution to Space-
Flight," C139.
The Electron by George Thomson,
"Epilogue," C584.
Electron Optics and the Electron
Microscope by V[ladimir]
K[osma] Zworykin et al., re-
view, C60.
"Electronic Library a Marvel of
the Future" [anonymous inter-
view], C512.
"The Electronic Revolution," C460.
"Electronic Tutors," C690.
"Electronics and Space-Flight,"
C84.
"An Elementary Mathematical Ap-
proach to Astronautics," C34.
"Encounter at Dawn," A143.
"Encounter in the Dawn," A60.
"The End of Night," C288.
"Envoi," C318.
"Epilogue," The Electron by
George Thomson, C584.
"Epilogue," The Lost Worlds of
2001, C564.

221

Intelligence in the Universe by
Roger A. McGowan and
Frederick I. Ordway III,
"Foreword," C465.
"The Interplanetary Approach,"
C37.
Interplanetary Flight: An Intro-
duction to Astronautics, C126.
"Interplanetary Navigation,"
C152.
"Interplanetary Politics," C135.
"The Interplanetary Project" by
A. V[alentine] Cleaver, re-
view [formal response], C82.
Interviews: B16, B19a, B24; C4,
C30, C74, C165, C195, C329,
C356, C416-17, C444, C472,
C488, C490-91, C493, C496,
C498, C500-06, C509, C520-
21, C544, C548, C588, C590,
C596, C598-99, C602, C605,
C611, C624, C636, C661, C664-
67, C669-71, C676-77, C682,
C694, C696, C698.
Interview by Dick Strout [title
unknown], B16.
"Interview: Arthur C. Clarke"
[by Malcolm Kirk], C682.
"Interview with Arthur C.
Clarke" [by Rex Malik], C698.
"An Interview with Arthur C.
Clarke" [by David Garnett],
C667.
"Interviews with Celebrities,
VI" [by "AGER"], C4.
"Interviews with Notorieties--
No. 1" [by "Ego"], C19.
"Into Space" (1937), C24.
"Into Space" (1947), C69.
Into Space: A Young Person's
Guide to Space [co-authored],
C553.
"Into the Abyss," C219.
"Into the Comet," A163.
"Into the Past," A11.
"Introducing Isaac Asimov" [re-
cording], B39.
"Introducing Isaac Asimov"
[transcript], C613.
Introduction to The Best of
Arthur C. Clarke, "1933: A

Science Fiction Odyssey," C597.
Introduction to "Computers and
Cybernetics," Section 2.14,
The Visual Encyclopedia of
Science Fiction, ed. Brian
Ash, C637.
Introduction to Islands in the
Sky, "Cities in Space," C142.
Introduction to The Unexplained
[film], B25.
"Introduction," Arthur C. Clarke's
Mysterious World, C692.
Introduction to "Astronautics at
the 'Palais de la Decouverte'"
by Robert Lencement, C27.
"Introduction," The Challenge of
the Spaceship: Previews of
Tomorrow's World, C303.
"Introduction," The Complete Venus
Equilateral by George O. Smith,
C628.
"Introduction," From the Earth to
the Moon and Around the Moon
by Jules Verne, C405.
"Introduction," From the Ocean,
From the Stars, C353.
"Introduction," The Invisible Man
and The War of the Worlds by
H.G. Wells, C372.
"Introduction," Journey to the
Center of the Earth by Jules
Verne, C300.
"Introduction," The Lion of
Comarre and Against the Fall
of Night, C499.
"Introduction," My Four Feet on
the Ground: Memories of Ex-
moor and Ballifants by Nora
Clarke, C673.
"Introduction," The Nine Billion
Names of God: The Best Short
Stories of Arthur C. Clarke,
C471.
"Introduction," No Place Like
Earth, ed. John Carnell, C166.
"Introduction" [interview], The
Panic Broadcast: Portrait of
an Event by Howard Koch, C544.
"Introduction," The Peculiar Ex-
ploits of Brigadier Ffellowes
by Sterling E. Lanier, C574.

The Best Short Stories of
Arthur C. Clarke, A186.
"1933: A Science Fiction
Odyssey," introduction [also
called preface] to The Best
of Arthur C. Clarke, C597.
"1965--Year of the Breakthrough,"
C464.
"1984 and Beyond" [panel dis-
cussion], C416.
"No Apologies for Science Fic-
tion," C151.
"No Morning After," A71.
No Place Like Earth, ed. John
Carnell, "Introduction,"
C147.
"Not Yet Space-Minded," C350.
"A Note from the Author,"
Dolphin Island, C415.
Novae Terrae [fanzine], Asso-
ciate [Editor], C21.

"Observations Made above Hudson
Bay," C202.
"Observations of Markings on
Ganymede" [review of "Four
Independent Simultaneous
Drawings of Ganymede"], C117.
"The Obsolescence of Man," C400.
"Octogenarian Observations" [by
"Clericus"], C3.
"Of Metaphysics and Moonshots"
[interview by Mary Blume],
C509.
"Of Mind and Matter," C278.
"Of Space and the Spirit," C317.
Of Time and Stars: The Worlds of
Arthur C. Clarke, A206.
"Of Whales and Perfume: Secrets
of the Sea," C322.
"Off the Moon Talk III" [inter-
view by Lois Solomon], C329.
"Oh for the Wings. . . ," C301.
"On Moylan and The City of the
Stars" [letter], C663.
"On the Morality of Space," C252.
"An Open Letter to the Science
Fiction Writers of America,"
C685.
"Opening the Doors of Memory,"
C260.

"'Orbital Refueling' Held Key to
Interplanetary Journeys"
[Part 5, The Exploration of
Space serialized], C150.
"An Orchid for Auntie," A218.
"The Other Side of the Sky"
[series], A122.
"The Other Side of the Sky"
["Special Delivery"], A172.
The Other Side of the Sky, A132.
The Other Side of the Sky [record-
ings], B27, B64.
"The Other Tiger," A60.
"Our Correspondence Column" [by
"A Real Old 6th Former"], A2.
"Our Dumb Colleagues," C261.
"Our Future in the Sea," C434.
"Our Noble Heritage" [by "ARCH"],
C15.
Our World in Colour, ed. William
MacQuitty, "Foreword," C612.
"Our World Will Never be the
Same," C463.
"Out from the Sun," A131.
"Out of the Cradle," A141.
"Out of the Cradle, Endlessly
Orbiting," A161.
"Out of the Sun," A135.
"Out of this World" [1947], C66.
"Out of this World" [1972], C581.
"Outer Space: What is Out
There?" C292.
"Outer Space: Worlds Without
End," C295.
"Outer-Space Vacation," C191.

"The Pacifist," A92.
The Panic Broadcast: Portrait of
an Event by Howard Koch,
"Introduction" [interview],
C494.
"The Parasite," A58.
"Passer-by," A120.
"Patent Pending," A101.
"Peak of Promise," A189.
The Peculiar Exploits of Brigadier
Ffellowes by Sterling E.
Lanier, "Introduction," C574.
"People of the Sea," A168.
"The Perfect Pet," C217.
"Pioneering Space Flights Coming

"Radar and Astronomy," C57.
"Radar Echoes from the Moon," C55.
Radio Astronomy by B[ernard] Lovell and J[ohn] A[therton] Clegg, review, C159.
"Radio Propagation and the Sun," C61.
"The Radio Telescope," C98.
"Radio Transmission from the Moon," C102.
"The Radio Universe," C316.
Reach for Tomorrow, A82.
Reach for Tomorrow [recording], B44.
"Recent Astronomical Observations in Ceylon," C287.
"Recent Measurement of Lunar Temperature" [review of "Microwave Thermal Radiation from the Moon"], C116.
"The Reckless Ones," A91.
"A Recursion in Metastories," A184.
The Reefs of Taprobane: Underwater Adventures Around Ceylon [co-authored], C240.
"Refugee," A133.
"The Reluctant Orchid," A92.
Rendezvous with Rama, A207.
Rendezvous with Rama [recordings], B37, B57, B65.
"Report of the Technical Committee" [co-authored], C40.
"Report on Planet Three," C313.
Report on Planet Three and Other Speculations, C565.
Report on Planet Three and Other Speculations [recording], B38.
The Report on Unidentified Flying Objects by Edward J. Ruppelt, review, C232.
"Rescue!" A198.
"Rescue Party," A19.
Rescue Party [film], B48.
"Retreat from Earth," A10.
"Reunion," A196.
"Reverie," C41.
"The Reversed Man," A36.
Reviews by Clarke [list includes

written and oral reviews of books, films, papers and talks], C23, C44, C49, C52, C59-60, C71-72, C75, C77-78, C82, C87, C89, C93, C95-96, C100, C102, C106-08, C111-18, C120, C125, C130-32, C138, C140-41, C144, C155-56, C159, C170, C176-77, C181, C185, C190, C192-93, C196, C232-33, C297, C334, C617, C652.
"Revised Preface," The Challenge of the Sea, C335.
"Riding on Air," C325.
"The Road Between the Worlds" [filmscript], B67.
"The Road to Lilliput," C397.
"The Road to the Planets," C178.
"The Road to the Sea," A167.
"Robin Hood, F.R.S.," A95.
"Robin Hood on the Moon," A216.
"The Robot Space Explorers," C380.
"Robots in the Nursery," C274.
"The Rocket and the Future of Astronomy," C169.
"The Rocket and the Future of Warfare," C56.
"Rocket Exploration," C85.
"Rocket Flight in Space" [Part 2, "Principles of Rocket Flight"]. C67.
"A Rocket for Romeo," A173.
"Rocket History Provides Striking Instance of Weapon's Comeback" [Part 3, The Exploration of Space serialized], C150.
"Rocket Ship to a Space Station," C168.
"Rocket to the Moon," C90.
"Rocket to the Renaissance," C328.
"Rocket Tours to Mars," C127.
"Rockets" [unsigned], C110.
Rockets and Jets by R[obert] Bernard [sic, Barnard] Way and Noel Greene, review, C118.
"Rockets and Orbits," C65.
Rockets and Space Travel: The Future of Flight Beyond the Stratosphere by Willy Ley, reviews, C77-78.
Rockets: The Future of Travel

Beyond the Stratosphere by
Willy Ley, review, C49.
"Royal Prerogative," A98.

"S.O.S. . . Adrift in Outer
Space," A125.
[The] Sands of Mars, A51.
The Sands of Mars/Prelude to
Space, A225.
"Satellite Communication," C632.
"Satellites and Saris," C647.
"Satellites and the United
States of Earth," C573.
"Saturn Rising," A148.
"Saved . . . ! by a Bow and
Arrow," A85.
"Say Hello and Good Morning to
Mr. Chips," C693.
"The Scent of Treasure," C641.
"Schoolmaster Satellite," C554.
"Schoolmaster Who Foresaw Space
Flights," C419.
Science Abstracts, Assistant
Editor, C91.
"Science and Spirituality," C423.
"Science Fiction and Space
Flight," foreword to The
Authentic Book of Space,
C210.
"Science Fiction for Beginners,"
C28.
Science Fiction--Past, Present
and Future," C22.
Science Fiction--Points the Way
Ahead," C510.
"Science Fiction: Preparation
for the Age of Space," C173.
"Science Fiction--The World's
Nightmare" by Victor
Bulkhovitinov and Vassilij
Zakhartchenko, review, C94.
"Science Fiction v. Mr. Youd,"
C25.
"Science in Ceylon," C332.
"Science Without Trimmings" [re-
view of Profile of Science],
C144.
The Scottie Book of Space
Travel, C258.
Sea Diver: A Quest for History
Under the Sea by Marion

Clayton Link, review, C297.
"The Sea of Sinbad," C648.
"Seas of Tomorrow," C450.
"The Second Century of the Tele-
phone," C655.
"Second Dawn," A47.
"The Secret," A203.
"The Secret of the Men in the
Moon," A170.
"Secret of the Sphere," A213.
"The Secret of the Sun," C237.
"The Secret Weapon," A72.
"Secrets of the Sun," C249.
"Security Check," A114.
"Seeker of the Sphinx," A42.
"The Sentinel," A68.
"The Sentinel" [recording], B49.
"Sentinel of Eternity," A44.
"[The] Servant Problem--Oriental
Style," C363.
Seven Miles Down: The Story of
the Bathyscaph Trieste by
Jacques Piccard and Robert
Dietz, review, C334.
"Shall We Find Life on Other
Planets?" [Part 5, "Space
Flight"], C189.
"The Shape of Ships to Come," C99.
"The Shape of Things to Come"
[interview by Frank Henry],
C165.
"Shaver's Regress," C324.
"Shaw and the Sound Barrier,"
C321.
"The Shining Ones," A176.
"The Shining Ones" [recording],
B11.
"Ships for the Stars," C361.
"Short History of Fantocracy--
1948-1960," A15.
"A Short Pre-History of Comsats,
or: How I Lost a Billion
Dollars in My Spare Time,"
C454.
"A Shortcut Through Space," C280.
Short-Wave Radio and the Ionos-
phere by T.W. Bennington, re-
view, C132.
"Sigiri--Fortress in the Sky,"
C408.
"Sigiriya--Some Modest Proposals,"
C481

"Signals from the Stars," C143.
"Silence, Please [!]" [originally by "Charles Willis"], A39.
"Silver Reef," C435.
"Sinbad in a Spaceship," C167.
The Sky and Its Mysteries by E. Agar Beet, review, C181.
"Slab It to 'Em, Arthur" [anonymous interview], C488.
"Sleep No More," C284.
"Sleeping Beauty," A107.
"A Slight Case of Sunstroke," A165.
"The Snows of Olympus," C610.
"So Long, Earth," A126.
"So You're Going to Mars?" C306.
"The Social Consequences of the Communications Satellites," C349.
"Some Startling Predictions for the 21st Century," C475.
"Son of Dr. Strangelove," C557.
"Son of Dr. Strangelove: or, How I Learned to Stop Worrying and Love Stanley Kubrick," C571.
"Songs of Distant Earth" [screenplay], B18.
"The Songs of Distant Earth," A136.
"Sources and Acknowledgements," The Fountains of Paradise, C679.
"Space Age Decade No. 2: A Prophecy," C485.
"Space and Ceylon," C421.
"Space and the Spirit of Man," C286.
Space: Communications [film], B21.
The Space Dreamers, A193.
Space: Earth Resources [film], B22.
Space: Education [film], B23.
"Space Flight" [series], C189.
"Space Flight and the Spirit of Man," C342.
"Space Flight to the Stars," C226.
"'Space Odyssey'--A Realistic Myth, Appropriate to Our

Times" [interview by Deloraine Brohier], C503.
"'Space Odyssey' in Science Fact" [interview by William A. Payne], C502.
Space Research and Exploration, ed. D[avid] R[obert] Bates, assoc. ed. Patrick Moore, "Introduction," C218.
"Space Ships Will Change Your Life," C234.
"Space Shuttle: Key to Future" [letter], C551.
"Space, the Unconquerable," C392.
Space the Unconquerable, C547.
"Space Travel and Human Affairs," C339.
"Spacecrews Will Fly to the Stars in Deep-Freeze," C381.
"Spaceflight Cargoes of Pure Oxygen" [preview title, Part 8, The Exploration of Space serialized], C150.
"Spaceships" [pictorial], C681.
"The Space-Station: It's [sic] Radio Applications," C484.
"Spacesuits Will Be Worn," C146.
"Space-Travel in Fact and Fiction," C135.
"Spark of the Second Industrial Revolution," C406.
"Special Delivery," A115.
"Speculations of a Space Man" [interview by Alan Bradford], C506.
"Speech Delivered in Columbus [Ohio]," C529.
"Spinoff from Space," C527.
"Springboard to Space," C238.
"Sri Lanka--A Land Without Enemies," C608.
"Sri Lanka and Me," C634.
"Sri Lanka--Land of No Sorrows," C600.
Sri Lanka: Past, Present, and People [film], B66.
"Sri Lanka--Pearl of the Orient," C688.
"Stairway to the Stars," C279.
"Standing Room Only," C265.
"The Star," A78.

"Transit of Earth" [recordings], B50, B58.

"Transit of Earth" and "The Nine Billion Names of God"--"The Star" Read by the Author, Arthur C. Clarke [recording], B50.

"Transit of Earth" and "The Nine Billion Names of God"--"The Star" Read by the Author, Arthur C. Clarke [untitled record liner notes], C672.

"Transition--From Fantasy to Science," C270.

"Travel by Wire!" A8.

"Treasure Hunting on the Sea Floor" [review of 4000 Years Under the Sea], C196.

"Treasure of the Great Reef," C420.

The Treasure of the Great Reef [co-authored], C429.

The Treasure of the Great Reef [recording], B8.

"A Trip to the Moon" [preview title, Part 9, The Exploration of Space serialized], C150.

"Trouble in Aquila, and Other Astronomical Brainstorms," C413.

"Trouble with the Natives," A83.

"Trouble with Time," A164.

"Twelve Months Reviewed" [unsigned], C109.

"Twilight in Tibet," A208.

"The Twilight of the Sun" [poem], B4.

200 Miles Up by J. Gordon Vaeth, review, C156.

Two Leagues Under the Sea by Jacques Piccard and Robert S. Dietz, review, C334.

"2001" [interview by Charles Power], C482.

"2001: A Space Odyssey" [essay], C489.

"2001: A Space Odyssey" [screenplay], B10, B12.

2001: A Space Odyssey [comic books], B45-46.

2001: A Space Odyssey [documentary film], B13.

2001: A Space Odyssey [feature film], B19.

2001: A Space Odyssey [novel], A188.

2001: A Space Odyssey [recordings], B41, B59.

"2001: An Earth Odyssey," C552.

2001 . . . And Even Beyond [interview by Poul Anderson], B19a.

"2001: The Book Behind the Movie . . . and the Man Who Wrote It" [book review and interview by Roger P. Smith], C498.

2001 Revisited: An Interview with Arthur C. Clarke [by Stephen Banker], B24.

"The Tyranny of Time," C366.

The UFO Controversy in America by David Michael Joseph, review, C617, C652.

UFOs Explained by Philip J. Klass, review, C617, C652.

"U.S.A.: A Spaceman Rides the Lecture Circuit," C277.

"Ugliest Fish in the World," C229.

"[The] Ultimate Melody," A102.

"Undersea Holiday," C197.

"Underwater Holiday," C700.

The Unexplained [film], introduction, B25.

"The Unforgettable Sight of Treasure," C430.

"An Unheard Melody Keeps Mona Smiling," C589.

"A Universal Escape-Velocity Mass-Ratio Chart," C76.

"The Uses of the Moon," C341.

"V2 for Ionospheric Research?" [letter], C51.

"Vacation in Vacuum," C304.

"The Vandals--of the Past and Future," C480.

"Venture to the Moon," A90.

Venus Equilateral by George O. Smith, "Foreword," C477.

The View from Serendip, C638.

Index 2:
Works about Arthur C. Clarke

ence Fiction Writer," Godfrey Smith, D41.

At the Edge of History: Specula-tions on the Transformation of Culture, William Irwin Thompson, D119.

"The Authentic Vision: A Study of the Writing of Arthur C. Clarke," Bud Parkinson, D71.

The Author's and Writer's Who's Who [unsigned vita], D20.

Authors of Books for Young People, eds. Martha E. Ward and Dorothy A. Marquardt, D121.

The Ballantine Teacher's Guide to Science Fiction: A Practical Creative Approach to Science Fiction in the Classroom, L[ouis] David Allen, D163.

"Bibliography: Books by Arthur C. Clarke" [unsigned], D125.

Billion Year Spree: The True History of Science Fiction, Brian W. Aldiss, D138.

"Biological Themes in Modern Sci-ence Fiction," Helen Nethercutt Parker, D207.

"The Blown Mind on Film," Walter Breen, D56.

The Blue Book: Leaders of the English-Speaking World [un-signed vita], D99.

"British Science Fiction," Christopher Priest, D256.

"Caution! Science Friction [sic] Causes Heat," Gene Snyder, D214.

"Chain Reaction," Jeremy Bernstein, D53.

"Childhood's End," David N. Samuelson, D260.

"Childhood's End: A Median Stage of Adolescence," David N. Samuelson, D148.

"Childhood's End" Excerpts Read by the Author Arthur C. Clarke [untitled liner notes], Isaac Asimov, D243.

"Childhood's End Hits Legal Snag," Jordan R. Fox, D230.

The Cinema of Stanley Kubrick, Norman Kagan, D131.

"The City and the Stars," Jack Williamson, D263.

"Clarke, Arthur C.," Judy-Lynn Benjamin del Rey, D153.

"Clarke, Arthur C.," P[eter] N[icholls], D252.

"Clarke, Arthur C(harles)," Curtis C. Smith, D136.

"Clarke of Ceylon" [unsigned pro-file], Newsweek, D24.

"Clarke's Law and Asimov's Corol-lary," Isaac Asimov, D193.

Classics of Science Fiction [film-strip/recording], Educational Dimensions, D165.

The Coast of Coral [unsigned un-titled note], D50.

"Coin Haul" [unsigned news article], Times, D101.

"The Comic Sense of 2001," F. Anthony Macklin, D85.

"Comment from the Editors," Elks, D26.

A Comprehensible World: On Modern Science and Its Origins, Jeremy Bernstein, D31, D40.

Contemporary Authors: A Bio-Bib-liographical Guide to Current Authors and Their Works [1967], ed. James M. Ethridge and Barbara Kopala, D47.

Contemporary Authors: A Bio-Bib-liographical Guide to Current Writers in Fiction, General Non-Fiction, Poetry, Journal-ism, Drama, Motion Pictures, Television and Other Fields [1980], ed. Ann Every, D268.

Contemporary Literary Criticism: Excerpts from Criticism of Today's Novelists, Poets, Playwrights, and other Creative Writers, ed. Carolyn Riley, [1973] D147, [1975] D170; ed. Dedria Bryfonski, [1980] D266.

Contemporary Novelists, ed. James Vinson, D136.

"Fountains of Paradise" [sic]
Read by the Author Arthur C.
Clarke [untitled liner notes],
Buckminster Fuller, D246.

"From Folded Hands to Clenched
Fists: Kesey and Science
Fiction," Edward J. Gallagher,
D197.

"From Icarus to Arthur Clarke"
[unsigned], Forbes, D61.

From Jules Verne to "Star Trek",
Jeff Rovin, D210.

"From Man to Overmind: Arthur
C. Clarke's Myth of Pro-
gress," John Huntington, D156.

The Future as Nightmare: H.G.
Wells and the Anti-Utopians,
Mark R. Hillegas, D48.

"The Future is Already Here,"
Jeremy Bernstein, D31.

"The Future is Practically Here:
A Tribute to Arthur C.
Clarke," Jeremy Bernstein,
D31.

"The Future Isn't What It Used to
Be," Gary Goshgarian and
Charles O'Neill, D144.

Future Tense: The Cinema of Science Fiction, John Brosnan,
D225.

"Gentle Prophet Behind the Man on
the Moon," Michael Deakin,
D129.

Getting Hooked on Science Fiction
[filmstrip/recording], D180.

A Handbook of Science Fiction and
Fantasy, Donald H. Tuck, D8.

A History of the Cinema from Its
Origins to 1970, Eric Rhode,
D187.

"Homer in 2001: Comparisons be-
tween The Odyssey and 2001:
A Space Odyssey," Phillis
Drake, D102.

"How They Made 2001," Richard
Dempewolff, D46.

"Ideological Contradictions in
Clarke's The City and the
Stars," Tom Moylan, D204.

The Illustrated Book of Science
Fiction Ideas and Dreams,
David Kyle, D200.

"Imperial Earth," Donald L.
Lawler, D250.

"In Response to Mr. Astle"
[letter], R[ichard] Dale
Mullen, D239.

In Search of Wonder, Damon Knight,
D12.

In Search of Wonder: Essays on
Modern Science Fiction, Damon
Knight, D49.

International Celebrity Register
[unsigned profile], ed.
Cleveland Amory, D18.

International Who's Who [unsigned
vita], D64.

Intersections: The Elements of
Fiction in Science Fiction,
Thomas L. Wymer et al., D241.

"An Interview with Charles
Sheffield," Karl Pollock, D255.

"Introduction" to Across the Sea
of Stars, Clifton Fadiman, D19.

"Introduction" to Alien Creatures,
Boylston Tompkins, D240.

"Introduction" to The Challenge of
the Sea, Wernher von Braun,
D23.

"Introduction" to Islands in the
Sky, Patrick Moore, D116.

"Introduction" to The Lost Worlds
of 2001, Foster Hirsch, D248.

"Introduction" to Of Time and
Stars: The Worlds of Arthur
C. Clarke, J.B. Priestley,
D135.

"Introduction: An A B C of
British Science Fiction--
Apocalypse, Bleakness, Catas-
trophe," Peter Nicholls, D146.

An Introduction to Film, Thomas
and Vivian C. Sobchack, D277.

"It is Ceylon that Now Seems Home"
[unsigned], Horizons, profile,
D114.

Journal of the World Science Fiction Society, Bill Donaho

K. Hutchens [profile/interview], D4.
"1001 Interpretations of 2001," Robert Plank, D86.
"The Outsider from Within: Clarke's Aliens," E. Michael Thron, D215.

"Party of One," Clifton Fadiman, D14.
Passages About Earth: An Exploration of the New Planetary Culture, William Irwin Thompson, D161.
"Pathfinder," R.B., Incentive/68, D54.
"Perhaps the Mysterious Monolith is Really Moby Dick" [film preview], Albert Rosenfeld, D74.
"Personalia" [unsigned news brief], Huish Magazine, D1.
"Persuasive Functions of Science Fiction: A Study in the Rhetoric of Science," Ray Lynn Anderson, D52.
A Pictorial History of Science Fiction, David Kyle, D183.
"Playboy Interview: Stanley Kubrick," Eric Norden, D71.
"The Politics of Survival: Science Fiction in the Nuclear Age," Andrew Feenberg, D229.
"The Possible Gods: Religion in Science Fiction," Jean Babrick, D123.
"Profiles: How About a Little Game?" [Kubrick interview], Jeremy Bernstein, D40.
"Profiles: Out of the Ego Chamber" [profile/interview], Jeremy Bernstein, D82.
"A Prophet Honored" [unsigned], Triton profile, C35.
"A Prophet of Hope" [unsigned], Asiaweek profile, D257.
"Prophet of the Space Age," Cedric French, D33.
"Prophet of the Space Age Comes Home to Ceylon" [unsigned news article], Ceylon Travel

Newsletter, D90.
"Publisher's Note," Against the Fall of Night, D22.
"Pulps," Michael Ashley, D221.

Quasar, Quasar, Burning Bright, Isaac Asimov, D193.

Random House Encyclopedia [unsigned profile], D208.
Reader's Guide to Science Fiction, Baird Searles et al., D275.
"Religious Dimensions of Representative Science Fiction," David Thomas Martin, D251.
"Religious Themes and Motifs in Science Fiction," Lyssa Dianne Bossay, D245.
"The Remarkable Adventure" [introduction to "Before Eden"], Philip José Farmer and Beverly Friend, D228.
"Rendezvous with Rama," William H. Hardesty, IV, D247.
"Return to Melies: Reflections on the Science Fiction Film," Harry M. Geduld, D62.

"SF: Literary Frontiers," Kenneth John Atchity, D140.
SF: The Other Side of Realism, ed. Thomas D. Clareson, D81, D88, D111.
"A Sampler of Science Fiction for Junior High," Jeanne K. Smith, D137.
Science Fiction Aliens, Ed Naha, D205.
Science Fiction: A Critical Guide, ed. Patrick Parrinder, D256.
Science Fiction: An Illustrated History, Sam J. Lundwall, D202.
Science Fiction: An Introduction, L[ouis] David Allen, D139.
Science Fiction and Fantasy [filmstrip/recording], Educational Audio-Visual, Inc., D189.
Science Fiction and Fantasy Literature: A Checklist: 1700-1974, with Contemporary Science Fiction Authors II,

D. Clareson, D128.

"Sri Lanka Finally Gives Writer Tax-Free Status," Sharon Rosenhouse, D209.

Stanley Kubrick: A Film Odyssey, Gene D. Phillips, D169.

Stanley Kubrick: A Guide to References and Resources, Wallace Coyle, D267.

Stanley Kubrick Directs, Alexander Walker, D120.

Stella Nova: The Contemporary Science Fiction Writers, "R[obert] Reginald," D105.

The Stellar Gauge: Essays on Science Fiction Writers, eds. Michael J. Tolley and Kirpal Singh, D277.

"The Stellar Parallels: Robert Silverberg, Larry Niven and Arthur C. Clarke," Alexander Nedelkovich, D271.

Stories into Film, eds. William Kittredge and Steven M. Krauzer, D249.

"Strange Odyssey: From Dart and Ardrey to Kubrick and Clarke," Richard D. Erlich, D175.

"Studies in the Contemporary American and British Science Fiction Novel," David Norman Samuelson, D93.

The Study of the Future: An Introduction to the Art and Science of Understanding and Shaping Tomorrow's World, Edward Cornish et al., D195.

"A Study of the Impact of Technology on Human Values as Reflected in Modern Science Fiction," Mary Jane Greenlaw, D104.

Survey of Science Fiction Literature, ed. Frank N. Magill, D247, D250, D260, D262-64.

"That Starlit Corridor," Alan Madsden, D36.

Things to Come: An Illustrated History of the Science Fiction Film, Douglas Menville and "R[obert] Reginald," D203.

"Three Journeys: One Tradition," A.J. Weidemann, D218.

"Three Styles of Arthur C. Clarke: the Projector, the Wit, and the Mystic," Peter Brigg, D194.

Three Tomorrows: American, British and Soviet Science Fiction, John Griffiths, D269.

Time of Need: Forms of Imagination in the Twentieth Century, William Barrett, D124.

"Time, Transplants, and Arthur Clarke," Phillip Strick, D118.

"Transit of Earth" and "The Nine Billion Names of God"--"The Star" Read by the Author Arthur C. Clarke [untitled liner notes], Ward Botsford, D223.

The Twentieth Anniversary Playboy Reader, ed. Hugh Hefner [unsigned untitled profile], D155.

Twentieth Century Authors: A Biographical Dictionary of Modern Literature, First Supplement, ed. Stanley J. Kunitz, D9.

Twentieth Century Writing, ed. Kenneth R. Richardson, D92.

"2001: A Critique," David MacDowall, D69.

"2001--A Masterpiece by Accident?" Roger Ebert, D59.

"2001: A Metaphysical Fantasy," Ted White, D77.

"2001: A New Myth," Don Daniels, D57.

"2001: A Parable Detailed, and a Devilish Advocacy," Alex Eisenstein, D60.

"2001: A Space Obfuscation," "Marshall Delaney," D58.

"2001: A Space Odyssey," Tim Hunter, Stephen Kaplan and Peter Jaszi, D64.

"2001: A Space Odyssey," P[eter] N[icholls] and J[ohn]. B[rosnan], D253.

"2001: A Space Odyssey," Robert O'Meara, D87.

Index 3: Register of Names

This index includes the following:

    1) authors of published or recorded comments about Clarke and his writing, including book reviews and interviews

    2) people whose books, papers or lectures Clarke has reviewed in print

    3) people for 'whose books or talks he has written a foreword, epilogue, or introduction

    4) people with whom he has co-authored books or articles or appeared on panels

    5) narrators of recordings of Clarke's work

    6) producers of audio-visual media involving Clarke

    7) interviewers of Clarke

    8) pseudonyms, for Clarke and for others, listed in the main bibliography. Clarke's are also indicated next to his name.

It does not include anonymous interviews, reference book articles, and magazine pieces (editorial introductions or publicity releases); they may be found in Index 2.

    Multiple entries for one "author" are alphabetized by title of work, beginning with items for which no title is listed, and ordered chronologically if entries are otherwise identical. References to "film" mean 2001: A Space Odyssey if not in brackets. Reviewers of Clarke's books (alphabetized by book title in Section E) are indicated by "rev."

Brown, Roger, B43.
Brown, Steve, E25.
Browning, D.C., D21.
Brunt, P., E61.
Bryfonski, Dedria, D266.
Budrys, Algis, C416; E25(2).
Bulkhovitjnov, Victor, C94.
Bulman, Learned T., E28.
Burgess, Michael R. See
    R[obert] Reginald.
Burns, Stan, E50.
Byrnes, Asher, E22.

Calder, Ritchie, C144.
Cameron, A.G.W., E61.
Campbell, H.J., ed., C210.
Canever, R.B., C13, C17.
Cant, Gilbert, E21.
Carmody, F.C., E28.
Carnell, John, C166; D7, D25; E9,
    E21-22, E28, E32, E52.
Carr, Archie, E12.
Cary, Meredith, D127.
Case, Peter, B40.
Cavallini, Jeanne, E24.
Chelton, Mary K., E25.
Chilson, Robert, E17.
Clareson, Thomas D., D81, D88,
    D100, D111, D128, D151, D176,
    D219.
Clark, Collin, E47, E58.
Clark, Eugenia, E12, E49.
Clarke, Arthur C. See pseudonyms:
    A. Munchausen, ARCH, Batsin
    Belphry, Charles Willis,
    Clericus, Court, De Profundis,
    DIL, E.G. O'Brien, One-Time
    Sixth Former, Professor
    Brittain and A Real Old 6th
    Former.
Clarke, Nora, C673.
Claussen, Joseph, E25.
Cleaver, A. V[alentine], C82;
    E32, E45, E52.
Clegg, J[ohn] [Atherton], C159.
Clericus, ACC pseudonym, A4; B1;
    C2-3, C5-6, C8-9, C14, C18,
    C20.
Cohen, P., E31.
Cohn, Victor, C501.
Cole, E.J., E28.

Cole, E.M., E12.
Colimore, Vincent J., E54.
Collins, Michael, C541.
Colvin, James, E46.
Commire, Anne, D226.
Conklin, Groff, E2, E10, E17, E19,
    E21, E33, E45(2), E52.
Conquest, Robert, E14, E58.
Cooney, Thomas E., E49.
Cooper, Edmund, E17, E29, E50,
    E62.
Cornish, Edward, D195.
Cotsworth, Staats, B15.
Cotts, S.E., E8-9, E43, E54.
Court, ACC pseudonym, A7.
Cowen, Robert C., E6-9, E21, E23,
    E30-31, E37, E43, E46, E60.
Cox, Arthur Jean, E2.
Coyle, Wallace, D267.
Craven, Tom, B13, B17, B21-23,
    B42, B47, B66; D196.
Crispin, Edmund [pseud. for Robert
    Bruce Montgomery], E17, E24.
Crockett, Edith S., E39, E55.
Cross, M.S., E58.
Cruickshank, Ken, E29.
Culpan, N., E15.
Curtis, Mike, E29.
Cutcheon, Billye, C676.

Dailey, Jennie Ora Marriott, D152.
Dalgleish, Alice, E30.
D'Ammassa, Don, E50.
Daniels, Don, D57, D110.
Davenport, Basil, E10, E48.
Davidson, Avram, E26, E54, E57.
Davidson, Mark, C661.
Davidson, Martin, C152; E16, E32.
Davy, Charles, E21.
Deakin, Michael, B30; D129.
de Bolt, Joe, D177.
De Profundis, ACC pseudonym, A6.
de Sola Pool, Ithiel, C633.
de Vaucouleurs, G., C89.
De Vries, Daniel, D142.
De Weese, Gene, E29.
del Rey, Judy-Lynn Benjamin, D153.
del Rey, Lester, E17, E21, E29.
Delaney, Marshall [pseud. for
    Robert Fulford], D58.
Dempewolff, R[ichard] F., D46.

Greenberg, Martin Harry,
    D206, D228.
Greene, Noel, C118.
Greenlaw, Mary Jane, D104.
Griffiths, John, D269.
Grimmer, George. See Grimminger,
    George.
Grimminger, George, C95.
Grosch, H.R.J., E32.

Hall, Hal W., E51.
Hall, Stanley B., E14, E49-50.
Halle, Morris, C633.
Halzour, J.E., E24.
Hamblin, Dora Jane, C541.
Hamilton, Alex, E46.
Hankenson, Alberta L., E35.
Hardesty, William H., IV, D247.
Hardy, David A., C577.
Hardy, Melody, E50.
Harfst, Betsy, D198.
Harman, Gordon, E28.
Harpenau, Lou, B31.
Harper, Harry, C72.
Harris, Leo, E14.
Harrison, Harry, D232-33.
Harrison, M. John, E58.
Hartman, William K., E39.
Haslett, A.W., E13.
Hass, Walter, C117.
Haviland, Virginia, E7, E23, E36.
Hawkins, R.R., E21.
Hayes, Sarah, E15.
Hefner, Hugh, ed., D155.
Heinlein, Robert A., C416.
Helfand, Esther, E24.
Henderson, C.J., E25.
Henderson, Dan, E29.
Henderson, R.W., E49.
Henniker-Heaton, Peter J., E1,
    E10, E19, E24, E51.
Henry, Frank, C165.
Herbert, Rosemary, E25.
Herget, Paul, C141.
Hess, Carl, B29.
Hill, Douglas, D234.
Hill, Horace B. [L.H.S.], E22,
    E43.
Hillegas, Mark R., D48.
Hirsch, Foster, D248.
Hodgens, Richard, D63.

Hogan, William, E12, E15, E37, E60.
Hollow, John, D181.
Holmes, H.H. [pseud. for William
    Anthony Parker White], E1-2,
    E10-11, E14, E17, E19, E21,
    E28, E33, E43, E45, E48, E51.
Hone, Ralph E., E39.
Hood, Robert, E30.
Horgan, Michael, B8.
Horgan, Patrick, B54.
Hornish, Rudy A., E10.
Hough, R.L., E24, E39.
Houston, David, C666.
Howes, Alan B., D199.
Hoyle, Fred, C125; E21.
Hubbard, Henry W., E8.
Hunter, Tim, D64.
Huntington, John, D156.
H[usband], R[ichard] F., E14.
Hutchens, John K., D4.
Hutchinson, Tom, E5, E25.
Hyman, Earle, B37.

Ikin, V., E62.
Ives, Vernon, E8.

Jacob, David,Michael, C617, C652.
James, Clive, D66.
Jameson, Frederic, E58.
Janser, A. co-author,C26,C33,C40
Jastrow, Robert, E47.
Jaszi, Peter, D64.
Jenkins, Will F., C75.
Johnson, Connie, C356.
Johnson, William, C491.
Jonas, Gerald, E25(2), E29(2),
    E59.
Jones, Brenda, E29.
Jones, Langdon, E61.
Jukes, Thomas H., E47.
Jun, K.M., E32.

Kafka, Janet, D167.
Kagan, Norman, D131.
Kagle, Steven Earl, D115.
Kahn, Barbara, E29.
Kaiser, Hans K., C130.
Kaplan, Stephen, D64.
Katz, John Stuart, D132.
Kauffman, Stanley, D67.
Keller, Elaine J., D133.

Meredith, Scott, C674.
Merril, Judith, E13, E38, E44,
    E56, E58.
Merrill, G., E62.
Merwin, Sam, Jr., E2.
Meyers, Walter E., D270.
Miles, Betty, E23.
Miles, Howard, E47.
Miller, Dan, E29(2).
Miller, H[enry] A[rthur], C59.
Miller, P. Schuyler, E2, E8-11,
    E14, E44, E45(3), E46, E48
    (2), E50, E52, E53(2), E54,
    E56-57, E61-62.
Miller, Ron, E58.
Millies, Suzanne, D168.
Millman, P[eter] M., C102, C112.
Mines, Samuel, E32, E46.
Minett, H.C., C116.
Minudri, Regina, E29, E51.
Mitchell, P.M., E28.
Modder, Jan, C599.
Molnar, A.K., E29.
Molnar, Robert, B56.
Molson, Francis J., D185.
Molyneux, Robert, E28, E50.
Monteleone, Thomas F., E62.
Montgomery, Robert Bruce. See
    Crispin, Edmund.
Moore, Patrick, C242, C577; D116,
    D237; E20.
More, Anthony, E10.
Morgan, Chris, D238.
Moritz, Charles, ed., D41.
Moritz, Jo., B38.
Morley, Derek Wragge, E21.
Morrison, Philip, E24, E39.
Morrison, Phylis, E24, E39.
Morse, C.R., E1.
Moskowitz, Sam, D34; E21, E33.
Mount, Ellis, E39, E55.
Moylan, Tom, D204.
Mullen, R[ichard] Dale, D239.
Munchausen, A., ACC pseudonym,
    A5.
Murray, Bruce, C594.
Myers, Tim, E25.

Naha, Ed., D205.
Nathan, Paul, D70.
Necker, W., E57.

Nedelkovich, Alexander, D271.
Newton, I. Allen, A173.
Newton, James R., E62.
Nicholls, Peter, D146, D158, D252-
    53.
Nicolson, Marjorie Hope, C104.
Nightingale, Benedict, E58.
Nonweiler, T.R.F., E32.
Norden, Eric, D71.
North, Sterling, E21.
Northrup, E.F. See Pseudoman,
    Akkad.

Oboler, E.M., E1.
O'Brien, E.G., ACC pseudonym, A22.
Ogan, Jane, D134.
O'Gorman, Edmundo, C614.
Olander, Joseph, ed., D206, D228.
Oliver, Curt, D132.
O'Meara, Robert, D87.
O'Neill, Charles, D144.
One-Time 6th Former, ACC pseud-
    onym, A1.
Ordway, Frederick I., III, C465.
Ostermann, R., E44.
O'Toole, Thomas, E24.
Otten, Terry, D272.
Otterburn-Hall, William, C590.
Ovenden, Michael W., C113, C116;
    E32.
Ower, John B., D159.
Ozanne, Ken, E33, E43, E54.

J.L.P., E21, E52.
Pal, George, C138, C155.
Panshin, Alexei, E35.
Parker, Helen Nethercutt, D207.
Parkinson, Bud, D72.
Parrinder, Patrick, D256, D273.
Patten, Brian, E62.
Payne, William A., C502.
Pendray, G. Edward, C52, C87; E21.
Perakos, Peter S., D254.
Perry, G.E., E6.
Pervesler, Kurt, C120.
Peterson, Clarence, E56, E58.
Pfeiffer, John, D177; E37.
Pfoutz, Daniel R., E47, E51.
Phillips, Gene D., D169.
Piccard, Jacques, C334.
Piddington, T.H., C116.

Small, R.W., C10-11.
Smith, Curtis C., D136.
Smith, George O., C439, C628;
    E33, E52.
Smith, Godfrey, D43.
Smith, Jeanne K., D137.
Smith, R.A., C26, C40, C199,
    C204.
Smith, Roger P., C498; E54.
Snow, C[harles] P[ercy], C515.
Snyder, Gene, D214.
Sobchack, Thomas, D278.
Sobchack, Vivian C., D278.
Solomon, Charles, E25.
Solomon, Lois, C329.
Sommer, Ronald J., E10, E58.
Sragow, Michael, D107.
Staicar, Tom, E25.
Stair, Douglas, E25.
Starr, Carol, E50.
Starr, Catherine, E33.
Stever, David, E50.
Stine, G. Harry, D75; E58.
Strachan, Don, E59.
Strick, Philip, D76, D118.
Strout, Dick, B16.
Sturgeon, Theodore, C416; E11,
    E14, E22, E50-51, E54, E62.
Sullivan, Walter, C594.
Sutherland, James, E50.
Sutton, Marilyn, D94.
Sutton, Thomas C., D94.

P.J.T., E32.
Taggart, Joseph, E52.
Temple, Robert, B18, B36.
Temple, William F., C30, C35.
Tenn, William [pseud. for Philip
    Klass], C416.
Theall, Donald F., E59.
Thomas, Shirley, C490.
Thompson, Don, E58.
Thompson,William Irwin,D119,D161
Thomson, George, C584.
Thron, E. Michael, D215.
Thyness, Gustave M., C100.
Tilney, Henry, E5, E36, E42, E50,
    E62.
Tolley, Michael J., ed., D277.
Tompkins, Boylston, D240.
Totton, Nick, E25.

Tranzy, Eugene, D216.
Travolga, W.N., E49.
Tuck, Donald H., D8.
Tucker, Anthony, E61.
Turner, Alice K., C596, C605.
Turner, George, E58(2).
Tutihasi, R. Laurraine, E5.
Tyler, T.E., E31.

Vaeth, J. Gordon, C156.
van Reyk, Peter, C433.
Van Vogt, A[lfred] E[dward], C416.
Verne, Jules, C300, C405.
Videan, David, E47.
Viggiano, Michael, E58.
Vinson, James, ed., D136.
Vogel, Mike, E29.
von Braun, Wernher, C192, C233;
    D23.

Waddington, R., E33.
Walker, Alexander, D120.
Walker, Martin, C669-71.
Walker, Paul, E29, E50, E59.
Ward, A.C., D108.
Ward, Martha E., D121.
Warga, Wayne, C521.
Warrick, Patricia, D217, D228.
Wathen, Richard, E54.
Watson, Ian, E25.
Watts, Alan, C548.
Way, R[obert] Barnard [sic:
    Bernard], C118.
Weems, David, E50(2).
Weereraine, Neville, C417.
Weidemann, A.J., D218.
Weinberger, Caspar, E9.
Weinkauf, Mary, D149.
Weiss, Myron, E32.
Welfare, Simon, C619.
Wells, Angus, ed., A209.
Wells, H.G., C372.
Wendt, Gerald, E9.
Wenger, Milton B., E21, E56, E60.
Westerback, Colin L., Jr., D150.
Weston, Peter, E29.

Weyl, A[lfred] R[ichard], C108,E32.
Whipple, Fred L., E21.
White, Edward M., E50.
White, Jean, C588.